Resurrecting Interpretation

Resurrecting Interpretation
Technology, Hermeneutics, and the Parable of the Rich Man and Lazarus

SIMON PERRY

◥PICKWICK *Publications* • Eugene, Oregon

RESURRECTING INTERPRETATION
Technology, Hermeneutics, and the Parable of the Rich Man and Lazarus

Copyright © 2012 Simon Perry. All rights reserved. Except for brief quotations in critical publications or reviews, no part of this book may be reproduced in any manner without prior written permission from the publisher. Write: Permissions, Wipf and Stock Publishers, 199 W. 8th Ave., Suite 3, Eugene, OR 97401.

Pickwick Publications
An Imprint of Wipf and Stock Publishers
199 W. 8th Ave., Suite 3
Eugene, OR 97401

www.wipfandstock.com
ISBN 13: 978-1-61097-611-4

Cataloging-in-Publication data:

Perry, Simon

   Resurrecting interpretation : technology, hermeneutics, and the parable of the rich man and Lazarus / Simon Perry.

   x + 264 p. ; 23 cm. —Includes bibliographical references and index(es).

   ISBN 13: 978-1-61097-611-4

   1. Bible—Hermeneutics. 2. Rich man and Lazarus (Parable)—Criticism, interpretation, etc. 3. Bible. N.T. Luke XVI, 16–31—Criticism, interpretation, etc. I. Title.

BT378 D5 P45 2012

   Manufactured in the U.S.A.

For Rachel

Contents

Acknowledgments ix

Introduction: The Prominence of Technologist Interpretation 1

1 Demythologizing the Text 26
2 Democratizing the Text 49
3 Defacing the Text 76
4 Resurrection as the Chiasmus of History and Biblical Interpretation 108
5 Christological Reading as Humility 140
6 Somatological Reading as Charis 178
7 Eschatological Reading as Sabbath Celebration 208

Conclusion: Resurrection as the Pulse of Scripture 230

Bibliography 237
Index of Scripture References 253
Index of Names 257
Index of Subjects 261

Acknowledgments

THIS PROJECT BEGAN IN 1998 in Tim Bradshaw's study at Regent's Park College, Oxford. Having taken an optional course on "The Integration of Biblical and Theological Studies" at the end of my undergraduate degree, Tim encouraged me to pursue postgraduate work at the University of Bristol where I was soon to move.

Lloyd Pietersen, who sparked off my interest in Stanley Fish, was my first supervisor; while Philip Jenson's interest in biblical hermeneutics led him to become my official supervisor. Eventually, however, my main teacher and source of encouragement was Robert Forrest, whose energy and interest in my work went way beyond what would normally be expected of a supervisor. The thesis was finally examined by John Nolland and Craig Bartholomew, both of whom were deeply encouraging and offered good advice on preparing the text for publication. In a less official capacity, weekly telephone conversations with Brian Brock really laid the foundations for the structure of the thesis and secured an interest in Heidegger and Barth. In fact, it was from Brian that I picked up on the relationship between Barth's notion of Sabbath and Heidegger's of technology. That relationship is brought out far more comprehensively in his own PhD Thesis for King's College, London, "Discovering Our Dwelling."

Through the years of study that were needed for a multi-disciplinary thesis like this, a basic competence in handling texts in their original language was picked up from Rex Mason. Having recently retired from Regent's Park College, he moved to a house across the hill from me in the wilds of Somerset and agreed to take me, week by week, through an entire course of Hebrew Study, for which I remain very grateful. The other help in this regard, was my eldest son, Willem. From being just a few months old, we would sit for countless hours in the very early morning, as I slowly rocked him back to sleep with inflections in Ancient Greek.

The bulk of the research for this work was completed while serving as part time minister at Fivehead Baptist Church, in Somerset. Learning to be a minister in this setting, making huge mistakes and having great fun in the process, was perhaps the most significant lesson in drawing together the reading of Scripture with the shape of daily life in all its messiness. The five good years I spent at Fivehead taught me more theology than I was likely to learn from any book. In particular, friendships with Steve and Wendy Cutts, Dave and Rachel Moffat, David and Caroline Gauld, Eric and Rose Cook, Lewis and Molly Misselbrook, Adrian and Judy Male, Tim and Lisa Westlake, and Sheila, Graham and Charlene Land, have ensured that the ideas stated here didn't descend any further than they have, into pretentious theoretical pointlessness.

But above all, this thesis is the fruit of conversation with my wife, Rachel. She has been a constant source of encouragement and inspiration, as I see in her so much of what I have struggled to articulate here. This thesis was written at the same time as building a family, and I hope this is reflected in the content. Learning to be a husband and father, have, I hope, kept the theoretical components of this book rooted in the grittiness of real life.

INTRODUCTION
The Prominence of Technologist Interpretation

For the influential biblical scholar Albert Schweitzer, engaging with a text affects the way the reader engages with the world. His own life story was profoundly reshaped by his encounter with the text of scripture, which led him to interpret scripture (most particularly, his reading of the parable of the Rich Man and Lazarus (Luke 16:19–31)) by abandoning the academy for the missionary hospital. He introduces his autobiographical work with the conviction that

> The parable of Dives and Lazarus seemed to me to have been spoken directly of us! We are Dives, for, through the advances of medical science, we now know a great deal about disease and pain, and have innumerable means of fighting them. yet we take as a matter of course the incalculable advantages which this new wealth gives us! Out there in the colonies, however, sits wretched Lazarus, the coloured folk, who suffers from illness and pain just as much as we do, nay, much more, and has absolutely no means of fighting them. And just as Dives sinned against the poor man at his gate because for want of thought he never put himself in his place and let his heart and conscience tell him what he ought to do, so do we sin against the poor man at our gate.[1]

The rest of Schweitzer's life may be read as an enacted interpretation of that parable. The burden of the present argument is to read this parable in detail, allowing it to show that scripture, like any other text, is best understood when it is lived. Hermeneutics, as the term is generally

---

1. Schweitzer, *On the Edge of the Primeval Forest*, 7.

used, is a crucial part of that process, but cannot yield all that is necessary for a full-blown understanding of scripture.

The interpretation of scripture, or for that matter of any text, is wholly (but not solely) determined by the wider context in which the reader encounters a text. This wider context is not simply a question, for instance, of historical location or social perspective of readers, horizons that might help or hinder the discovery of an ancient author's intent. Rather, it is a context that embraces the reader's life when she is not actually reading a text, i.e., a world beyond the text that is nevertheless—at least in the case of scripture—addressed by the text. There is significant convergence here with H. G. Gadamer's monumental volume on hermeneutics, *Truth and Method*. One of Gadamer's important moves is to broaden the notion of hermeneutics from exclusively addressing textual interpretation, to incorporate wider extra-textual considerations embracing the life of the reader more generally.[2]

Even for Gadamer, however, hermeneutics is a discipline that attempts to bridge the historical distance between modern readers and ancient writers.[3] I argue that such a practice is better described as "historicist hermeneutics,"[4] that is, a particular sub-category of a wider discipline. Nevertheless it will be shown that hermeneutics as a whole is often mistaken for its historicist sub-category. When biblical interpretation is confined by the structures of historicist hermeneutics, its theological integrity is compromised.[5] This is because a very particular conception of

---

2. The first part of *Truth and Method* is taken up largely with this question, as Gadamer surveys the importance of aesthetic understanding as one that embraces the entire life of its observer, such that observation is no longer considered an adequate category. Gadamer concludes with the belief that hermeneutics must be even more widely embracing than the aesthetic encounter with art: '...hermeneutics must be so determined as a whole that it does justice to the experience of art.' (Gadamer, *Truth and Method*, 164.)

3. Gadamer, *Truth and Method*, 460–91.

4. Historicism as a term is discussed more fully on p. 111–15 below. In brief, it is based on a linear conception of history from which divine action is excluded. One consequence of this is that cultures and people separated from one another by the passing of centuries are thereby mutually alienated. A hermeneutics based on this historicist view is then preoccupied with overcoming the alienating distance of culture and time. For a clear narrative outlining the development of historicism, see Colin Greene ("In the Arms of the Angels" in Bartholomew et. al, *Behind the Text*, 198–238)—although there is a question to be asked how far he can distinguish between Enlightenment and historicism.

5. Contra Jeanrond, *Theological Hermeneutics*.

Introduction: *The Prominence of Technologist Interpretation* 3

history, one in which God's action in the world is drastically minimised, is allowed to determine the way that a biblical text is heard. The result is that hermeneutics becomes excessively preoccupied with the historicist problem of historical distance (between first century author and twenty first century reader). One cannot deny that historical distance demands humility from the interpreter, but it is not the only, or even the most important problem to be addressed by the reader of scripture. Other issues that are important for biblical interpreters, such as the manner in which the text is enfleshed in the lives of believers, are often regarded as subsidiary concerns. Only when a text has already been properly understood, so the logic runs, can it subsequently be properly applied.[6] The chapters below will therefore seek to allow wider issues in biblical interpretation to determine the framework for hermeneutics. In this sense, the character of the arguments offered below may be situated within the broad stream of "Biblical Theology." That is, inasmuch as they examine contemporary philosophical and theological patterns of interpretation in the light of scripture, they assume the general validity of a history of salvation whose climax is the resurrection of Israel's Messiah.[7] It is this event, whose effects stretch beyond the texts that report it, that demands interpretive approaches that engage the extra-textual world of those who engage the written text.

STRUCTURE OF THE ARGUMENT

The "worldly" environment will be the focus of the first part of the book, with special attention paid to the insights of Martin Heidegger, arguably

---

6. Kevin Vanhoozer's approach to hermeneutics comes dangerously close to such a position, with his endorsement of the belief that while a text may communicate a single *meaning*, this *meaning* will have different *significance* for different readers as they seek, with the help of the Spirit, to apply this original meaning in their present life (Vanhoozer, *Is there a Meaning in this Text?*, 421–24). Nevertheless, Vanhoozer does attempt to retain an emphasis on the importance of "embodied" interpretation in the life of the Christian disciple (Vanhoozer. *Is there a Meaning in this Text?* 441).

7. The Biblical Theology Movement cannot be described as a simple and unified tradition. For instance, Brevard Childs lists eight different models for Biblical Theology. (See Childs, *Biblical Theology of the Old and new Testaments*.) In his introduction to the Scripture and Hermeneutics Seminar's volume on Biblical Theology, Craig Bartholomew helpfully offers six important aspects of Childs's own Canonical approach that are indispensable for theological interpretation (Bartholomew, *Out of Egypt*, 12–15).

the most influential writer on the subject of hermeneutics in the twentieth century.[8] Heidegger had much to say about the ways in which the individual engages with the world, and what follows here relies upon his analysis of the environing power wielded by one's host culture as articulated in his later writings on the subject of technology.

Heidegger emphasized in his earlier work, *Being and Time*, that the detached observation of the thinking subject is a mis-description of humanity's place in the universe. Instead he argued that the thinking subject finds herself embedded in a complex set of relationships and cultural practices that shape the way she encounters the world and, we may infer, the text. In reading, as in any activity, "we begin in the middle,"[9] that is, our lived context of belief and practice shapes the range and type of responses available to us. It is for this reason that the key chapter of this book, the interpretive significance of the resurrection, stands at the centre rather than the beginning, and serves as the centre point between the first and second parts. The first three chapters that comprise Part I focus upon the philosophical and theological implications of the interpretive strategies offered by Rudolf Bultmann, Stanley Fish, and Jacques Derrida respectively, and demonstrate the dominance of what Heidegger described as technology. In this sense, the first part of the book is formally negative, in that it prepares the way for the displacement effected by the advent of Christ.

These three strategists are not theologically determinative of the argument that follows, but simply highlight interpretive issues that are directly challenged by Christology, Somatology, and Eschatology. The second part of the argument explores these three interpretive apperceptions, each of which are already in place when scripture is being read. All readers of scripture adopt a stance towards Christ, they read from within the confines of a community and they have a particular eschatological orientation. From a Christian perspective these ways of reading are rooted in resurrection, which is not simply an event that occupies a particular place in history. It is also an event that is appropriated in the

---

8. Gadamer and Ricoeur were both students of Heidegger, and their works, along with those of Bultmann and Derrida, are to a great extent dependent upon his insights.

9. Bonhoeffer, *Creation and Fall*, 12. See also Dilthey, "we centre on the mid point," quoted in Gadamer, *Truth and Method*, 291. See also Gadamer, *Truth and Method*, 301–2.

Introduction: The Prominence of Technologist Interpretation

lives of those who would engage with scripture as *Holy* Scripture, that is, as a text that presents a profound and particular form of otherness.

Throughout the book allusion is made to this often ambiguous category of "otherness," so the particular manner in which it is employed here must be outlined. The term is not used as a relativistic dogma pronouncing the equal validity of all viewpoints, although in the first instance it does affirm the notion that there exist other peoples and perspectives whose very existence stand over against any pretension to the absolutism that may be assumed of one's own perspective. In this sense there is some coherence to be found with Derrida's description of other people and of God himself as *tout autre*.[10] But although it is not a biblical category, the sense in which the phrase is used in the present argument is to be defined theologically, not least because no one embodies such profound otherness as God himself.[11] The technological environment as described below, relates to such otherness simply by assimilating it into oneself, collapsing the tension of an I-Thou encounter.[12] The otherness of the other is thus flattened by technologism, presenting a fundamental problem for Christian interpretation, in that Christ *is* otherness, but not in an abstract sense. In order to counter the exclusive dominance of technologism, openness to the other is not to be pursued as an abstract openness *per se*. The readiness to welcome the other is not a perpetual desire for novelty whose result saint Paul might describe as being "tossed to and fro and blown about by every wind of doctrine." (Eph 4:14).[13] Rather it lies in the readiness to welcome the content-full presence of Christ. This cannot be achieved negatively, that is by clearing space for the Spirit then to fill. (Such an activity might well lead to occupation by seven demons more fierce than the first [Mt 12:43–45]). The tenacity of interpretive spirits is demonstrated by the three chapters below. For Bultmann, the desire to exorcise presuppositions fails to reckon with the sheer inescapability of one's wider interpretive horizons that quietly

---

10. See Derrida, *Gift of Death*, as discussed in section 3.3 below.

11. Isa 55:10–11.

12. See Buber, *I and Thou*.

13. Such doctrines are generated in Pauline terms by a 'readiness to do anything' (πανουργία|) through deceitful methodologies (μεθοδείαν) that are merely human. In this precise context (Eph 4:15) Paul urges the alternative of an active truth, employing the verbal form (ἀληθεύοντες) with which Heidegger's notion of truth resonates. Paul's notion of *aletheia* is not a "readiness for anything," but an openness firmly directed toward the content-full otherness embodied in the presence of Christ.

determine one's (often) unacknowledged presuppositional stance (chapter 1). For Fish, the mystery and challenge embodied by otherness is exorcised, only to be replaced by the power of rhetoric (chapter 2). For Derrida, the openness to the other is ultimately an activity that regulates divine interference in human life and interpretation (chapter 3). In each case, it will be argued, a genuine attempt to liberate interpretation theory from serious historical obstacles has resulted in those obstacles being quietly replaced by others. Clearing space for otherness subsequently to inhabit, is to decide in advance the scope of its influence, and in so doing subjecting the other to insidious domestication even while maintaining a belief that genuine (rather than a pseudo) otherness is thereby experienced. Stated positively, engagement with otherness is the symbiotic relationship between human listening (an activity demonstrating the readiness to be transformed by an encounter with an other) and God speaking, in that God's voice can make itself heard.[14] The capacity to embrace the otherness of Christ is not one that is forged by autonomous human activity (i.e., in accordance with technologism) but is an act of the Holy Spirit. The otherness assumed by this argument is thus a Trinitarian otherness.

Chapter 4, the center of the book, describes resurrection as an event whose effects emanate throughout history to visit the challenge of a content-full otherness upon the extra-textual lives of readers. As such it assumes the Spirit's presence who effects the personal, social, moral regeneration of the individual reader.[15] This transformation of the reader by definition presupposes the encounter with genuine otherness by which it is effected, and thus highlights a sharp contrast between resurrection and the all-pervasive technological environment identified by Heidegger, an environment that is oriented towards conquering otherness, as outlined below. This contrast is to be addressed as each chapter in Part II is read against its counterpart in Part I.

Chapter 1 traces Bultmann's program of existential hermeneutics, and his concern that those who read scripture be exposed to the transforming demands of the *kerygma*. If, following Heidegger, to exist is to

---

14. This issue will be addressed in more detail in chapters 3 and 5 below.

15. The individual here is not to be understood in an autonomous sense, but as chapter 6 will show, within the body of Christ a believer's individuality is derived from her interpersonal relationships with other members of the body (Rom 12:6). Scripture is the canon of the church.

ek-sist, to "stand out"¹⁶ of history so as to be transformed, the result is a de-historicised Christian faith. That is, the primal hermeneutic encounter is located in the decisions made by the existential reader, an engagement in which the Jesus of history is eclipsed by the Christ of faith. Chapter 7 however, takes up Bultmann's existential concern by appeal to Sabbath celebration, a communal activity in which one is re-oriented within the purposes of God, encountering a divine otherness without negating the otherness of history.

Chapter 2 addresses the authority of the interpretive community as heralded by Fish, and is complemented by Chapter 6, which explores more fully the constitution of the Christian community and the manner in which it embodies the authority (and the otherness) of Christ. Fish argues against the very notion of otherness, claiming that the moment it becomes intelligible it is thereby assimilated into the community's own constitution and bereft of any otherness to which it might lay claim. This leaves the authority of one's own community absolute, and the possibility of a transforming *ek-sistence* unavailable. Conversely, chapter 6 focuses upon Bernd Wannenwetsch's reading of Romans 12 that accentuates the political importance of being "members of one another" (Rom 12:5), in such a way as to be transformed from beyond the schematising power of the age (Rom 12:2).¹⁷ We are social beings, but how we read depends on whether we inhabit "flesh" without reference to God, or whether we live in faith of the promise of Christ's body.

Chapter 3 on Derrida's readiness for the Messiah is set against chapter 5 on the implications of Christology. These two chapters explore in more detail the concept of otherness as outlined briefly above. Derrida's deconstructive approach to the text is thus described not merely as a method that can be activated or deactivated at will, but as an attitude that is inevitably brought to bear on the text. His avowal of messianic readiness and openness to the other is devoid of content, and thoroughly at odds with the Christology described by Bonhoeffer, who pictures a Christ whose transforming presence deconstructs people rather than texts.

---

16. Heidegger, "On the Essence of Truth," 26; see also *Being and Time*, 302. Heidegger's "standing out" in this sense, is not to dehistoricize oneself permanently. It is rather the sense of taking one's bearings in the world as it is encountered, in order to re-insert oneself resolutely back into that world with greater awareness of one's *telos*.

17. Wannenwetsch, "Members of One Another," 210.

Thus part I of this book will offer a critique of these three key hermeneutic strategists from the perspective of the technological problem as portrayed by Heidegger. These three reading strategies have each been pressed into the service of biblical interpretation but the argument running through these chapters will be that this service by no means automatically emancipates them from the technological environment but rather serves to exemplify its dominance. This is neither to reject the importance of some particular insights offered by the proponents of such strategies, nor to ignore the questions they pose for biblical interpretation. Nevertheless it is important to ask of these strategies whether and how they may surreptitiously silence the otherness presented by the text. If the strategy of our age is dominated by technology as described by Heidegger, Part II argues that if resurrection is taken seriously, it heralds for biblical interpretation a necessary exodus from technological dominance. It is a necessary exodus because without it, regardless of what convictions or intentions are brought to the text, those prior concerns are prone to impose themselves without being exposed to the transforming divine otherness.[18] Overall then, the argument hangs upon a chiastic structure as follows.

> Chapter 1 –Bultmann and demythologizing the text.
>
> > Chapter 2—Fish and the power of interpretive communities.
> >
> > > Chapter 3—Derrida and deconstructive reading.
> > >
> > > > Chapter 4—Resurrection as the chiasmus of interpretation.
> > >
> > > Chapter 5—Christological reading as humility.
> >
> > Chapter 6—Somatological reading as *charis*.
>
> Chapter 7—Eschatological reading as Sabbath celebration.

The Chiasm itself is integral to the argument, since the first three chapters describe the environment that is transformed by the last three. Resurrection denotes both continuity and contrast as it engages the worldly environment of a technologism that drives the incessant quest to conquer otherness. Those who inhabit this environment might be transformed in the light of a particular content-full otherness that

---

18. As discussed below, this is not to deny the Holy Spirit's role as *didaskolos*, and his freedom to overcome the scriptural hearing impairment of technologized humanity.

enables one to *ek-sist* without negating one's environment. Heidegger's description of our environment is *technologism*.

HEIDEGGER AND TECHNOLOGY

Heidegger's writings on technology can appear abstract and elusive, largely because they underwent an extended period of development that began as early as the mid 1920s when he compiled *Being and Time*. His later explicit writing on technology[19] is inseparable from his wider philosophical concerns and presupposes familiarity with the complexities of Heideggerian vocabulary. His ambiguity is also related to the stance he adopts toward the political turbulence of his day. He had not only witnessed but experienced the awesome technological feats of the American and Soviet military machines as they overpowered his native Germany and its National Socialist dream (by which he had earlier been captivated).[20] He was not favourably disposed to the advent of a so-called technological age,[21] and as discussed below, attempted to deconstruct the dominance of technology with an emphasis on art and poetry. To achieve this he constructed an original conception of the essence of technology.

Heidegger perceived in technology a danger that threatened humanity in its very being. However, he was neither a Luddite opposing a lamentable over-reliance on the expansion of technological power, nor a technophile trying to get more dangerous technologies "intelligently in hand."[22] He understands technology not as an object (or plethora of objects) that can be mastered and used, but as a means of interpreting the world. It is not to be thought of as the modern manufacture of devices that is enabled by scientific progress, but as an ancient mode of knowledge. Technology is a way of encountering truth, or in Heideggerian terms, it is an "unveiling." Derived from the Greek *techne* it denotes a

---

19. Most notably the revision of four lectures delivered in 1949/50, that was published in 1953 as the "The Question Concerning Technology".

20. On the relation between his political experience and technology, see the brief discussion in Macquarrie, *Heidegger and Christianity*, 112–21. Much of the main documentary evidence, including an interview with Heidegger himself, along with a spectrum of insightful critique is to be found in Wolin's *The Heidegger Controversy*.

21. Neither did he regard technology as a social evil, as discussed further below.

22. Heidegger, "The Question Concerning Technology," 313.

disclosive practice in which Heidegger notices two principle features. Firstly, *techne* "is the name not only for the activities and skills of the craftsman but also for the arts of the mind and the fine arts. *Techne* belongs to bringing-forth, to *poiesis*; it is something poetic."[23] Secondly, he notes that *techne* "is a mode of *aletheuein*. . . It is as revealing, and not as manufacturing, that *techne* is a bringing-forth."[24] Elucidation of these two points will help clarify what Heidegger means by technology.

Firstly the notion of *aletheia* is crucially important for Heidegger. Returning to a purportedly pre-Platonic conception of truth, he emphasises the alpha-privative and reads it *a-letheia*, where *letheia* refers to that which is concealed. This insight enables him to portray truth as an active and dynamic event of emergence and withdrawal, dis-closedness and closedness, revealing and concealing.[25] Truth as conceived by Heidegger, necessarily embraces both partners of these dualisms. As it brings some things out of concealment, it thereby conceals others, in much the same way as tuning into one radio frequency automatically silences all others. Furthermore, the awareness of our very *attunement* to one frequency alerts us to the existence of other frequencies. One cannot focus exclusively upon that which is unconcealed but must rather be aware of the concealment that accompanies and enables such manifestation. Only as such will one be exposed to the play of differences highlighted by *a-letheia*.[26]

Secondly, this conception of *aletheia* sheds lights upon what Heidegger means by *poiesis*, a term which he describes as a "bringing-forth."[27] It is best understood in relation to his 1935 lecture, "The Origin of a Work of Art,"[28] in which Heidegger introduces a bipolar opposition between the historical activity of people (world) and the ontological stuff of nature (earth).[29] World is human conquest and discovery; earth is nature's resistance and revealing. However, the distinction between the

---

23. Heidegger, "The Question Concerning Technology," 318.

24. Heidegger, "The Question Concerning Technology," 319.

25. Heidegger, "Plato's Doctrine of Truth," 168–69.

26. This is even true as we walk around an object and survey its different sides. In order to see it at all, we must see one aspect of it at a time. That aspect emerges out of unconcealment. Concealment, in Heidegger's view, is more primordial than unconcealment.

27. Heidegger, "The Question Concerning Technology," 318–19.

28. Heidegger, "The Question Concerning Technology," 143–203.

29. Heidegger, "The Question Concerning Technology," 174.

two does not render them separate but mutually engaged. Nevertheless earth and world are not simply contraposed but interdependent, since earth needs world in order for its being to be made manifest, and conversely world needs earth since it provides its ontological basis.[30] The perpetual strife that reverberates between earth and world may thus be understood as the site of *poiesis*, human "bringing forth," not merely in the sense of manufacturing but in the fuller sense of revealing.[31] In this sense the work of art is an aspect of work that engages both earth and world, as it reveals elements of earth in such a way as to disrupt and create history in the world. Art brings forth the being of earth as a revelation to and reshaping of world. The most fitting example used by Heidegger is that of the Greek temple.[32] The temple is the site of active truth, a place of revelation, which, though crafted by worldly human hands, is wholly dependent upon the earth that yields itself in *this* particular way at *this* particular time. Emerging from the *fourfold* essence of earth, sky, gods and mortals, the clearing opens so that offerings can be made by mortals to the gods, beneath the heavens, using vessels of earth. The space opens up not so much for some human initiative to take place, but rather is the "destining" that prompts the offering. Mortals participate in freedom by this means, but this means that they are freed to participate; not that they have free choice to make use of the temple site in whatever way appeals to them at the time. In this way mortals achieve their full destiny and dignity, whereas in technology they are reduced to numerical components, or "human resources." As a human construct the temple embodies particular interpretation of human life, and equally it opens up a clearing, a space in which interpretations are reconfigured as they are exposed to the ontological separateness of earth in a new way. Thus *techne*, as a human work and a property of *poiesis*, "is

30. Heidegger, "The Question Concerning Technology," 174.

31. Heidegger, "The Question Concerning Technology," 319.

32. This raises the tangential question of Heidegger's option for Greek paganism (which was construed as part of Aryan civilisation by the Nazis—something which the Greek people profoundly chose not to appreciate in their armed resistance of 1941–43). The mention of the offering cup is deliberate because it allows Heidegger not to lose the theological student constituency of which he was thoroughly aware, even while treating of a perfectly respectable pagan source. Comments he made in his lecture on *Time and Being* and again in 1962 in relation to calling a New Testament Seminar show his ready awareness of the Theological Faculty, quite apart from the fact that he lectured on New Testament writings in the early 1920s—undertaking his own exegeses of writings like 1 Thessalonians. See Kisiel, *The Genesis of Heidegger's Being and Time* 173–91.

a mode of *alethuein*."³³ Hence, for Heidegger technology is defined as "a mode of revealing. Technology comes to presence in the realm where revealing and unconcealment take place, where *aletheia*, truth, happens."³⁴

This definition may appear to be a long way from modern technology with its use of machines rather than skilled craftsmen and artisans, a phenomenon that has developed in relation to scientific progress rather than in the poetic bringing forth of earth. But it is precisely in this apparent disjuncture between ancient revelatory technology and modern scientific technology that Heidegger locates the most acute technological danger. Modern technology cannot be so readily dislocated from its ancient counterpart. "It too is a revealing," he claims. "Only when we allow our attention to rest on this fundamental characteristic does that which is new in modern technology show itself to us."³⁵

If modern technology is a means of unveiling then according to Heidegger it has become devoid of *poiesis*. "The revealing that rules throughout modern technology has the character of a setting-upon, in the sense of a challenging-forth."³⁶ The earth-world distinction is obliterated by a desire to seize upon nature for the sake of controlling it. In what Nietzsche might have called "the triumph of the will," Heidegger perceived a new form of enslavement.³⁷

> [T]he revealing that holds sway throughout modern technology does not unfold into a bringing-forth in the sense of *poiesis*. The revealing that rules in modern technology is a challenging [*Herausfordern*], which puts to nature the unreasonable demand that it supply energy which can be extracted and stored as such. But does this not hold true for the windmill as well? No. Its sails do indeed turn in the wind; they are left entirely to the wind's blowing. But the windmill does not unlock energy from the air currents in order to store it.³⁸

---

33. Heidegger, "The Question Concerning Technology," 319.
34. Heidegger, "The Question Concerning Technology," 319.
35. Heidegger, "The Question Concerning Technology," 320.
36. Heidegger, "The Question Concerning Technology," 321.
37. Leni Riefenstahl directed a 1935 Nazi propoganda film entitled *Triumph Des Willens* (*Triumph of the Will*). It documents the Sixth Nazi Party Congress at Nuremberg so that future generations would be able to witness the genesis of the Third Reich. Ironically it now stands as a testament to the awesome potency of rhetoric to reduce human beings to human resources, evangelising the masses by technological means.
38. Heidegger, "The Question Concerning Technology," 320.

Introduction: The Prominence of Technologist Interpretation

Challenging, or "setting upon" nature in this way yields a particular understanding of the earth. Such challenging discloses things as objects that are utterly at our disposal. Entities are unconcealed in a manner that renders them readily available for consumption, ready to be simply unearthed, extracted or manipulated. The earth now stands as an inventory waiting to be utilised, and is bereft of its capacity to stand over-against us. Heidegger's own example is the Rhine, which is transformed by technology into a "standing reserve" (*Bestand*).[39]

> The hydroelectric plant is set into the current of the Rhine. It sets the Rhine to supplying its hydraulic pressure, which then sets the turbines turning. This turning sets those machines in motion whose whole thrust sets going the electric current for which the long-distance power station and its network of cables are set up to dispatch electricity. . . . the energy concealed in nature is unlocked, what is unlocked is transformed, what is transformed is stored up, what is stored up is, in turn, distributed, and what is distributed is switched about ever anew. In the context of the interlocking processes pertaining to the orderly disposition of electrical energy, even the Rhine itself appears as something at our command.[40]

This passage elucidates in a twofold sense the danger Heidegger perceives in technology. Firstly it highlights that the modern technological disposition towards nature reveals it as "standing reserve" to the point where it becomes the *only* way of engaging nature. However, secondly and more importantly, in order to maintain this disposition, further technological manipulation is inevitable. That is, the abuse of the Rhine, of nature, is not a technological problem for which one might find a technological solution. As Hubert Dreyfus summarizes, "[t]he threat is not a *problem* for which we must find a *solution*, but an *ontological condition* that requires a *transformation of our understanding of being.*"[41] Both Dreyfus and John Macquarrie note that in the passage cited above, the hurried succession of activities creates the impression of an endless treadmill of technological frenzy that drives humanity from one goal to another but remains devoid of any ultimate purpose that would reveal

---

39. Heidegger, "The Question Concerning Technology," 322.
40. Heidegger, "The Question Concerning Technology," 321.
41. Dreyfus, "Heidegger on the Connection between Nihilism, Art, Technology and Politics," 305.

the earth in a different way—say, for instance, the desire to worship God.[42] The confinement in such an ontological condition is described by Heidegger using the notion of *Gestell*, or "enframing." What Heidegger is getting at is the reduction of nature to numbers. This reduction is evident in Galileo's statement that there are two books—scripture, which is written in words, and nature, which is written in numbers. As soon as nature is reduced by modern physics (and by a narrow focus on physics, or mechanics, or biological analysis, or whatever) it certainly reveals itself with relentless uniformity, and enables itself to be manipulated with ruthless efficiency (for the homogenised is always easier to handle than a mixture of types), but much is thereby concealed. And herein lies the danger.

In the technological *Gestell*, what Heidegger describes as *poiesis* is silenced and the capacity for the earth to resist or to stand over against a humanity compelled simply to manipulate it, is suspended. Active *a-letheia* grinds to a halt as humanity becomes forgetful of its attunement, and (unwittingly) comes to conceive of itself along with all else, as standing reserve. As an example Heidegger uses the notion of an airliner sitting on the tarmac.[43] It does not simply stand as an object ready for use. As an integral part of a complex transportation system, it also subsumes people who become passengers—another cog in the wheel of the transport mechanism—serving it rather than merely being served by it. To press Heidegger's analogy further, passengers might contend that they had chosen to fly, and had therefore used the system simply as its masters, in free choice. But this would not take into account the factors that led to such a choice. (Even if the flight were being used for instance as a holiday, the question of why the need for such a holiday, and indeed, why the need for a holiday at all?) The wider factors leading to such decisions (e.g., advertising strategies) may always be seen as further cogs to keep the transportation system active, leading human resources to keep it running by shaping the way they choose to travel. Considered in such a way, a technological mindset so deeply pervasive cannot be controlled by humans. Humanity so enframed loses its freedom, as it loses its ability to receive *poiesis* and is thereby consigned to a surreptitiously truncated exposure to *aletheia*.

---

42. See Dreyfus, "Heidegger on the Connection between Nihilism, Art, Technology and Politics," 306; and Macquarrie, *Heidegger and Christianity*, 68–70.

43. Heidegger, "The Question Concerning Technology," 322–23.

Introduction: The Prominence of Technologist Interpretation

It is precisely this "destining of revealing" that constitutes the real danger of enframing.[44] Such destining is not to be confused with "a fate that compels."[45] By fate, is meant "the inevitableness of an unalterable course."[46] Destining on the other hand, refers to our capacity to receive revelation, our freedom to encounter *aletheia*. The "destining" of the technicist *Gestell* maintains the illusion that humankind, as master, tames the jungle of otherness by ordering, regulating and securing with the effect that the dominance of the *Gestell* is perpetuated. Destining that compels such an ordering of nature radically restricts the play of *a-lethia* and constitutes extreme danger. Heidegger is here grappling for a way of demonstrating both the sheer weight of the technological *Gestell*, its inescapable force and extensive reach, (it is our destiny) and at the same time to show that the *Gestell* does not wield absolute or ultimate power (it is not—necessarily—our fate).[47] Salvation from this *Gestell* is to be found at the heart of this danger. Although technology defines the manner in which things are interpreted, a true questioning of the essence of technology might offer the opportunity of transformation as *aletheia* is reconceived in its dynamism. *Aletheia* is a path that is sequentially discovered, broadening out so that one might encounter unconcealment in a way different from that determined by technologism. How is this to be done? By enticing the *poiesis* that is concealed within the technological *Gestell* into emergence. Rather than seeking to escape from technology, Heidegger appeals to the question of its essence. Technology is not essentially prone to the conception of the universe as subject to the human will. The self-disclosing nature of earth might be highlighted by *poiesis*. Thus Heidegger turns to the *poiesis* of Hölderlin in order to draw attention to what he deems a more primal call to truth:

> But where danger is, grows
> The saving power also.[48]

---

44. Heidegger, "The Question Concerning Technology," 331.
45. Heidegger, "The Question Concerning Technology," 330.
46. Heidegger, "The Question Concerning Technology," 330.
47. This is because a path of *aletheia* is one which we follow at an invitation. It invokes our voluntary assent. In this sense it is not a blank compelling but a sequentially discovered path. But it may lead into murky depths of the forest where it is hard to retrace our steps and where light is increasingly eclipsed.
48. Hölderlin, quoted by Heidegger, "The Question Concerning Technology," 333.

Heidegger interprets "saving" here as a bringing home, i.e., as humanity is brought into the free space in which *aletheia* may be active again. Once one is alerted to the essence of technology as enframing, the seeds of salvation have already been sown. The awareness of one's enframing, of "the destining . . . that holds sway,"[49] demonstrates one's very *attunement* and thereby alerts us to the reality that the technological way of encountering the world is not the only way. *Poiesis* revisits itself upon those who question the essence of technology. The questionability of technology thus addresses itself to thinkers, within the opening horizon.

TECHNOLOGY AND BIBLICAL INTERPRETATION

The importance of Heidegger's analysis of the modern ontological condition has enormous implications for questions concerning the nature of biblical interpretation. If, as this book maintains, Heidegger's diagnosis is substantially correct, then the weight of this "technologist" condition is one that is virtually impossible to overestimate, and will inexorably manifest itself in the ways that readers engage with texts. Some preliminary remarks about how the technologism outlined above brings itself to bear upon biblical interpretation will serve both to clarify Heidegger's ambiguous intentions, and to plot in advance the course trodden by this argument. If all that is encountered in the "world" includes the text, the propensity to handle the text as a resource to be mined for meaning is inevitable. Interpretive models and programs are legitimate, indeed unavoidable and only to be joyfully affirmed. Just as humans are subjects in a technological world, so it is the fate of all would-be hearers of texts to bring their presuppositions to bear upon the words that are read. The practice of our daily lives is inseparable from the logic of our exegetical practices. However, when *poiesis* is silenced so too is the textual capacity to stand over against the reader, and the text itself, whilst being "used," is treated effectively if unwittingly as "standing reserve,"[50] i.e., as a source of truths whose proper meaning will be revealed given the right interpretive technique. Such an approach is problematic for a theological

---

49. Heidegger, "The Question Concerning Technology," 331.
50. Heidegger, "The Question Concerning Technology," 322.

Introduction: The Prominence of Technologist Interpretation 17

discourse that wishes to acknowledge the presence of the Holy Spirit in and through the interpretive endeavour.

The Spirit's role is explicitly indispensable in the interpretive process if the enormous extent of technological influence is acknowledged. The role of the Spirit in the reading process is presented throughout this book in direct relation to the resurrection. John Webster makes the point well when he states:

> a Christian theological anthropology will envisage the act of reading Scripture as an instance of the fundamental pattern of all Christian existence, which is dying and rising with Jesus Christ through the purging and quickening power of the Holy Spirit.[51]

To appropriate Heidegger's insights, biblical interpretation cannot be conceived of as an exclusively human task because the compulsion to treat the world in general, and the text in particular as mere "standing reserve"[52] is not simply a theoretical problem to be associated with a perception one may or may not choose to adopt. It is deeply ingrained in the ontological condition that may be equated with what the apostle Paul had deemed, "the schematising power of the age" (Rom 12:2).[53] This is why Romans 12 is a crucially important text: it contrasts the deeply pervasive power of the interpretive environment not with a technological escape route, but with the economy of grace.[54] Even the most intelligent hermeneutical strategy cannot get the technological problem "intelligently in hand"[55] because to do so would simply exacerbate the problem. Heidegger himself felt the human incapacity to overcome the technologist dominance he identified, leading him eventually to the pronouncement that "Only a God can save us."[56] For Heidegger, the omni-

---

51. Webster, *Word and Church*, 11.

52. Heidegger, "The Question Concerning Technology," 322.

53. Heidegger felt free to transmute the Christian category of fallenness, via Augustine, into his own transcendental ontology of *Being and Time*, 156–57.

54. Discussed in chapter 6 below.

55. Heidegger, "The Question Concerning Technology," 313.

56. (Noch nur ein Gott Kann uns retten) Heidegger, *Der Spiegel*, May 31, 1976. This text is an almost confessional interview, conducted in 1966 with the proviso that it be published only posthumously. It is printed in full [translated by Maria P. Alter and John D. Caputo] in Wolin 1993, 91–116. See also Philosophy Today XX (4/4): 267–85. Heidegger had always railed against the construction of "God," and held that his own atheism in 1929 was for this reason more theological and less idolatrous than the "theism" of the theologians. In the same way, this is one reason why he found Holderlin so

pervasive influence of the technologist condition cannot be overstated. It constitutes the contemporary human environment, and remains as all-embracing (and almost as imperceptible) as the air that we breathe.

It is in relation to the sheer pervasiveness of the technologist condition that this argument is structured as described below, and is contrasted with the similar approach of Kevin Vanhoozer's study of postmodern reading strategists, *Is There a Meaning in This Text?*[57] Vanhoozer builds extensive critiques of Stanley Fish and Jacques Derrida, two of the main subjects of Part I below. Describing such postmodernists as "users" or "undoers" of the text, Vanhoozer confronts his readers with "a choice,"[58] i.e., to adopt such unbelieving approaches, or to engage in a more Trinitarian hermeneutic. In contrast, the present book does not offer such a direct exit from the compulsion to be a "user" of scripture because to use scripture in the manner propounded by Heidegger is not a conscious option that is made on the basis of simple choice, and consequently one need not be an "unbeliever" to be a "user" of the text.[59] In accord with Vanhoozer, it will be argued that the practice of reading Scripture is rooted in the wider self-communicative nexus of relationships between God and his people, locating readers in the disclosive practices of Christian discipleship. Against Vanhoozer, it will be argued that these disclosive practices play a substantive role in the interpretive process. It is here, in the transforming experience of Christian discipleship that the dominance of the technological *Gestell* is most seriously threatened.[60] Technologist dominance and its compulsion to make use of all, including Scripture, is simply endorsed by the hermeneutic strategy propounded by Vanhoozer because his strategy fails to address the monstrous grasp of the *Gestell*. The structure of this book reflects the primal textual determinacy of the reader's life outside the text, a life

---

attractive—for Holderlin suggested that "the gods have withdrawn" and "we can only await whether they shall return."

57. Vanhoozer, *Is There a Meaning in this Text?*

58. Vanhoozer, *Is There a Meaning in this Text?*, 457.

59. Augustine's *On Christian Doctrine* exploits the notion of the *use* of scripture (esp. book I), but unlike Heidegger's conception, for Augustine 'use' is related to a hermeneutic of love and a capacity also to be used by God.

60. This is why Romans 12, as addressed in chapter 6, is an important passage. Chapter 6 below will argue that the economy of grace outlined there disrupts the technological *Gestell*.

Introduction: The Prominence of Technologist Interpretation 19

anchored in communicative practices that predetermine the manner in which the text itself is engaged.

Lest this argument on biblical interpretation should be construed as the "practice of reading scripture without bothering to read scripture,"[61] interwoven through its constructive (second) part will be a careful reading of the parable of the rich man and Lazarus (Luke 16:19–31). The point of this argument is to read this parable, and in our technologist context reading this, like any other text, requires the transformation of presupposed technologist convictions in order that it may be heard. This parable suggests itself as an appropriate textual focus mainly because it climaxes with the implicit declaration that one's encounter with a text is inseparable from the way in which one encounters others in the world outside the text, or in Luke's words, "if [the rich man's brothers] do not listen to Moses and the Prophets, neither will they be convinced even by someone who rises from the dead" (Luke16:31). Reference will be made to this aspect of the parable throughout the critiques of Part I, and in Part II it will be viewed through the lenses of the three fundamental apperceptions that cannot be ignored by any contemporary theological theory of biblical interpretation. As mentioned above, the first way of reading is Christological, i.e., focussing upon the manner in which expectation of encounter with Christ governs one's encounter with a text. Secondly is the slightly cumbersome notion of "somatological" reading, which refers to the manner in which the world in general, and the body of Christ in particular, can shape one's construal of the text. Thirdly is the question of how the reader's eschatology determines her structure of reading. As the first part of the book explores the enormous influence of the technologism identified by Heidegger, and the second upon how resurrection influences interpretation in a totally different manner, the entire argument may be summarized in a sentence: *Resurrection displaces technologist reading categories that seek to make use of scripture, with the cultivation of an attentive disposition which enables the reader to be transformed by the God encountered in scripture.*

A brief defense of the importance of each of these apperceptions must now be offered. An initial question must be why these three, and not some others? Given the endless perspectivalism of contemporary hermeneutics, this is an important question. Why not some form of liberation theology perspective, a historical-critical interpretation or

61. A danger highlighted in conversation with Dr. John Day.

a literary-critical reading? To adopt any of these approaches however would necessarily, though often unwittingly, incorporate the three apperceptions identified in pursuance of their method. As methodological perspectives, these varied and valid models would not be sufficient to address the problems identified in the wider phenomenon of technologism, largely because it is quite probable that, as textual theories they remain exclusively focussed upon the text. Even the liberationist perspectives of feminist and third world readings, perspectives which do aim to embrace a world outside the text, in practice may easily remain domesticated textual theories that fail to awaken the otherness of the text. One need only consider that the majority of those in the West sophisticated enough to employ liberationist reading strategies are simply not reading from the perspective of the poor.[62] Similarly, half of those embracing feminist critiques are probably not feminine. This is by no means to disparage the importance of such critiques but to take them with the utmost seriousness, that is, by questioning what impact they actually have upon readers. There is a crucial distinction to be made between perspectives and apperceptions.[63] Focussing upon the apperceptions of readers is not to dismiss the notion of other perspectives, but rather addresses the question of whether and how those other perspectives are allowed to reshape one's ownmost interpretive structures. As apperceptions, Christology, Somatology, and Eschatology necessitate a readerly capacity for transformation in that the biblical text is engaged as an entity that may stand over against the reader.[64]

From a Christian perspective, all communication is Christological. If Christ is worshipped as the Cosmic Christ, his absence from communicative acts is inconceivable, unless of course one has assented to a historicist view of the world.[65] Those for whom the Christological titles

---

62. The parable of the rich man and Lazarus is pertinent in this respect. It is far from inconceivable that a group of exegetical scholars could read the parable from a liberationist perspective, without ever taking positive action towards the plight of the Lazarus beyond the gates of their seminary.

63. A perspective here refers primarily to a point of view one may easily choose to adopt, whereas an apperception is a deeply ingrained way of seeing.

64. If however, scripture is viewed through technologist configurations, then the applicability of Heidegger's comment is obvious: 'Whatever stands by in the sense of standing-reserve no longer stands over against us as object.' (Heidegger, "The Question Concerning Technology," 322.)

65. This is a point considered in chapter 5 below, in which it is argued that Christ is

are not only textual artefacts but contemporary affirmations of faith face all the questions of how the world outside the text shapes one's encounter with the text. If Peter declared to the early church, ". . . let the entire house of Israel know with certainty that God has made him both Lord and Messiah, this Jesus whom you crucified" (Acts 2:36), then the apparently dichotomous relationship between the Jesus of history and the Christ of faith is to be understood within the wider framework of the authority of the Cosmic Christ. Those who worship Christ as such cannot then expect to engage in any form of communication without an ear open to the Christ who as Cosmocrator underwrites the very possibility of communication in the first place. His presence cannot then be conceived as extrinsic to everyday acts of communication. The manner in which the reader responds to the text is thus inseparable from the manner in which she encounters the world at large (cf. Prov 20:12), which means that any discussion of Christian textual interpretation cannot ignore the question of what stance towards Christ is reflected in such interpretation. All reading is irreducibly Christological.

The second apperception is "somatological." It is now commonplace to note that the environment in which readers have learned to communicate is largely determinative of how texts are encountered. Again, the questions of encounter with the text in particular and the world in general cannot be mutually quarantined, as reflected in the reading of Heidegger outlined above. However, given the readiness to speak of the authority of the interpretive community, in hermeneutical discourse there remains an overwhelming reluctance to define community. This is despite the fact that in Heidegger for instance, the ontological forgetfulness of the they-self wields an awesome communal authority, but authentic existence itself is by no means necessarily individualistic. If the community has authority over the reader, the questions of which community, how the community is characterised and how it exerts its authority are essential for Christian interpretation. If "the body of Christ" is the primary communal context for Christian interpreters of scripture, the manner in which that community embodies Christ is a crucial question, since communities can also embody characteristics that are at odds with Christian conviction.

---

anonymously present in the interpretive process. (See also Taylor, *Go-Between God*, 17; Luke 24:13–35.) A historicist conception of the world however would firmly refute such divine immanence. (See p. 111–15 below).

Finally, eschatological assumptions and claims are never absent from the reading process. One cannot talk of the reader's aims, purposes or goals without thereby adopting some form of eschatology. To read is to realise eschatology,[66] that is, to bring to bear upon the text the ends to which the life of the reader are oriented. Again, this highlights the seriousness of the technologist condition in which the frenzied rush from one activity to another is bereft of any end beyond unceasing change itself.[67] In this light, eschatology then is not exclusively the study of events that constitute the climax of the space-time continuum. As Stephen Travis concludes, "Eschatology concerns the vindication of God's purposes for all creation. It calls people not so much to contemplate their individual destinies, as to allow the perspective of hope to influence the whole of life."[68] The activity of reading reflects one's general orientation towards the world as a whole, which is why chapter 7 will explore the eschatological implications of the Sabbath command as a means of being obediently oriented within the created order. As such, Sabbath is an extremely different means of awakening *poiesis* than that offered by Heidegger himself.

The chapters of Part II, each of which takes up one of these apperceptions, are coupled with a complementary chapter in Part I. As a whole they approach the question of reading from different perspectives, complementing one another whilst by no means remaining mutually exclusive. Chapters 1 and 7 address the end or purpose *for which* one reads, chapters 2 and 6 identify the community *in which* one reads, and chapters 3 and 5 assess the messianic readiness *with which* one reads.

READING AS ETHICAL ACTIVITY

These apperceptions each imply that reading a text involves more than reading a text. It is an action, and therefore always embodies an ethical dimension as it reaches into a world beyond the text. The argument will demonstrate that historicist hermeneutics, often understood simply as

---

66. At least in the sense of bringing eschatology to bear upon the present. (Not at all what C. H. Dodd meant by "realised eschatology." See Dodd, *The Parables of the Kingdom*.)

67. Heidegger, "The Question Concerning Technology," 321.

68. Travis, "Eschatology," 231.

Introduction: The Prominence of Technologist Interpretation 23

the science of interpretation,[69] is ill-equipped to engage a world beyond the text. This, it is argued, is largely attributable to the fact that it remains preoccupied with the historical distance that stretches out between modern readers and ancient writers. Consequently, other gaps, such as that which separates the life of the reader from the words of a text, are regarded as peripheral to the real business of interpretation.[70] This book will argue however, that reading is essentially an ethical activity.[71] This is by no means to assume that interpretation is fully explained by the reader's ethical comportment, although the ethical life fully affects the reader's interpretation. Rather, for the fully engaged reader there exists an ethical simultaneity between reading and living, between the world of the text and the world beyond the text.[72] There is nothing new to such a claim. It was assumed in the thought of Augustine, who regarded pride as a serious obstacle to apprehending scripture, a pride that issues in

---

69. Hamilton (*Historicism*), Jeanrond (*Theological Hermeneutics*), and even Thiselton (*The Two Horizons*) struggle to evade this critique.

70. Brian Stock draws attention to the variety of gaps identified by Augustine. Not only is Augustine aware of the gap between a reader and an author. Stock notes that according to Augustine, "We are separated from each other by a gulf that our external and internal senses cannot bridge [*De Libero Arbitro* 2.7.15; *Corpus Christianorum, Series Latina* 29.247.1–11; 36.183.23–27; 38.470.20–22; 39.1416.28–29]. We are like sojourners in a foreign land [*In Iohannis Euangelium Tractatus* CXXIV, 6.2; *Corpus Christianorum, Series Latina* 36.53.15–16], participants in a 'pilgrimage of the flesh,' in which 'hearts are closed off from each other' [*Enarrationes in Psalmos* 55.9; also *Corpus Christianorum, Series Latina* 39.684.8–9] . . . We are estranged from our 'native land' by an 'ocean': we are able to see the distant shore but not to reach it [*In Iohannis Euangelium Tractatus* CXXIV, 2.2; also *Corpus Christianorum, Series Latina* 36.12.20–25]." (Stock, *Augustine the Reader*, 15)

71. Reading the bible "ethically" is a concern taken up by the Scripture and Hermeneutics Seminar in the volume, *A Royal Priesthood?* (eds. Bartholomew et al.). Though the present thesis makes good use of some of the essays that comprise this compendium, it differs from the main focus of that volume in one important respect. The emphasis of the book is on reawakening the ethical and political demands of scripture, and as such brings a valuable and refreshing challenge to biblical interpretation. The argument of this thesis however, is not so much that reading should highlight both implicit and explicit ethical contents of scripture but that the very act of reading itself is inseparable from the *active* (as opposed to the *thinking*) life of the reader. By the term "ethical" is not meant a person's relation to a body of moral principles, but is used rather to describe the general *ethos* of the reader that predetermines the manner in which she approaches a text. This thesis argues that there is an ethical simultaneity in reading scripture in which the reader shapes and is shaped by the text.

72. An insight demonstrated by Schweitzer not so much from his writings, but from his missionary activity as described above.

a refusal to yield to the demands of scripture.[73] This book argues that such demands are not to be understood merely in the sense of theoretical assent to certain strategies to overcome the perceived chasm between ancients and moderns. On the contrary, they are demands which threaten, embrace and claim to transform the entire ethical orientation of the reader, addressing her Messianic orientation, her orientation towards others within and beyond her community, and her own personal teleological orientation. These considerations, fundamental to a full-blown engagement with scripture, tend to be marginalised by historicist hermeneutics and its exclusively textual focus.

Those who would import historicist hermeneutical theory into theological interpretation are left with an extremely limited scope for the Spirit's role as *didaskalos*.[74] The Holy Spirit's role in interpretation is then rather awkwardly inserted as a legitimization for a particular hermeneutical program.[75] Biblical interpretation however, is fundamentally not an exclusively textual enterprise, but as an activity that implicates

---

73. Augustine's notion of pride was based on the existence of a yawning chasm between the human quest for understanding and God himself, a chasm that is bridged only by the grace of God. For Augustine scripture has the effect of breaking the pride and sparing the reader from boredom (*De Doctrina Christiana* II:5 and 7. See also: I:23, 36; II:20; III:29, 33, 53).

74. E.g., Lategan produces a worthy overview of hermeneutical approaches, but the only "Spirit" that is mentioned is the "Spirit of the Enlightenment" (Lategan, "Hermeneutics").

75. The third person of the Trinity can sometimes make an appearance in biblical hermeneutic theory as the unwelcome relative that one is compelled to invite, but often has no substantive role (e.g., Macquarrie, *The Scope of Demythologising*.) It is in this context that Thiselton takes issue with Barth's emphasis on the Spirit's capacity to stand over-against (rather than merely to underwrite) one's interpretive endeavour (Thiselton, *The Two Horizons*, 88–90; Barth, *Word of God*, 28–50). Thiselton's critique of Barth is surprisingly wide of the mark. Chapter 6 below will distinguish between different aspects of communication in a manner that highlights Thiselton's misunderstanding (see Wannenwetsch, "Communication as Transformation"). Thiselton assumes that technical communication, the impartation of information from a sender to a receiver, is the only aspect of communicative practice. His critique of Barth betrays this assumption. However another aspect of communication, one that is transformative for communicators who are themselves exposed to the message communicated, is adopted by Barth, whose emphasis on the transforming capacity of the Spirit then makes perfect sense. Thiselton and Barth pass like ships in the night. One argues that the Spirit underwrites technical communication; the other that the Spirit stands over against the reader in transformational communication. Barth may be justly criticized for overstating the Spirit's role to threaten the reader's position, but Thiselton fails to reckon with Barth's wider notion of communication.

Introduction: The Prominence of Technologist Interpretation

the reader's entire life is one in which the reader is slain and raised by the Spirit. Does this mean that readers who have not been apprehended by the Spirit cannot participate meaningfully in reading scripture? Does this criterion threaten to undermine the public character of knowledge? This argument follows Barth in arguing that the necessary discipline of human listening does not restrict the freedom of God to speak when, where and how he wills.[76] The Spirit is no more incarcerated within the Christian community than within the temple.[77] As John V. Taylor argues, there is a level of communication that is enabled anonymously by the Spirit.

> What makes a landscape or a person or an idea come to life for me and become a presence towards which I surrender myself? I recognise, I respond, I fall in love, I worship—yet it was not I who took the first step. In every encounter there has been an anonymous third party who makes the introduction, acts as a go-between, makes two beings aware of each other, sets up a current of communication between them.[78]

This aspect of life in the Spirit is not extrinsic to the act of reading, but absolutely crucial if the sheer weight of the technological *Gestell* is to be taken seriously by those reading within the confines of the technological society. The Spirit's role as *didaskalos* is addressed by this book in the widest sense because, as Part I will now show, for those who inhabit this *Gestell*, "only a God can save us."[79]

---

76. Barth, *Church Dogmatics* I.1, 55.

77. See ch. 6 below.

78. Taylor, *Go Between God*, 17. Taylor however does not fall into the trap of presuming that the Spirit merely provides a hidden buttress to one's hermeneutical edifices, but draws attention as well to the Spirit's explicit transforming capacity.

79. Heidegger, *Der Spiegel*, May 31, 1976, (recorded in a 1966 interview with the proviso that it be published only posthumously). It is printed in full (translated by Maria P. Alter and John D. Caputo) in "Only God Can Save Us."

1

Demythologizing the Text

EARLY INFLUENCES ON BULTMANN'S THOUGHT

THE THREE CHAPTERS IN the first part of this thesis explore the extensive reach of the phenomenon identified by Heidegger as technologism, considering whether and to what extent its influence may be detected in various models of interpretive theory. This chapter focuses upon the biblical scholar Rudolf Bultmann (1884–1976), who consciously and carefully fostered a hermeneutical theory to shape his biblical interpretation. What follows cannot amount to a thoroughgoing critique of Bultmann's theological achievements, a task that is both beyond the scope of this thesis and one that has been thoroughly conducted by a host of incisive theological minds from a variety of perspectives.[1] The limited aim of this chapter is rather to locate Bultmann's interpretive theory, and some established critiques of his hermeneutics, in relation to the concerns of Heidegger as outlined in the introduction.

Structurally this chapter is coupled with chapter 7, which explores Barth's exposition of the Sabbath command and its relation to biblical interpretation. Though Bultmann and Barth shared many theological convictions, and indeed, a longstanding friendship, their approaches to hermeneutics were significantly different, a difference that clarifies the concerns of each thinker and one that is highlighted by chapters 1 and 7

---

1. E.g., Schmithals *Introduction to the Theology of Rudolf Bultmann*; Ogden, *Christ Without Myth*; Johnson, *The Origins of Demythologizing*.

taken together. (Chapter 7 will relate existential reading to the parable of the rich man and Lazarus [Luke 16:19–31], but this chapter will simply allude to the parable to highlight the shortcomings of Bultmann's notion of history). One of the major differences between Barth and Bultmann was their association with philosophy. Bultmann sought to embrace philosophy as an aid to theological understanding, whereas Barth saw it relativized by the revelation of Christ. In this light, Barth criticised Bultmann for being too attached to Heidegger.[2]

Given the collaboration between Heidegger and Bultmann, Marburg companions from 1923–28, it is hardly surprising that the former's influence upon the latter is often perceived as the chink in Bultmann's armor. But the mutual influence between the two thinkers was not a one-way street,[3] nor was Heidegger the only or even the major influence upon Bultmann's thought. Nineteenth century Lutheranism had a tremendous effect on his theological concerns, clearly leading Barth to note—albeit in a devastating critique of Bultmann's theology—that those who throw stones at Bultmann are likely to hit Luther.[4] It should also be noted that Barth and Bultmann both sought to respond to Nineteenth century Liberal Protestantism, and it is in this context that Dialectical Theology also made its mark upon Bultmann. The list could go on to include other figures and movements including the History of Religions School and the Marburg Neo-Kantians.[5] Treatments of these influences are offered by a variety of Bultmann commentators,[6] and demonstrate that Heidegger by no means set the agenda for Bultmann's concerns or for the program of demythologization.[7] In sum, Bultmann's demythologizing program is not properly understood as a theological version of Heidegger's existentialism.

Bultmann's importance as a biblical interpreter hardly needs stating, but is of particular interest for this thesis because of the several concerns

---

2. Barth and Bultmann, *Letters*, 65.

3. Safranski's biography of Heidegger notes Bultmann as having contributed to the structure of *Being and Time* (Safranski, *Heidegger*, 40).

4. Barth, "Rudolf Bultmann," 126.

5. Thiselton tracks the influences upon Bultmann's thought in a brilliant and lucid chapter in his *Two Horizons* (205–26). The paucity of reference to Kierkegaard in Thiselton's chapter however, is rather curious. See further below.

6. E.g., Johnson, *Bultmann*; and Schmithals, *Rudolf Bultmann*.

7. This is the point made by Thiselton, *Two Horizons*, 226; and Jeanrond, *Theological Hermeneutics*, 137–41.

he consistently pursued throughout his career. He was acutely aware of the dangers designated by technologism, and remained committed to the belief that the Jesus of the Gospels should not be innocuously restricted to the world of the text. Biblical interpretation for Bultmann is inescapably self-involving, engaging the subjective world of the reader with the stark challenge of otherness. The twentieth century reader, with a scientific worldview was automatically thought to be dislocated from the world in which the New Testament was forged, a world informed by and dependent upon what today is called mythology. Bultmann rejected the liberal notion that the mythological elements of the New Testament could be discarded, as he also rejected the notion that they could be reduced to the attempt to articulate human moral ideals and filtered down into some form of a social Gospel. Bultmann rather insisted upon taking seriously the myths, seeking to hear their essential challenge for the modern reader and to do so by interpreting them. In the light of subsequent research Bultmann's particular interpretation of perceived myths may appear dated, but as demonstrated below, if his core interpretations have been largely superseded, essential elements of his interpretive methodology remain central to the concerns of contemporary mainstream biblical hermeneutics.

OBJECTIFICATION

If Bultmann's program of "demythologization" is to be fully appreciated, then clearly in the first instance his concept of "myth" must be unpacked. Across the span of his prolific writings, the constitution of myth takes different forms and appears to serve different purposes.[8] Before exploring the role of myth in Bultmann's thought, however, a prior question must also be addressed, namely the question of why myths present a problem in the first place. This was a major source of contention in the dialogue with Barth. After Barth's famously provocative lecture, "*Rudolf Bultmann, Ein Versuch ihn zu verstehen*," the heated correspondence that ensued led to a conclusion that helps to clarify the reason for Bultmann's overriding concerns about mythology: "It was materially impressive

---

8. Thiselton, *Two Horizons*, 252–58.

to me," writes Barth, ". . . that for you the really irksome thing about 'mythological thinking' turns out to be its 'objectifying.'"[9]

Bultmann's theological rejection of "objectification" was a constituent element of his own thought from the earliest stage, and as Roger Johnson points out, is most likely attributable to Marburg Neo-Kantianism in general and the influence of his teacher, Wilhelm Herrman in particular.[10] The term is used almost exclusively by Bultmann in a pejorative sense,[11] since by it he does not mean to criticize the mind's orientation to its object. Far from it, rather, he is fiercely opposed to the mind's own *construction* of objects, objects that do not in fact exist. Such construction serves to achieve the clarity of structured thought. While this activity is valid in a provisional sense for certain disciplines, it is wholly inappropriate for a mode of thought which seeks to engage the wholly other.[12] The contrast with Cartesian idealism is obvious. For Bultmann, the thinking subject does not encounter a world of detached objects awaiting investigation, because—and this parallels Heidegger's early work—the subject is always already interconnected with the objects it encounters. The illusory activity of creating objects that serve to secure one's position in the world is what Bultmann signifies with the term "objectifying." The reasons for the repulsion he adopts towards objectifying thought in relation to theology are obvious: A God construed as Wholly Other cannot at the same time be encountered in objectifying thought, because for Bultmann the movement of such an enterprise is always in one direction. Without exception, the God of objectification is nothing other than an idol forged by human hands.

Bultmann counters the objectified God of myth, with an extensive, if idiosyncratic, use of eschatology. Eschatology certainly does not refer to a planned sequence of chronological events in which God himself is destined to bring an end to human history. Eschatology, in line with the entire pattern of Bultmann's theological program, is de-historicized;[13] that is, it

---

9. Barth, *Letters*, 106.

10. See Johnson, *Bultmann*, ch. 3.

11. A notable exception appears to be found in a lecture delivered in 1925 entitled "The Problem of a Theological Exegesis of the New Testament," published in Johnson, *Rudolf Bultmann*, 129–37.

12. A rather troubled concept as outlined in the Introduction above, and discussed further below.

13. See further below p. 211.

becomes a decisive event in the life of the subject. This version of eschatology[14] is set up deliberately over against the eschatological machinations of objectification. Johnson makes the point with succinct perception:

> When I think in an objectifying way, I give a certain permanence to the objects of my thought, whether they are ideas or things, physical or spiritual. But eschatology apprehends God without any taint of permanence. God's word happens in a moment, an eschatological moment, which cannot be fitted into chronological time.[15]

In Bultmann's 1926 portrayal of Jesus,[16] the future is invoked only to compel decision in the present. The kingdom of God (supposed by Bultmann to signify the irruption of God's rule at the end of time) is an eschatological mythology that deconstructs itself as it serves its purpose, bringing the crisis of the future to bear upon the present life of the believing subject.

Eschatology then is interpreted out of the future and into the crucial moment of the believer's decision.[17] Conversely, since eschatology presupposes the otherness, or more precisely the otherworldliness of God, he cannot be casually regarded as the hidden shaper of natural events in the everyday world because to do so is once again to fall into the objectivist pattern of thought. The Wholly Other does not provide security for, but rather provokes crisis in the believing subject. As Johnson has shown most clearly,[18] objectifying thought and eschatology are exclusively alternative means of engaging with the world. As a version of objectification, the concept of mythology is inevitably going to be a major target for the incisive challenge of Bultmann's theology.

MYTHOLOGY

There is no single, unified conceptuality for the notion of myth as it functions within the Bultmann corpus. Three distinct and apparently

---

14. Prefigured in the writings of Nietzsche (*Will to Power*, 1053–1067).

15. Johnson, *Bultmann*, 25–26

16. Bultmann, *Jesus and the Word*, 33–40.

17. Again, anticipated in Nietzsche's notion of eternal recurrence, teleology without telos. Nietzsche, *Will to Power*, 1053–67.

18. Johnson, *Bultmann*, 29.

incompatible uses of the term "myth" are detectable in Bultmann's writings, as Thiselton has shown.[19] First, and most importantly, myth designates the desire for objectification—as outlined above. While objectification is necessary for human thought, to bring God into the realm of time (in accordance with the mythological eschatology mentioned above) or space (resulting similarly in the objectified permanence of a triple-decker universe) is essentially an idolatrous scheme. The supposedly wholly other is thereby subsumed by the patterns of the this-worldly, and the dynamic event of God's self-revelation is displaced by the predictable and controllable notion of permanent guaranteed familiarity forged by the hands of objectified knowledge.[20] As Barth had perceived, it was this objectification that lay behind Bultmann's desire to interpret rather than to accept the mythological conceptions of scripture.[21]

Secondly, there is the apparently more innocent observation that the entire "worldview" in which the New Testament was forged was "mythological"; that is, a particular way of making sense of everyday phenomena. In a pre-scientific era, it is supposed, events that would one day be described within a strict cause and effect nexus (e.g., a thunderclap as a meteorological inevitability given a natural and predictable set of causal conditions), were primitively described as this-worldly manifestations of divine action (e.g., a thunderclap expresses divine anger). As such, it may be inferred, particular myths are merely expressions of this much wider framework for making sense of humanity's place in the cosmos. Since myths are the product of a pre-scientific worldview, it is necessary to mine through the pre-scientific deposits beneath which their essence is hidden in order that the dynamic event of their kerygmatic challenge may be encountered. In other words, the mythological worldview of the New Testament dangerously distracts the modern reader from that challenge to authenticity that profoundly configures its writings.

To harmonize these two approaches to myth is no easy task because the former treats myth as the idolatrous objectification of the divine, whilst the second is the inevitable action of those who lived with a pre-scientific worldview. It forms a tension in Bultmann's writings that has

---

19. Thiselton, *Two Horizons*, 252–58.

20. The notion of Crisis in Luther's theology fulfils this same function, as he sought to reawaken the crises encountered in his own conversion in the lives of his fellow Germans (see Beutel, "Luther's Life," 8–9).

21. Barth, *Letters*, 106.

been criticized at some length,[22] but is outlined here to highlight the question of why he committed such a sustained assault upon mythological thought. If objectification was indeed his main target, then he cannot, as is often supposed, be regarded simply as a theologian battling to make Christianity relevant for the modern world. Far from it, his overriding purpose was not to make biblical claims palatable to those with a post-mythological worldview, but rather to expose the scientific world to the discomforting call to decision issued by the New Testament from behind the veil of mythological language. From this perspective, and in the light of the first two conceptions of mythology Bultmann's third use of myth makes perfect sense. The first conception of myth shows how Bultmann wished to remove the superstitious hindrances to hearing the New Testament accounts (such as the three decker universe, physical healings and the like). The second view of myth suggests that he was neutral about the worldview of the New Testament writings (since every age, including our own, is bound to have *some* projected objectification of its environing realm) and merely wanted to ensure that readers of the New Testament are exposed to its essential challenge. In this second case, demythologization is only an attempt to make us conscious of the elaborate picture frame (the myth) so that we can now look past it into the eyes of the portrait. Although in both cases, Bultmann regards mythology as a problem, in the first case it is a *vicious* problem (revealing a need for false security amongst the communities that produced the New Testament writings), while in the second case it is a straightforward hermeneutical problem (that of understanding a message which has been uttered within a past horizon which is unfamiliar to us). The thought that *keeping the mythology intact* might be a necessary part of receiving the message is specifically rejected by Bultmann in both cases.

Here Kierkegaard's influence upon Bultmann also comes to the fore with the third function of mythological thinking, namely its call to existential decision.[23] In view of the concerns already present in Bultmann's

---

22. E.g., Henderson, *Myth in the New Testament*; R. W. Hepburn, "Demythologising and the Problem of Validity"; both quoted in Thiselton, *Two Horizons*, 254.

23. While Paul Ricoeur very much approved of Bultmann's emphasis on demythologization to the extent that it enlarged interpretive questions beyond authorial intention, he highlighted an important weakness in Bultmann's acceptance of Heidegger: he did not follow Heidegger far enough (Ricoeur, *Essays*, 72). The later Heidegger's turn to language was not followed by Bultmann, leaving unaddressed a series of questions raised by demythologization. Chief among them, is the question of why a sophisticated

theology, existential categories lend themselves readily to his interpretive proposals. Bultmann states that

> [the] real purpose of myth is not to present an objective picture of the world as it is (*ein objectives Weltbild*), but to express man's understanding of himself in the world in which he lives. Myth should be interpreted not cosmologically, but anthropologically, or better still, existentially.[24]

Bultmann has not, as is sometimes supposed, become so infatuated with existentialism that he chooses to impose Heideggerian categories upon the New Testament.[25] Rather, in existentialism he identifies a means of making sense of the subject in the world that lends clarity to the New Testament's own call for repentance. His radical attempt to liberate the readers of scripture from enslavement to objectified conceptions of God and the world makes him an important figure in relation to the technologism outlined above. Bultmann's call to *ek-sist* is certainly consistent with a desire to 'stand outside' what Heidegger would later call the technologist *Gestell*. To consider fully the significance of this existentialist interpretation for Bultmann, it is necessary to hear it within the context of his understanding of history.

HISTORY IN BULTMANN'S EXISTENTIAL INTERPRETATION

The role of history in Bultmann's thinking is ambiguous to say the least. On the one hand he discusses his interpretive proposals as "de-historicized," while on the other he takes with utmost seriousness the historical context in which the New Testament was compiled. Bultmann's view

---

hermeneutic is applied to those elements of the New Testament deemed "mythological," and not to other apparently straightforward kerygmatic calls to existential decision.

24. Bultmann, *Kerygma and Myth*, 10; quoted by Thiselton, *Two Horizons*, 256.

25. It is debatable whether Heidegger, even in the apparently anthropocentric *Being and Time*, was not rather a philosopher of Being than an existentialist. He addressed the question of being via an anthropological route, but subsequently sought the question of Being through poetry, and later still through apophatic waiting. Bultmann's interests, being invested primarily in the human condition, were more anthropocentric than Heidegger's. In his 1966 book *Heidegger, Being, and Truth*, Lazlo Versenyi criticizes Heidegger for *not* being primarily interested in the human condition. Heidegger's primary interest in Being renders his thought more theocentric than Bultmann (see Heidegger, *Being and Time*).

of history is largely attributable to his Lutheran conceptions.[26] In *The Freedom of a Christian* (1520) Luther himself had argued, "I believe that it is now become clear that it is not enough or in any sense Christian to preach the works, life, and words of Christ as historical facts, as if the knowledge of these would suffice for the conduct of life . . ."[27] Far from discarding the importance of history, Luther instead argued that to take history seriously is to be subjectively confronted by Christ, not as Christ is in himself, but as he is in relation to me.[28] Bultmann follows Luther in accentuating the present encounter with Christ, but is then left with an ambiguous notion of history. Unlike Luther, Bultmann seems to nullify history in ways that become problematic for biblical interpretation.

First, Bultmann was heir to the tradition of the *religionsgeschichtliche Schule*, with its emphasis on the awesome historical distance between the New Testament and the twentieth century. The influence is clearly perceived in Bultmann's identification of the sheer incompatibility between the scientific era of his contemporaries and the mythological worldview through which the *kerygma* is processed. (The extent to which the New Testament is saturated with mythology is another insight attributed by Bultmann to the History of Religion School.)[29] This movement was a major influence in this respect, and the distance it sought to identify between the contemporary reader and the biblical Jesus is to be understood in the light of late nineteenth century assumptions about access to the historical Christ.

Regarding Jesus as an example of moral goodness and timeless ethics meant that he was in danger of becoming thoroughly domesticated by the modern world.[30] It was in order to de-familiarize him that the

26. Luther's influence upon Bultmann is widely recognized, although Johnson points out, it was mediated via nineteenth-century Lutheranist filters, leaving an emphasis on the dualism of an individual / threatening world rather than of the sinner / judging God (see Johnson, *Bultmann*, 33–35). Lutheran influence upon Bultmann came not only through his deliberate study, but more subtly through the general theological context of his day, mediated largely by Bultmann's own father (see Schmithals, *Rudolf Bultmann*, 3).

27. Luther, "Freedom," 282.

28. Luther, "Freedom," 284. This will be explored in more detail when considering Bonhoeffer in chapter 5.

29. Bartsch *Kerygma and Myth*, 14.

30. There is a complex history behind this belief. Religious wars—most notably the 30 Years War (1618–1648) and the English Civil war (1641–45/49)—created a popular discontent with doctrinaire religion. Combined with this was the Newtonian

History of Religion School focused on the otherness of the apocalyptic Jesus. The existence of this gulf is taken for granted in all historicist hermeneutical models and was one source of Bultmann's historical distantiation. Another figure worthy of mention is Martin Kahler (1835–1912) who believed that the historical Jesus was of no importance, emphasizing instead the present experience of Christ as encountered in preaching.[31] In his view, the historical critics of his day obscured the real Christ by rendering him accessible to a privileged elite only. Although there are important differences between Kahler and Bultmann (in that the former rejects the problem of the historical Jesus whilst the latter faces it readily), Thiselton claims that "Kahler provides Bultmann with his radical contrast between objective past-history (*Historie*) and history which is significant for the present (*Geschichte*)."[32] Thiselton's reading of Kahler's influence here is somewhat misleading, in that this was a distinction both Kahler and Bultmann would have found in Kierkegaard, and was a well circulated topic by their era.[33] It was a distinction central to Bultmann's

---

Revolution. Natural science and reason—since it so successfully unravelled nature's mysteries—evidently cohered with the (rational) structure of the universe and overwhelmingly proved the existence of a rational supreme being. A result of this was a strong Unitarian tendency (manifested especially in Deism but also in the philosopher Locke), which tended to reduce Jesus to the level of a divinely authenticated moral teacher. Kant reinforced the notion that religion is about morality and the moral will, but the rational and moral Jesus, in the gospels was encrusted in primitive Judaic myth. Thus in the nineteenth century many theologians felt the superstitious element of the Jesus story needed to be stripped away to reveal the core divine impulse. This was the argument, for example of J. G. Eichhorn (1752–1857), and other early Romantic theologians. The anti-Semite, E. Renan (1823–1892), who wrote a widely influential *Life of Jesus*, offered a later Romantic foray into this kind of religion (In the attempt to discover the needle of religious truth in the haystack of semitic culture). The Hegelian, D. F. Strauss (1808–1874), took a similar route in his *Life of Jesus* (1835), turned into English by George Eliot, who lost her faith as she translated. By contrast, there were a few theologians like Bishop Robert Lowth (1710–1787) who instead argued that the "mythological" outlook of the Hebrew OT writers was a thoroughly appropriate medium for poetically rendering truths about God.

31. Kahler, *Historical Jesus*, 66.

32. Thiselton, *Two Horizons*, 215.

33. E.g., Kierkegaard: "When the question [of the relation between studying the gospels as history and appropriating or being appropriated by their message] is treated in an objective manner it becomes impossible for the subject to face the decision with passion, least of all with an infinitely interested passion." Kierkegaard, *Concluding Unscientific Postscript*, 32. The whole of Part 1 of this book (is devoted to this problem "The Objective problem of the truth of Christianity," and it is then developed in Part 2.

claims about history, as discussed below, and the great void (of *Historie*) that separates modern readers from the historical Jesus forms the basis of his hermeneutical schema.[34]

It is this apparently unbridgeable historical chasm that Bultmann seeks to span with his model of existential interpretation. Secondly, however, to do so Bultmann refuses to work within the parameters set by what would later be termed "historicism," a phenomenon considered in chapters 2 and 4 below. This is an issue addressed in a 1925 Marburg lecture entitled "Das Problem einer theologischen Exegese des Neuen Testament,"[35] in which Bultmann rejects the validity of historical interpretations that do not seriously engage the subject.

> From texts so interpreted, the attempt is made to understand history without asking whether there are perhaps fundamental realities in history which may be grasped only by giving up a detached position, only by being ready to take a stand. To be sure, New Testament exegesis does not say that what is there is no ultimate concern to a person. However, exegesis itself is not determined by this *tua res agitur* (your interest at stake), but proceeds on the basis of the expectant, neutral attitude of the exegete. Historical and psychological exegesis establish primarily that this or that has been thought, said, or done at a particular time and under such and such historical circumstances and psychological conditions, without reflecting on the meaning and demands of what is said. For these views, to the extent that a particular aspect has a significance beyond the moment, that significance is only from the viewpoint of regularity (mostly causal) of events, and thus history becomes a great relational connection in which every particular manifestation is only relative.[36]

From here it becomes clear that, as for the early Barth, for Bultmann to take history seriously means to be confronted by it. Anticipating much later theological hermeneutics,[37] and indeed one of the central claims of this thesis, Bultmann insists that one cannot take a text seriously by engaging with it on merely historical grounds. To take history seriously

---

34. Again, it was Kierkegaard again that forced this issue and engaged Lessing (Kierkegaard, *Concluding Unscientific Postscript*, 86–87).

35. See Johnson, *Bultmann*, 129–57.

36. Bultmann, *Jesus and the Word*, 131.

37. Kierkegaard again.

is to be confronted with "the problematic character of our existence"[38]; and, equally, to address the question of our existence seriously is to be confronted by history, almost as though it were a person. This means that to listen to history and to listen to the biblical text is to "confront the text just as we confront other men to whom we stand in living relationship and with whom we first achieve any existence at all, that is, in the relation of I and Thou."[39] Here Bultmann approaches the very essence of existentialist interpretation, arguing that because encounter with a text is not merely an exercise but an event, any attempt to reconstruct history will result in some form of objectification consistent with the manner in which it viewed.[40] Instead, since humans have their being in dynamic encounter with others, so history itself constitutes an 'other' that can stand over against its inquirer in critical relationship with them. "Just these relations," he continues, "are temporal events for us, events which bear the character of decision, so then the existential encounter of history takes place in temporal moments which demand our decision."[41]

Therein lies the critical insight of Bultmann's brand of existential interpretation, which highlights its third and most controversial historical claim, namely that history, in order to be truly historical, must be dehistoricized. Bultmann states his case most clearly in his *Theology of the New Testament*, where he claims that Jesus himself "'dehistoricized' God and man; that is, released the relation between God and man from its previous ties to history (history considered as the affairs of nations)."[42] What may be deemed as political history is utterly superfluous and perhaps even a hindrance to the message of Jesus. Simultaneously, however, Jesus also "radically 'historicized' God in a different sense of history."[43] Judaism he claims, had already de-historicized humanity and God by placing one high above the heavens and the other deeply rooted in the earth, a disjointed relationship exacerbated by the ritual and legal systems which only served to accentuate the distance between divinity

---

38. Bultmann, *History and Eschatology*, 23.

39. Bultmann, *Jesus Christ and Mythology*, 134. Not surprisingly, Buber himself was associated with Marburg Neo-Kantianism.

40. Interesting examples of how this can be done were provided by Bornkamm *Jesus of Nazareth*; and Bornkamm, *Paul*.

41. Bultmann, *Jesus Christ and Mythology*, 134.

42. Bultmann, *Jesus and the Word*, 25.

43. Bultmann, *Jesus and the Word*, 25.

and humanity. Into this context, Jesus places the word of God before humanity, "which tears [humanity] out of all security of any kind and places him at the brink of the end."[44] Jesus' portrayal of an eschatological God who confronts each individual with the stark realization of his or her own end, lifts human being from its historical context into direct relation to God. Bultmann summarizes the paradoxical nature of this de-historicization:

> Precisely that God, who stands aloof from the history of nations, meets each man in his own little history, his everyday life with its daily gift and demand; de-historicized man (i.e. naked of his supposed security within his historical group) is guided into his concrete encounter with his neighbour, in which he finds his true history.[45]

Thus existential encounter with the divine takes precedence over the triviality of historical context and history is understood in terms of interpersonal relationships to the exclusion of national political contexts. Naturally this has enormous implications for biblical interpretation, and Bultmann's entire approach to history is fraught with difficulty as discussed below. A full blown critique of Bultmann is out of the question here, but the narrative in which his thought has been placed above enables some of his key hermeneutical moves to be clearly seen and critiqued in light of Heidegger's description of technologism. Several aspects of his interpretive thought will now be traced in light of what has been said above, and within an appreciation for the overall intention of Bultmann's lifelong concern to allow scripture to be heard in a technological age.

THE INSUFFICIENCY OF BULTMANN'S CONCEPT OF HISTORY

To be sure, Bultmann's dogged insistence that historical exegesis cannot be conducted from the safe position of a detached observer can only be affirmed. What is to be questioned is that, given Bultmann's strategy for ensuring existential encounter with scripture, what does history look like after he has finished with it? When history as regards the political aspirations of nations and kingdoms is excluded from the realm of

---

44. Bultmann *Jesus and the Word*, 25.
45. Bultmann, *Theology of the New Testament*, 1:25–26.

genuine history, how far can the remainder of history then claim to be history at all? This is not a question meant to deny the importance of individual decision within the stream of history, but if the context in which personal identity is forged is supplanted by an existential history that reveals political contexts as distractions from genuine existence, surely one has pre-ordained the extent to which history as a whole can confront the individual as Bultmann intends. There are several key elements of these historical problems that are not easily disentangled, but which need to be addressed on their own terms.

The existential nature of Bultmann's theology is often too hastily attributed to Heidegger,[46] even though Bultmann's own thought was quite far advanced by the time he and Heidegger became colleagues in 1923. A more prominent source for Bultmann's understanding of history is to be found in Kierkegaard, whose anti-Hegelian polemic was well known in the early twentieth century Germany academy.[47] The first part of the *Concluding Unscientific Postscript* is devoted to 'the objective problem,' which as outlined above is of enormous significance for Bultmann.[48] For Kierkegaard, Christianity is rooted in the historical life, death, and resurrection of Jesus. In contrast to Hegel's idea of a generative seed of human consciousness, God incarnate is the basis of Christianity. But as a historical event, this incarnation can only be appropriated by an act of faith.[49] In his sustained critique of Christendom, leveled against the view that Christian faith could be considered in purely historical terms, Kierkegaard emphasized with dramatic effect the importance of faith. He deliberately attempts to precipitate a crisis of faith in his reader, resulting in an individuated notion of history—the historical becomes actual in the faith-encounter of the believer.[50]

It is only a small step from Kierkegaard to Bultmann's notion of history. For Bultmann the significance of history arises from the more

---

46. For instance, Thiselton is right to note that much of Bultmann's conceptual framework was derived from Heidegger, other strong influences—including that of Kierkegaard—are under-emphasized in the overall course of his analysis.

47. In this discussion, Heidegger's own conception of history was doubtlessly influential for Bultmann, but as a participant in a tradition that flows from the pen of Kierkegaard.

48. Kierkegaard, *Concluding Unscientific Postscript*, 13–55.

49. E.g., Kierkegaard, *Concluding Unscientific Postscript*, 208–9.

50. Many of his statements are provocative and challenging, drawn from curious standpoints (hence his masks or pseudonyms).

primal position of the existing individual.[51] The historical nature of biblical texts is then drastically reconfigured by Bultmann's relentless call to individual decision. The elements that comprise salvation history, the importance of a national community and their fate, the climax of prophetic fulfillment and the very notion of messiahship are all simply the disposable wrappings that once contained an essential kerygma geared to evoke individual decision. Historical texts effectively become the raw material from which a Christ who calls for existential decision in the present may be technologically manufactured anew. Whatever narrative biblical texts may be conceived as embodying, regardless of what may appear to be the most natural and obvious reading, this must be mined through in order to extract the truer, more essential existential core. The result is that the supposedly true meanings are extracted from their historical context and relocated in a radically different historical framework. The text, so it seems, has become what Heidegger was later to term "standing reserve."[52] As such it is comprehensively shorn of its capacity to stand over against those who would en-counter, and thereby be challenged by it. Demythologization, then, may be regarded as a tool; but when it is the only tool with which one approaches every text, one already knows what the text contains before having to read it. (To a man with a hammer everything looks like a nail!) History may be discarded as disposable objectification, prophecy as primitive attempts to frame a cause and event nexus, and myths expelled as the exhaust fumes of the kerygmatic machine.

In Bultmann's defense, such an unqualified technologization was certainly not his intention. Indeed, he argued for the provisional nature of any reading strategy that is taken to scripture[53]. In practice however, demythologization, though a useful way of reading, effectively made impossible—or at least pronounced as illegitimate—other ways of approaching the text.[54]

51. A thoroughly Kierkegaardian phrase (e.g., Bultmnn, *Existence and Faith*, 106–8) which points again to the common source of much of Bultmann and Kahler's thought.

52. Heidegger, "The Question Concerning Technology," 322.

53. Bultmann, *Theology of the New Testament*, 349–350.

54. In his assessment of how theological hermeneutics evolved, Werner Jeanrond (*Theological Hermeneutics*) assumes (with Bultmann and against Barth) that one's theoretical openness to a variety of philosophical hermeneutical models can remain in place as one adopts an existentialist reading of the text. (See Bultmann *Existence and Faith*, 342–52.) Jeanrond attempts to support such a view by forcing a sharp dis-

Chapter 7 below provides an eschatological reading of the parable of the rich man and Lazarus (Luke 16:19–31) that addresses Bultmann's concerns to allow history to engage the personal life of the reader. From the parable we may infer this necessity, as the rich man is condemned for his inability to hear Moses and the Prophets (Luke 16:31), separated as they were from him by the chasm of centuries. But what Bultmann fails to take seriously enough is just how such hearing might take place, that is, just how readily one's presuppositions can be recognized, let alone abandoned. This in turn raises the question about whether responsible individuals are prone to create their own histories, thus determining in advance a diminished capacity to "ek-sist." The celebration of the Sabbath, it will be argued, allows the reader to be personally confronted, but not in so individualistic a manner as Bultmann's hermeneutics suggest.[55] Sabbath remains a corporate activity[56] that nevertheless requires the "ek-sistence" of the believing individual.

Bultmann's readiness to allow history to be grounded in the existing individual is largely a reaction to the historical skepticism of his context.[57] The vital importance of taking seriously the historical void

---

tinction between one's pre-held hermeneutic convictions as *determining* (Barth) on the one hand and as *conditioning* (Bultmann) on the other. In our view those words will simply not bear the distinction Jeanrond foists upon them. More importantly, Jeanrond sides with Bultmann as he criticizes Barth's interpretive starting point which lay in the transformative presence of the Holy Spirit rather than in the philosophical location of the reader. Jeanrond's conclusion to this defense of Bultmann unwittingly yields all the ground to Barth, when Jeanrond states that "as long as our discussion of the interpretative conditions is a truly open discussion, one fails to see why God's Spirit should not be able to lead us towards an always deeper appreciation of the truth of the Bible precisely through such a discussion" (*Theological Hermeneutics*, 137). The question of this "openness" is taken far too lightly by Bultmann and by Jeanrond, both of whom fail to take into account the determinative nature of sin, a problem that the present thesis follows Barth in addressing (see Part II below). More ironically Jeanrond here unwittingly affirms Barth by making the guiding presence of the Holy Spirit a prior condition for subsequent philosophical discussion.

55. Bultmann's particular form of individualism is addressed below.

56. Ch. 7 below.

57. If it is in any way dependent upon Kierkegaard's critique it was grounded in the need to allow the scriptures to have a subjective impact on the reader. Kierkegaard, like Martin Kahler was concerned that the application of historical criticism to scripture was not only whittling away the content of the Christian faith, but endlessly deferring the crisis of being genuinely encountered by the text. Only when the last word was written by the skeptical historical critics would we (apparently) have permission to believe whatever was left. Kierkegaard cut through this historico-critical skepticism and

between contemporary readers and New Testament authors cannot be denied,[58] and since it appears that Bultmann accepted the centrality of this void for the sake of humility towards history, his intent can only be praised. The question to be asked of Bultmann is whether in fact, this apparently humble stance towards history resulted in a surreptitious arrogance towards historical possibility.

Bultmann's 1926 reading of the parable of the rich man and Lazarus demonstrates both his good intentions and their unfortunate effects. His commentary comes within the context of a comprehensive denial about Jesus' demand for anything that resembled a social reform. By this stage Bultmann is already heralding the primacy of individual decision over any particular social qualities or ascetic techniques.[59] There is no call for a reformed social order in the preaching of Jesus. On such issues as the imbalance of wealth and social injustice, claims Bultmann, Jesus has nothing to say—a point deliberately intended to deny the portrait of him as a great social reformer.[60] With Bultmann one can only agree on this issue, but there is one awkward biblical passage that he thinks does not accord with the claims about social reform:

> There is only one passage in the gospel record in which a rich man is declared deserving of hell-fire simply because he is rich, and a poor man simply because he is poor is found worthy to be carried by the angels to Abraham's bosom—the story of the rich man and Lazarus. (Luke 16.19–26) This is unique, and is probably not a genuine part of the preaching of Jesus.[61]

From this claim several questions may be raised,[62] but the focus here is the problem that arises from historical skepticism. The merits

---

declared all that such historical attempts to establish "what happened" miss the point that confronts the individual. That is, that I, *here and now, am challenged to the root of my being* by *this* gospel text.

58. Lessing's *ugly historical ditch* that Kierkegaard wanted to bridge by the existential leap of faith. See, as above, Kierkegaard, *Concluding Unscientific Postscript*, 86–97.

59. Bultmann, *Jesus and the Word*, 77.

60. E.g., Adolf von Harnack (1851–1930).

61. Bultmann, *Jesus and the Word*, 78–79. Conversely Luke 16:19–26 is regarded as authentic by Crossan, who instead rejects vv. 27–31 as inauthentic, as discussed in chapters 3 and 5 below.

62. E.g., the assumption that the parable is talking about social reform, and conversely the failure to discuss the historical context in which allusions were made apocalyptically to the political and social realities of the day. Such criticisms however arise

of historical distantiation are operative simultaneously with a bold re-writing of history that presumes no historical distance whatsoever. Bultmann burns the hermeneutical bridge of social reform that links an ancient Jesus with a modern concern, only by hurling himself across the unbridgeable chasm of history to burn that bridge from the far side. In order to support the historical portrait of an apocalyptic antagonist with no interest in socio-political realities, he retains sufficient confidence to discard the parable's originality on the lips of a historical Jesus as improbable.[63] This highlights something of an incongruity in Bultmann, in that one cannot accuse him of being uninterested in history on the basis of construing history itself existentially. Bultmann has plenty to say about the historical Jesus, even if he does so in an elusive manner. His brief reading of the parable rather demonstrates that, echoing the claims about existential history above, Bultmann has a preconceived notion of historical possibility, and one that is far from provisional or transformable because it leapfrogs the perceived void of history with a certainty (not only a probability) that goes wholly unacknowledged. Although one may object that Bultmann has simply portrayed his own version of history from his standpoint as an individual existentialist, it must again be noted that such a history is thereby mechanically sterilized, or in Heidegger's words, "technologically enframed." The existentialist may well remain unwittingly immune to any demands of history that would lead to the radical re-formation of personal existence.[64]

The third problematic aspect of history is inherited, represented and endorsed by Bultmann in a manner that escapes not only his attention but also that of all historicist hermeneutical programs that suppose themselves to constitute biblical interpretation. It is a problem that is a prime concern of this thesis, and one that is accentuated by Bultmann's

---

from research that has been conducted long after Bultmann wrote, so cannot constitute a very sharp critique of Bultmann himself. See the interpretation of the parable offered in chapter 5 below.

63. Bultmann, *Theology of the New Testament*, 77.

64. To be existentially challenged by Jesus, we must first surrender our historical judgment to Bultmann. Kierkegaard's is not a parallel case, partly because he does not reject the incarnation, and partly because he deliberately precipitates such a crisis in the reader, by paradoxes, shocking statements and masked perspectives. For example, he wrote under the pseudonym of St. John the Climacus (c. 579–649), the severe Christian ascetic hermit, who lived in solitude on Mt. Sinai and who wrote the challenging book *The Ladder of Divine Ascent*.

failure to address it. More precisely for Bultmann, it is not so much the problem as the proposed solution to the problem that is fundamentally problematic. Like Barth, Bultmann was acutely aware that to engage with a biblical text it must engage the extra-textual life of the reader, and Bultmann's interpretive program reflects this important concern fully. However, whilst Bultmann's whole existential strategy for hearing scripture is intended to resolve this issue, in reality it exacerbates it for the following reasons.

Bultmann rightly perceives a historical distance between reader and text, and yet invests such enormous significance in this gap, that it is regarded as the single most important gap between reader and text. This is far from the case. Of much greater theological import is the distance that stretches out between text and reader. This is not attributable to a set of moral principles to which readers strive to measure up, but refers rather to humanity's fallenness as manifested in its congenital propensity to resist the will of God as encountered in scripture. Attention might also be drawn to the relational distance between individual subjects in an era of individualism, an issue that is inextricably intertwined with the human capacity to be transformed by the otherness encountered in other people. This is a problem that is explored in the next chapter and for which a theological response is offered in chapter 6. Part of the implication of the parable of the rich man and Lazarus is clearly that the way that one responds to people is fundamentally linked to the manner in which one responds to a text. This, as discussed in part II of this thesis, is the climax of the parable: "If [the rich man's brothers] do not listen to Moses and the Prophets, neither will they be convinced even if someone rises from the dead" (Luke 16:31). This emphasizes the need not only for reading in community, with its commonplace exposure to other perspectives that is now in popular demand in contemporary hermeneutical theses, but also the question of whether community members are truly transformed by such communal reading practices. These are not the only distances that are relevant for the purposes of biblical interpretation, but they cannot be bracketed out from a consideration of how the text is to confront the reader. That a text cannot be fully understood from a historical-critical reading alone Bultmann had seen well enough. The problem that lies with his alternative strategy is that it still appeals to history in order to bridge gaps that are not of a historical nature.[65]

---

65. Bultmann was an individualist, but not necessarily in the negative sense implied

There is no refuge to be found in referring to Bultmann's reconceived notion of existential history. As discussed above, it remains necessary for Bultmann to portray a messianic figure to fit his purposes, but to do so by no means guarantees the existential transformation of the reader. In many cases the opposite effect is more than probable because whilst it may create the impression of a wild-eyed agitator of interpretive familiarity, such a portrait can be every bit as domesticated as gentle Jesus meek and mild. If anything this former conception of the historical Jesus is more dangerously impotent because the reader will be incapable of seeing that its supposedly provocative apocalyptic prophet is a mere docile fabrication. This is precisely the danger that lies at the heart of Heidegger's conception of technological enframing: namely, in conceptualizing otherness according to predetermined patterns, otherness is thereby silenced. Of course it may be noted that Bultmann's intent was that the existential reader have her interpretive frameworks perpetually reconfigured, but in practice as discussed above the parameters within which transformation might occur are unlikely to be redrawn. In sum, Bultmann has sought a historical solution to a problem that is only peripherally historical, and despite his attempts to precipitate a crisis in the individual reader of scripture, has left out of the picture questions that are crucially important for the biblical interpreter.

CONCLUSIONS: BULTMANN AS TECHNOLOGIST

One can only concur with Bultmann's efforts to ensure that the individual subject is transformed by encounter with scripture, but it has been the purpose of this chapter to highlight how Bultmann's own strategy is conceivable in terms of the technologist categories identified by his one

---

for instance in chapter 6 below. The individualism he espoused was leveled against the idea of the mass, or herd mentality. The great problem in modernity was that the individual was being sunk in the collective, where they no longer were responsible for what happened. Against this Bultmann, as Kierkegaard, thought of reading or preaching as a proleptic experience of the Last Judgment. As it will be then, so now as we hear the word, each of us is individuated and held to account by God (Rom 14:10; Rev 20:11–15). We cannot plead then that "he made me do it," or "they said it was all right to have that attitude." Hence, this individuation is the crisis that Kierkegaard and Bultmann sought to provoke throughout their writings. It is not merely a mindless acceptance of individualism on Bultmann's part, but a rejection of the mass consciousness of 19th–20th century life that suppressed individual responsibility.

time Marburg associate. The problems that Bultmann valiantly attempts to tackle are the problems of how an ancient authoritative text can stand over against the contemporary reader. It is in supposing that a solution to this problem can be achieved by means of methodology alone that render Bultmann's approach technologist. This is not of course to say that methods can be dispensed with, but Bultmann's existentialist historical method is based upon the untransformable assumption that it constitutes a full-blown means of interpreting scripture, even though it pays insufficient attention to how the individual reader herself may be ethically and communally transformed.[66]

While these questions of transformation are fully addressed in chapters 6 and 7 below, here it need simply be noted that the actual historical transformability of the existential interpreter is an essential element of biblical interpretation and is not taken as seriously by Bultmann as it might have been. Whilst his emphasis on the individual taking responsible decision is commendable, it remains vague and esoteric. The questions of whether and how God's grace is operative in the radical but apparently straightforward decision to abandon one's presuppositions, the actual "security" one is called to leave behind, and the lack of security one is invited to embrace, remain unaddressed by Bultmann. His emphasis remains textual, and one is left to infer that hermeneutic presuppositions are exclusively literary, that "securities" refer only to familiar ways of reading, and that the absence of security is a theoretical openness to textual challenge. Such criticisms hardly sound fair in the light of Bultmann's intentions, but he does little to widen the scope hermeneutics beyond the text itself to address the reader's historical location.

Francis Watson's account of Bultmann portrays him as a Neo-Marcionite[67] and asks just how far Bultmann's own historical facticity was truly addressed by his theological hermeneutics. Watson percep-

---

66. Nevertheless, for Bultmann, (as for Luther), is the compulsion of always and at every moment having one's existence radically turned again to God. For Luther, one is always as a Christian a baptized sinner, who is perpetually called to respond to God's word. The notion of being *progressively* transformed is not part of the Lutheran theological lexicon. It might imply accumulating some righteous merit of our own on which we can then stand before God—something Luther rejected vehemently.

67. By "Neo-Marcionite" Watson refers to the hypothesis "that the erasure of Scriptural texts from both Testaments is motivated by a desire for immediate encounter that seeks to dissolve all forms of textual mediation." (Watson, *Text and Truth,* 128)

tively and provocatively locates Bultmann within his historical context in the time of the Third Reich. On the one hand he observes that because Bultmann's redefinition of history (to exclude the hopes and destinies of nations) was made in a totalitarian setting, it is not so apolitically innocuous as it may appear. Bultmann effectively denounced the defamation of Jews and expressed unease at the attempt to subordinate the church to the God-given destiny of the German nation.[68] On the other hand, to de-historicize the Bible is to sever it from its Jewish context.

> What is the significance, at just this historical juncture, of Bultmann's call for the de-judaizing of Christian faith? Is the attempt to free theology and church from their Jewish roots entirely unrelated to current attempts to purify other areas of society and culture from alien, Jewish influences? Or is this—in effect if not in intention—a small contribution to the solution of 'the Jewish problem in Germany,' a problem whose 'complicated character' Bultmann acknowledges while courageously attacking the defamation of German Jews? A church that learned to distance itself from its Jewish roots, adapting its liturgical, homiletical and educational practices accordingly, would be recognizably a church in and for the Third Reich, whatever measures it otherwise took to ensure its essential independence.[69]

Unfortunately Watson's critique is too individualist and fails to take contemporary German academic life seriously enough as the context in which Bultmann's thought developed. Further, it assumes that his thinking took shape only in the Nazi period, whereas in fact it belongs to the period of the Weimar Republic and before.[70] Nevertheless Watson's comments place a question mark against the extent to which the Jesus of history conceived by Bultmann was able in fact to reach beyond the world of the text to effect the transformation of the reader's context. Bultmann's hermeneutic thus remains confined within the technological *Gestell*, predisposed to reduce history, scripture and personal transfor-

---

68. Watson, *Text and Truth*, 161.
69. Watson, *Text and Truth*, 162.
70. The problem was not Bultmann's personal culpability but the fact that by the 1920s, anti-Jewishness was built into German New Testament interpretation—for more than one reason. One is the Enlightenment project to de-historicize religion and make it universal, and the other (which was connected) was that German national aspirations sought to release German culture from Jewish influences.

mation to the terms of a scientific worldview, even while creating the impression that divine otherness has been genuinely encountered.

Chapter 7 below will seek to appropriate some of the major insights of existential categories in the light of Sabbath celebration. Existential reading may offer a useful and valuable interpretive framework for engaging the Gospels; however, all valid preconceptions become idolatrous when they unwittingly silence the otherness of scripture. This chapter has argued that Bultmann's particular historical method is fundamentally prone to this danger, because it uses scripture as the crude material from which a pure *kerygma* is technologically refined in accordance with a pre-determined conception of what counts as truth.

2

Democratizing the Text

If Bultmann had attempted to expose the whole life of the reader to the transforming otherness of the text, then in stark contrast, Stanley Fish represents the view that the text itself has no leverage whatsoever over the life of the reader. Writing as a lawyer and literary critic, Fish denies that there is such a thing as the "text-in-itself" and therefore also the possibility that it might confront the reader with the potential disruption of otherness.[1] If Bultmann's primary focus fell upon the individual reading subject, then for Fish the focus is rather upon the community in which the individual acquires the literary competence to engage a text. Immersion in this community renders impossible the manipulation of

---

1. Fish's denial that "texts" exist (e.g., Fish, *Is There a Text in this Class?* 305–21, 356–71) is fully exploited by Saye's comparison of Fish with Barth (Saye, "The Wild and Crooked Tree") in which Saye claims that for neither Fish nor Barth is there such a thing as the "text itself." Saye concludes his discussion of how the traditional model of demonstration is more suspect than its rhetorical counterpart, persuasion, by stating that "demonstration appeals to the neutral territory of the "text itself," but as Fish has helped us see, such an entity does not exist." While Saye happily attributes the same conviction to Barth he fails to note that in paragraph 19 of the *Church Dogmatics* Barth frequently refers to the text or the bible "itself" (e.g., Barth, *Church Dogmatics* I.1, 458, [492], 493, 497). Furthermore Barth frequently defends the capacity of the text to stand over against the church (i.e., the Christian interpretive community), for instance when he states, "Here as everywhere defence against possible violence to the text must be left to the text itself, which in fact has always succeeded in doing something a purely spiritual and oral tradition cannot do, namely, maintaining its own life against the encroachments of individual or total periods and tendencies in the Church, victoriously asserting this life in ever new developments, and thus creating recognition for itself as a norm" (Barth, *Church Dogmatics*, I.1, 106).

the text by the reader, who in reading remains inescapably subservient to the largely imperceptible conventions of that community.

This chapter forms a pair with chapter 6 which focuses on the nature of relationships within the body of Christ and the manner in which those relationships determine the way that one reads Scripture, with special reference to the parable of the rich man and Lazarus (Luke 16:19–31). In this sense, Fish is affirmed in his claim that one's day-to-day context is determinative of the manner in which one reads. But this chapter identifies in Fish a brand of the technologism outlined by Heidegger.[2] To read technologically is to protect oneself from the otherness that might disturb and disrupt one's entire moral comportment, and it is the burden of this chapter to show how a Fishian community demands the expulsion of such otherness from the reading process. The parable of the rich man and Lazarus features below, where Lazarus is conceived as the embodiment of the otherness which Fish's technologically shaped community, like the rich man's, cannot or will not encounter.

Fish's emphasis on the reading community as the prime determinant for textual interpretation has made him an attractive figure for biblical interpreters who quite rightly wish to herald the importance of the church's role in hearing scripture.[3] Fish, it may appear, offers an account of reading in which the reader is confronted with otherness in the form of the community, and the reading conventions of the Christian community—so the argument runs—are themselves shaped by the Holy Spirit, a view with which Fish himself is happy to concur.[4] The aim of this chapter is to explore this possibility in the light of Heidegger's insights about technology, and to see whether Fish's interpretive programme enables otherness to flourish, or whether it simply extinguishes it. This goal will be pursued firstly by offering an account of Fish's neo-pragmatist literary theory and secondly by critiquing some of its key features.

---

2. Se p. 9–16 above.

3. E.g., Hauerwas *Unleashing the Scripture*; Saye, "Wild and Crooked Tree"; Morgan and Barton, *Biblical Interpretation*.

4. E.g., Fish, *Is There a Text in this Class?*, 181–96.

OUTLINE OF FISH'S GENERAL ARGUMENT

A writer as aggressive and relentless as Fish naturally polarizes his readers' response. He is generally regarded as either brilliant in his simplicity or tedious in his predictability. Similarly, for some he is welcomed as harmless, since by his own rhetoric—his is a merely descriptive theory that can "go nowhere,"[5] because every description is an interpretation. For others he is opposed as a dangerous enemy of society in general and biblical interpretation in particular, as he paves the way for the tyranny of the rhetorician able to mould the community, i.e., stir the mob. If in previous chapters it was shown that a concise but fair summary of figures like Bultmann and Heidegger is notoriously difficult to construct, no such struggle is needed with Fish, whose entire interpretive thesis can be summarized with great simplicity: All interpretive constraints are derived from the community to which the reader belongs, and as such are neither absolute nor eternal but socially contingent through and through. Throughout his writings, Fish simply takes this notion and applies it to literature, law, and religion, with consequences (if he can tolerate such a thing) that are both provocative and predictable. This summary of Fish's strategy will proceed by examining three core features of his theory, namely intelligibility, contradiction, and social contingency.

For Fish, anything lying beyond the boundaries of the interpretive community is utterly alien, detached, irrelevant and unintelligible to the community. Any form of otherness, any person or object that is fundamentally different, is rendered intelligible only as it is filtered through the interpretive mechanisms of the community, but of course, in so doing it is made familiar and thereby jettisons any degree of otherness it may previously have embodied. Fish does not deny the possibility that entities beyond the community exist, but he insists that the force they may exert upon a community is decided in advance by communal consent:

> It is simply not possible even to conceive of a constraint ... without already having assumed a context of practice in relation to which it is intelligible ... and whenever a so-called outside or external or independent constraint is invoked, what is really being invoked is the interested agenda ... of a project already in (some other) place.[6]

---

5. Fish, *Doing What Comes Naturally*, 27.
6. Fish, *Doing What Comes Naturally*, 13.

This means that a text is utterly incapable of standing over against the reading community with a capacity to transform its interpretive mechanisms. If this is to happen at all, it will be under the authorisation of the community, not in obedience to a text.

Once one has abandoned the notion that the text itself has the capacity to offer the constraints by which it is interpreted, it may be objected that the individual reader within the community is free to make anything out of a text, to force the text to say whatever the reader wants it to say. But those who make such a claim have not understood Fish.[7] With the supposed abandoning of a singular textual meaning, the reader is not left with unconstrained liberty to construe his own meaning. Literary competence is necessary for a text to be understood, so for an individual reader it is quite possible to misread a text.[8] The reading subject cannot impose just any interpretation onto a text because she is constrained by the conventions of the community. If she misreads a text, although the text itself will be unable to resist, the community will determine (and in a sense has already determined) whether or not her reading is legitimate. By relocating meaning from the text to the community, Fish has not simply exchanged one singular eternal determinative entity for another, as will become clear. Instead he has simply argued that anything that is encountered in the world is rendered intelligible by nothing other than the community in which a person has learned to make sense of the world. Nothing that a person encounters is ever external to that community, but is always inevitably embedded in that context. Anything a-contextual is unintelligible because it has not been encountered.

> An infinite plurality of meanings would be a fear only if sentences existed in a state in which they were not already embedded in, and come into view as a function of some situation or other. That state, if it could be located, would be the normative one, and it would be disturbing indeed if the norm were free-floating and indeterminate. But there is no such state; sentences emerge only in situations, and within those situations, the normative meaning of an utterance will always be obvious or at least accessible,

---

7. Although this thesis converges with the conclusions of both Vanhoozer (*Is there a Meaning in This Text?*) and Thiselton (*New Horizons*), both thinkers tend to rush toward describing Fish as an interpretive anarchist for whom anything goes. This is far from Fish's intent. Both critiques would be stronger had they stated more clearly just what Fish means when he talks of interpretive constraints.

8. Fish, *Is there a Text in this Class?*, 48.

although within another situation that same utterance, no longer the same, will have another normative meaning that will be no less obvious and accessible.[9]

The meaning of a sentence, then, and of the words that comprise it, does not lie somewhere in the atmosphere above the down to earth lived context of communicants. Writers do not deposit meaning into a timeless language account from which subsequent readers from any time or context may simply withdraw, given the right credentials of literary competence. There is no context-free utterance, and no context-free means of apprehending the text. For Fish, a text without a context is a con. That is, whenever some supposedly a-contextual meaning is appealed to, such a meaning cannot be conceived of or imagined without the definite (even if quietly prescriptive) interpretive action that enables access to apparently uninterpreted fact. As he points out,

> . . . the text as an entity independent of interpretation and (ideally) responsible for its career drops out and is replaced by the texts that emerge as the consequence of our interpretive activities. There are still formal patterns, but they do not lie innocently in the world; rather, they are themselves constituted by an interpretive act. The facts one points to are still there (in a sense that would not be consoling to an objectivist) but only as a consequence of the interpretive (man-made) model that has called them into being. The relationship between interpretation and text is thus reversed: interpretive strategies are not put into execution after reading, and because they are the shape of reading, they give texts their shape, making them rather than, as is usually assumed, arising from them.[10]

Does Fish thereby claim that there is nothing beyond the interpretive norms of the community that can exert influence upon reading subjects? Not quite. It is impossible from Fish's position to lay claim to

---

9. Fish, *Is there a Text in this Class?*, 307–8. There is a "family likeness" here to Wittgenstein's discussion of forms of life and language games. Wittgenstein sought emancipation from pure formalism, just as Fish does. However, unlike Fish he does not pronounce a rigid either/or option between formalism and relativism. (This aspect of Fish's rhetoric invites an incisive critique by Thiselton [*New Horizons*, 540–47]). Instead, Wittgenstein's approach recognizes that formal concepts arise from everyday life. These "forms of life" are different for different people in different contexts, but there is nevertheless overlap between these forms, such as to suggest the possibility of trans-contextual norms. Wittgenstein, *On Certainty*, 281–325.

10. Fish, *Is there a Text in this Class?*, 13.

knowledge of anything that lies beyond the boundary of the community. From a theological perspective for instance, if anything from beyond the community is to be considered, encountered or even imagined—it will have only one way of achieving this: By providentially shaping the receptivity of the interpretive community.[11] Hence Fish is happy to entertain the possibility of God's existence, but if God is active in communicating with people it can only be by quietly shaping the interpretive framework of the interpretive community.

> In those cases in which meanings seem immediately available without recourse to anything but the words themselves, it is because the intentional structure—the conditions of intelligibility that limit the meanings words can have before they are produced—is so deeply in place that we are not aware of it and seem to experience its effects directly, without mediation.[12]

If God is active in the interpretive procedure, it is not as the transgressor of the community's boundaries, but as one who has intentionally shaped the community's internal norms.[13] If a divine being exists, then the divine seal of approval is antecedently placed on the interpretive community before it begins to read.[14] Whatever is beyond the community is thus conceived in terms consistent with technologism. That is, the world (or the God) beyond one's community is unable to challenge, reshape or surprise—the world loses its ability to stand over against the community, because for Fish the community is never mistaken. But if

---

11. This for instance, is the position of Saye in his attempt to portray Barth and Fish as hermeneutical allies. He succeeds in drawing out significant similarities between the two thinkers, especially the emphasis of one's immersion into a community that largely predetermines what one will hear in scripture. The two major problems with Saye's analysis are firstly, that Fish is by no means responsible for establishing the aspects of his own thought that cohere with those of Barth. A consideration for instance of Heidegger or Wittgenstein would readily reveal the importance of the reader's lived context. Secondly, a selective reading of Barth (a difficult danger to avoid given the prolific and varied nature of Barth's work) blinds Saye to Barth's own potentially devastating critique of Fish's thought as outlined for instance in above.

12. Fish, *Doing What Comes Naturally*, 295.

13. In such a view, texts such as Gen 6:5–6 and Matt 24:38–39 must be demythologized.

14. In effect, Fish would say to the critical realist Christian community almost exactly what the Matthean Jesus said to Peter: "whatever you [accept] on earth will already have been [accepted] in heaven, and whatever you [reject] on earth will already have been [rejected] in heaven"(Matt 16.19). God has proleptically placed his seal of approval on the Christian community. The community is predestined to be right.

this is so, how is it that contradictory but apparently valid readings of a single text can occur within the community?

The text's own inability to constrain the manner in or purpose for which it is read may yield an infinite variety (though not a limitless one since the community provides invisible interpretive constraints)[15] of apparently contradictory readings from a single text by a variety of communities. Fish himself rejoices in the diversity of incompatible readings that might be made of a single text. In the absence of context-free immutable renderings, every sentence uttered can be analysed with any number of presuppositions. He offers an intriguing example by explaining how he wrote on the blackboard of his classroom a column containing the names of authors his students were to study.[16] To the students of literary theory (a class constituting an interpretive community) the meaning of the text was naturally an academic assignment. When another class studying seventeenth-century religious poetry (a different interpretive community) later entered the room and were told that the list of names was in fact a poem, the class was able to extract the "natural" poetic meaning. Fish cites this rather crude example to illustrate how a text may be interpreted entirely differently by different communities.[17] Contradiction in reading is almost to be expected of communities in different contexts, but this leaves unanswered two crucial questions that must be asked about why contradiction occurs within a single community, and why convergence occurs between very different communities. These criticisms, which will be taken up below, highlight some of the difficulties that arise from regarding meanings as exclusively socially contingent.

---

15. Infinity can occur within limits (e.g., the number of possible numbers between 1 and 2). An infinite number of readings by no means equates with limitless polyvalence.

16. Fish, *Is there a Text in this Class?*, 323.

17. This infamous illustration is a focal point that has drawn a wide response of criticisms, the weaker end of the spectrum being represented by Scholes (*Textual Power*, 158–59), and the more convincing by Noble ("Hermeneutics and Postmodernism"). Noble for instance, argues that this type of analysis might be quite applicable to a poetic genre that invites polyvalent readings but would work less well for scientific or engineering documents. Even Noble however seems to have oversimplified this issue by failing to consider how those from beyond scientific communities interpret scientific texts.

"Interpretation," Fish declares, "is the only game in town."[18] Interpretation, it seems, is thus severed from the reality of entities existing outside the community, and therefore from anything inherent within the text that may represent radical otherness. In consequence, an ethnic group with xenophobic hostility towards outsiders might find its policy of community triumphalism vindicated by Fish's description of interpretation[19]—or at least Fish could provide no convincing objection to its communal self-assertiveness.[20] Does this not mean that a perceived Enlightenment absolutism (of the human subject) has been replaced by a thoroughgoing relativism that simply promotes the human subject in a different way?[21] If Fish is arguing for relativism, what is to protect him from the logical charge that his own position may therefore be relativized? To be sure, there is a sense in which Fish may be fully described as a relativist, since truth is at the disposal of the interpretive community, and different communities conceive of different truths, which—it may be argued—leads finally to having no truth at all. Fish concedes this point, but then describes it as irrelevant.

> It is unassailable as a general and theoretical conclusion: the positing of context- or institution-specific norms surely rules out the possibility of a norm whose validity would be recognized by everyone, no matter what his situation. But it is beside the point for any particular individual, for since everyone is situated somewhere, there is no one for whom the absence of an a-situational norm would be of any practical consequence, in the sense that his performance or his confidence in his ability to perform would be impaired. So that while it is generally true that to have many

---

18. Fish, *Doing What Comes Naturally*, 355.

19. As Adolf Hitler declared "... a philosophy can hope for victory only if the broad masses adhere to the new doctrine and declare their readiness to undertake the new struggle" (*Mein Kampf*, 91). Hitler was well aware of how the orator is a conductor who can play upon the emotional registers of the people, and defended the notion of cultural relativism "In the absolute, moreover, nothing is either great or small. Things are big or little by the standard one selects ... Man judges himself in relation to himself. What is bigger than himself is big. What is smaller is small. Only one thing is certain, that one is part of the spectacle. Everyone finds his own role" (*Hitler's Table Talk, 1941–1944*, 141, 144).

20. Richard Rorty acknowledged that his own pragmatist philosophy was open to use by nihilists and fascists but replied that, *aesthetically speaking*, he personally preferred kindness to cruelty (Rorty, *Contingency*, 65).

21. For instance, in the manner described by Graham Ward ("Barth, Modernity and Postmodernity").

standards is to have none at all, it is not true for anyone in particular (for there is no one in a position to speak "generally"), and, therefore it is a truth of which one can say "it doesn't matter."[22]

While relativism is a theory that might be levelled at Fish's sociopragmatic pattern of interpretation, it yields little. For every person who communicates is a historically situated person who belongs to a definite interpretive community, and since no one can see beyond their community to see that *with* which their own truth might be relative, the actual authority of the community is absolute. In turn of course, this precludes the possibility of a Fishian reader being a relativist—there is no way of stepping outside the absolutism of one's context. As Fish goes on to say, "while relativism is a position one can entertain, it is not a position one can occupy."[23]

If the authority of any given community is temporally absolute, how might some interpretive structures come into effect whilst others do not? Without a context-independent authority, what is to prevent interpretative principles from arbitrariness? Here Fish simply falls back on the primitive insight that might is right. "Does might make right?" he asks. "In a sense the answer I must give is yes, since in the absence of a perspective independent of interpretation some interpretive perspective will always rule by virtue of having won over its competitors."[24] However for Fish this is no cause for despair, because all that the community knows is the perspective that won, and this perspective is recognized as acceptable by the community. Might is right, interpretation is force, and force is all there is.[25] Whether in deliberate transgression of a community's law, or in the dutiful enforcement of that law, "*there is always a gun in your hand.*"[26] Whether it be in adherence to or rebellion against any idea, such as country, reason, honor, love, or God, the utter dependence upon force to establish that idea as normative is inevitable.

---

22. Fish, *Is There a Text in this Class?*, 319.

23. Fish, *Is There a Text in this Class?*, 319.

24. Fish, *Doing What Comes Naturally*, 10. Thrasymachus (a fascinating character in the Plato corpus) advocates, on the face of it, that "might is right," and in this way provides a headlong encounter between Socrates and himself on the subject of nihilism versus revealed good. His famous saying occurs at *Republic*, Bk 1, 338C (See also 336B, 348C).

25. E.g., Fish, *Doing What Comes Naturally*, 10; 503–24.

26. Fish, *Doing What Comes Naturally*, 520 (emphasis original).

Regardless of which force prevails, the victory establishes a communal tradition, which in turn generates a normative pattern of interpreting its own victory. For those who inhabit this tradition, this pattern will be one that appears "naturally" right, which conveniently dispels the fear of the anarchic consequences that are thought to arise from the final authority of the interpretive community.

For Fish, the community is inescapable, which is why he calls a halt to the valiant escape attempts made by those who have become aware of their utter situatedness and then seek liberty in the unconstrained quest for truth.[27] Fish is saying that the prison of the community is not so bad after all, and since every escape attempt is futile, readers may as well enjoy their communal confinement, or to put this in Fish's own rhetoric, to "stop worrying and enjoy interpretation."[28] With the deliberate segregation of community and otherness, of authority and text, Fish claims that he is in no way prescribing any particular hermeneutics, but rather is simply describing the way things are. "Since it is primarily a literary argument, one wonders what implications it has for the practice of literary criticism. The answer is, none whatsoever."[29] In practice, it has no implications because all he has done is to pronounce as superfluous issues he supposes to be superfluous. The normal practice of literary criticism may continue unhindered by Fish's insights, which are nothing other than a recapitulation of what is already happening in the endeavour of reading texts. This claim that mere description has no implications is a claim with very far reaching implications.

FISH THE TECHNOLOGIST

Fish's neo-pragmatist enterprise has been assessed from a variety of perspectives,[30] but one of the most incisive treatments of his work may

---

27. This is a recurrent theme of the section "Consequences" spanning several chapters of *Doing What Comes Naturally*.

28. See Fish's essay, *Is There a Text in this Class?*, 1–17 entitled, "Introduction, or How I Stopped Worrying and Learned to Love Interpretation."

29. Fish, *Is There a Text in this Class?*, 370.

30. E.g., Vanhoozer (*Is There a Meaning in this Text?*) regards Fishian communities as "using the text" in such a way as to be incapable of encountering otherness through a text. Thiselton (*New Horizons*) describes Fish as a socio-pragmatist who fails to appreciate the complexities of the philosophy of language, relying on rigid either/or

be found in the work of a critic who had never read Fish. In 1953 Leo Strauss's important work, *Natural Right and History*, opens with a discussion of what he calls historicism, in the course of which the general position that would later be adopted by Fish is substantially traced and thoroughly critiqued. By representing Strauss's views, the character of Fish's position will become apparent enough, but Strauss's analysis is valuable more importantly for the guise in which Fish is revealed, namely in terms of technologism. Strauss does not write specifically on the subject of technologism, but his discussion of historicism—as also argued in chapter 4 below—can be readily construed as an aspect of the technologism Heidegger describes. Three aspects of Fish's technologism will thus be identified in the light of Strauss's insights: Rhetoric as the science (rather than the "art")[31] of persuasion; Community, and its potential to consolidate individuals" self- interest; and History as an already interpreted narrative devoid of the capacity to make itself heard.

Strauss offers an intriguing critique because of his own political stature, not least as the intellectual founding father of the neoconservative movement contemporary US politics.[32] He is useful for the purposes

---

distinction between abstract truth and concrete reality. *The Postmodern Bible* (55–60) charges Fishian communities with an inherent incapacity to critique their own ideological ends and their effects upon other communities, a concern shared by Terry Eagleton ("The Estate Agent"). Eagleton's Marxist perspective highlights the damaging socio-political implications of Fishian theory for those who do not belong to a powerful community (See also Eagleton, *Ideology*, 148–49). Donelly (*Rhetorical Faith*) focuses on the Augustinian notion of *caritas*, which leads to a consideration not merely at the level of literary theory, but includes the question of how one embodies textual convictions in daily life and practice.

31. This distinction is meant to highlight a technological turn in the notion of rhetoric such as that observed by the Reformed sociologist Jacques Ellul (1912–1994): "It is the emergence of mass media which makes possible the use of propaganda techniques on a societal scale. The orchestration of press, radio and television to create a continuous, lasting and total environment renders the influence of propaganda virtually unnoticed precisely because it creates a constant environment. Mass media provides the essential link between the individual and the demands of the technological society" (Ellul, *Propaganda*, 22). See further below.

32. Strauss's own belief in eternal truths may lead to precisely the same brand of communal xenophobia that is attributed to Fish's brand of cultural relativism. For instance, an extreme example might be that one's community, if it believes it has exclusive access to eternal principles may perceive itself as justified in attempting world domination. After all, as Strauss had noted, "one ought not even to expect any real knowledge of natural right among savages" (*Natural Right and History*, 9). This critique of Strauss is pursued (seemingly beyond proportion) by Gilles Kepel (*The War for Muslim Minds*).

of this thesis because he offers not a technical critique of Fish's literary method, but a wider philosophical consideration of the world Fish describes (and by Fish's own logic, prescribes). Strauss was defending a traditional position that upheld belief in Natural Right understood as eternal principles of right and wrong, not dependant upon the perspective of human subjects, but nevertheless discernable to historically located human subjects. The opposing view was represented by conventionalists who regarded rights, laws or moral principles as having their basis not in a natural order but "on the arbitrary decisions . . . of communities: they have no basis but on some kind of agreement, and agreement may produce peace but it cannot produce truth."[33] Here Fish's literary theory may be located in a larger argument that predates Plato. In a country such as ancient Greece, comprised largely of city-states, could a single universal and apparently natural right or law be applicable to all city-states?[34] Plato's dialogue with Protagoras for instance, addresses such a question.[35] However, for Strauss, the classical distinction between nature (the world as it is in itself) and convention (the human world of ideas one seeks to transcend in order to grasp the eternal) which was accepted both by ancient conventionalists and their opponents, is obliterated by modern thinkers [including Fish] who deny

---

Such extreme critique nevertheless highlights the importance of a community's capacity to listen to those who are not its members, i.e., to "welcome the stranger" (See Heb 13:1–2). On Strauss's logic this remains wholly possible, but in the community heralded by Fish it is not. See further below.

33. Strauss, *Natural Right and History*, 11.

34. Aristotle thought not. He argued that a single universal has a variety of expressions in particular circumstances. (*Ethics* 1134b24–1135a8).

35. Fish, who is clearly familiar with Protagoras (Fish, *Doing What Comes Naturally*, 480; *The Trouble with Principle*, 307) has much in common with Plato's dialogue partner. For instance, in the *Theatetus* (166) Protagoras is heard to state that "whatever practices seem right and laudable to any particular State are so for that State, so long as it holds by them." In Plato's dialogue, Protagoras is no immoral rhetor but promotes commitment to one's traditions, and the submission of the individual to one's city-state. After all, in the absence of the gods and the consequent relative character of human judgements, one ought to find a temporal absolute authority in one's city [for Fish read "interpretive"] community. However, there are differences between Protagoras and Fish, the most important being that for Protagoras, good citizenship ought to be modelled and taught to students of rhetoric in order to assuage possible suspicion. There is no such compulsion to be found anywhere in the writing of Fish. Frederick Copplestone's 1961 commentary on Protagoras reads like a sympathetic summary of Fish. See Copplestone, *History of Philosophy*, 87–91.

either the importance or even existence of natural, universal principles of right and wrong.[36] Subjecting moral principles to the arbitrary flux of historical development in turn leaves the human subject acquiescing in Plato's cave[37]:

> Whereas, according to the ancients, philosophizing essentially means to leave the cave, according to our contemporaries all philosophizing belongs to a "historical world," "culture," "civilization," "Weltanschauung," that is, to what Plato had called the cave. We shall call this view "historicism."[38]

By historicism Strauss refers to a new edition of *conventionalism*, that is, the view that any conception of the eternal is subject to the arbitrary melting pot of historical developments, immune to interference from eternal truth. In support of the traditional belief in Natural Right, it was not Strauss but his historicist opponents that deserved the designation "conservative." The reason for their rejection of Natural Right was attributable to the desire to maintain the *status quo*. That is, insofar as the any political state will always fall short of eternal ideals, regardless of how such ideals take shape, they may alert those who are dissatisfied with the current order to the possibility of a more just order, and in so doing provide a potential hotbed for political revolution. By contrast, Strauss's natural rights critique of historicism leads to the *possibility* of mounting a genuine opposition to an "unjust status quo" and thus work in favour of change. The historicist school therefore focussed on local rather than eternal principles, to the extent that the latter were deemed either irrelevant or non-existent and were thus to be either ignored or rejected. Historical, local principles were then thought to offer the

---

36. Strauss, *Natural Right and History*, 14.

37. *Republic* VII.7. For Plato, the simile of the cave is designed to illustrate the fact that concrete human thought, speech and action can take place without reference to or awareness of the [eternal] Forms. However, all that humanity imprisoned within the cave is aware of are shadows, rather than the Forms that cast the shadows.

38. Strauss, *Natural Right and History*, 12. While Strauss offers a superb critique of historicism, he does not give a comprehensive genealogy of the movement. Prior to a fuller discussion (chapter 4) it may simply be noted that as a movement, it needs also to be considered in the light of Hegel's view of history, and the reaction to it advanced by Johann Gottfried Herder (1744–1803) and Leopold von Ranke (1795–1886). Whilst there exist a variety of "historicisms," Strauss himself defines it as the assertion that "all human thoughts or beliefs are historical, and hence deservedly [destined] to perish . . . "(Strauss, *Natural Right and History*, 25).

very same stability as those previously held by societies (or historical localities) that mistook their local principles for eternal laws. Strauss sees clearly that when history is thus bereft of eternal principles, the question then arises about the governance of history: This highlights the first aspect of Fish's technologism, namely that historical life is set adrift from any final cause or purpose, and left in the hands of human power-brokers.[39]

Rhetoric is often regarded as a mischievous alternative to truth, employed by those in sinister pursuit of some undisclosed scheme.[40] Fish offers an explanation for the way that rhetoric has been conceived in this negative sense, by listing a collection of binary opposites such as inner/outer, reason/passion, straightforward/angled, unmediated/mediated, etc.

> Underlying this list . . . are three basic oppositions: first between a truth that exists independently of all perspectives and points of view and the many truths that emerge and seem perspicuous when a particular perspective or point of view has been established and is in force; second, an opposition between true knowledge, which is knowledge as it exists apart from any and all systems of belief and the knowledge, which because it flows from some or other system of belief, is incomplete and partial (in the sense of biased); and third, an opposition between a self or consciousness that is turned outward in an effort to apprehend and attach itself to truth and true knowledge and a self or consciousness that is turned inward in the direction of its own prejudices, which far from being transcended, continue to inform its every word and action.[41]

Fish sets up these oppositions to suggest that those who adhere to the first partner of each dualism are regarded as faithfully pursuing the quest for truth, whereas those whose work falls under the second

---

39. P. 211..

40. Rhetoric—as the art of persuasion—is an ancient subject of education. For Plato, the Sophist teachers of rhetoric were not philosophers but peddlers of methods to deceive people. Aristotle took a different view and in his *Rhetoric* sought to codify the methods involved in the art of persuasion. So far as politics and the law courts were concerned rhetoric was vital. The subject therefore had a high reputation both in ancient and medieval times. As stated above in the 20th century, rhetoric became discredited because of the way propaganda developed from the *art* of persuasion to the *technique* of persuasion (Ellul, *Propaganda*).

41. Fish, *Doing What Comes Naturally*, 474.

partner of the dualisms are deemed mere peddlers of the suspicious science of persuasion, that is, rhetoricians. From here his move is a simple one. It is to argue that the former partner of each dualism is always already determined by the latter. Rhetoric embraces all, and all are rhetoricians, even if they are unwittingly so.[42] History has turned in favour of rhetorical humanity, and this history is welcomed by Fish[43] even as it was feared by Strauss who noted that "[h]istory teaches us that a given view has been abandoned in favour of another view by all men, or by all competent men, or perhaps only by *the most vocal men*; it does not teach us whether the change was sound or whether the rejected view deserved to be rejected."[44] As far as Fish is concerned, there is nothing but rhetoric to constrain history, even though rhetoric is at the mercy of history. However, his defence of an all-pervasive rhetoric,[45] far from bringing the feared danger of interpretive anarchy, simply offers a faithful description of the way things are (see 2.1.4 above); and, far from being anarchic or terrifying, "the way things are" is quite acceptable because it is all we have. Strauss goes on to question the purported historical provisionality of positions such as that adopted by Fish. That is, Fish's innocent description of the way things are is every bit as biased, as questionable and as universal as any other rhetorical claim. Pursuing Strauss's logic it might further be noted that despite having discussed the potential relativity of community members, Fish never discusses the potential relativity of his own time-spanning principle of a world with rhetorical foundations.[46] Fish might well reply that he is merely conducting an immanentist description of how things work; that is, simply an account from the inside of human discourse—in his view the only possible site from which any description could be conducted.[47] In this case he would simply concede

---

42. This is an ancient point of view and was articulated in a much more poetic way by Gorgias, in Plato's day, who in his only extant work, ("Encomium on Helen") suggested that language is a magic potion which we can use to seduce other people to do anything we want.

43. Fish, *Doing What Comes Naturally*, 484–85.

44. Strauss, *Natural Right and History*, 19 (emphasis added).

45. This is a general view shared also with Nietzsche, and many postmodern writers including Richard Rorty.

46. E.g., Fish, *Doing What Comes Naturally*, 499–502.

47. In this case he would find support in Nietzsche: No one can claim, because there is no possible verification of their claim, that they are uttering words from a transcendent "other." Any such claims to ecstatic, or mantic speech, would be a claim that my

that to defeat his case one must offer a more convincing alternative. Logically his position is indeed incontrovertible because he has decided in advance the legitimate criteria for debate, and that any appeal to trans-contextual evidence is just another rhetorical ploy. However, his denial of the eternal, of truth, of principle—remains a rhetorical move, because by his own admission, there is "no vocabulary not already laden with substance and therefore no neutral observation language . . . on the basis of which nonbiased action can be taken."[48]

What biased action might Fish be attempting with the denial of otherness? Far from being an inconsequential theory that can "go nowhere,"[49] there are definite benefits arising from his theory, which do affect the way interpretation works from day to day because they shape the general outlook of a convinced community. The excision of external constraints leaves the interpretive community defenceless against the rhetorician, and such a move can hardly yield a theory that is deemed to "go nowhere."[50] What it does, in fact, is to heighten the power that Fish believes he himself wields—rhetoric. Again, the absence of constraints and the exclusive influence of rhetoric, being all that there has ever been, have not resulted in untold moral catastrophe.[51] Rhetoric is quite simply all there is,[52] which is why he has gone to such great lengths to apply his single point relentlessly to philosophers, lawyers, literary critics and theologians. In short, his purportedly innocent principle of

---

spirit is stronger than your spirit—or, in Nietzschean terms, an attempt at "the triumph of the will" (e.g., Nietzsche, *Will to Power*, 173–75). How can any such claim be verified? Nietzsche would say, how do we know it is not uttered by the bulging sinews of the body, attempting to impose its organic needs on other bodies? Such terms are unnecessarily biologistic for Fish, who nonetheless implies that language is the natural history of human beings as Wittgenstien would say, like the chatter of squirrels (Wittgenstein, *On Certainty*, 287), an insistent noise intended to impress itself on other human beings.

48. Fish, *The Trouble with Principle*, 14.
49. Fish, *Doing What Comes Naturally*, 27.
50. Fish, *Doing What Comes Naturally*, 27.
51. Such a claim does not sit well even within his native North American Christian history. In fact it has been argued convincingly that the American Civil War (1861–65) was a clash of rivalling interpretive communities that took opposing stances in their interpretation of the legitimacy of slavery according to scripture. This integration of religious, political and moral action stamped an identity upon the nation. To regard this interpretive war as without consequences is not very convincing. Cf. Noll, Mark *The Civil War as a Theological Crisis*.
52. E.g., Fish, *Doing What Comes Naturally*, 485.

rhetoric serves him well as the weapon used to obliterate all resistance to his brand of rhetoric. Ultimately, in taking on the godlike task of naming reality, Fish is making absolute theological claims, and cannot be regarded as someone who merely offers theologians a helpful interpretive insight.[53]

The theology (and consequent anthropology) that Fish propounds is one that accords well with Heidegger's analysis of technologism. According to Richard Lanham, "Rhetorical man is trained not to discover reality but to manipulate it. Reality is what is accepted as reality, what is useful."[54] This use of reality described and thereby encouraged by Fish, whilst appearing to be severed from a-contextual morality, results in a morality that will not be convincing to all. This may be demonstrated by simple example. If a nameless child in a distant land dies as a result of the political or economic action of the wealthy interpretive community, there is no moral principle to be violated, just so long as the powerful community are comfortable with[55] that child's plight. Rhetorical strategies that reflect the will-to-power of a community and its members ensure that the community is happy with the suffering of others.[56] This is achieved by such means as de-sensitisation through media, binding communal moral principles (such as appealing to one's own children and their interests), thus creating the impression that one is helpless because "the poor you will always have with you"(Matt 26:11) or that one's taxes are already helping their situation. From the perspective of the parable considered in part II of this thesis, it may be noted that at the hands of Fish's rhetorician, poor Lazarus is destined to starve while the rich man's brothers sumptuously feast with absolute moral impunity. Everyone is happy, because the Fishian "everyone" does not include Lazarus, who as an alien from beyond the community is, in effect, nobody.

The power of persuasion is one that is substantively addressed by the parable itself, which climaxes with the question of whether the rich man's brothers can be persuaded (Luke 16:31). If they cannot be

53. To speak is to engage in metaphysics. This is an ancient argument and constitutes an important aspect of Aristotle's *Metaphysics*, surfacing most clearly in his discussions about contradiction (Bk I, 1005b, 1008a).

54. Lanham, *The Motives of Eloquence*, 4.

55. "Comfortable with" incorporating "ignorant of."

56. Happy is by no means too strong a word. Real life drama can entertain the spectator, creating the impression of an emotional response, whilst actually it is a mere sentimentalism that results in no positive action that would benefit those who suffer.

persuaded (πεισθήσονται) by (the text of) Moses and the Prophets, neither will they be persuaded by one who rises from the dead.[57] Here we may identify a marked progression of the ability to remain un-persuaded. Anticipating the identification of Christ with Lazarus that is suggested in chapter 5,[58] we may offer the following interpretation: An exasperated Abraham appears to lament that if, in the first instance, his "son" will not be persuaded by the presence of Christly otherness in Lazarus, then in the second, his "sons" will not even be persuaded by the otherness of Moses and the Prophets, and this in turn means that finally they would not be persuaded by a resurrected Lazarus. A suffering Christ or a suffering Lazarus are no more believable than a resurrected Christ or Lazarus.

May Fish's position be defended by arguing that a wider community (larger than the rich man's immediate household) might embrace the outsider? The short answer is that theoretically yes, it might—but (since theoreticians have no influence in a rhetorical economy) actually it will not and cannot. The Fishian community is defined solely by its rhetoricians, and rhetoricians belonging to a privileged minority are not going to win any debating points by arguing for a global community. Throughout Fish's writings the notion of community remains obscure and indefinable.

The primary criticism levelled at Fish is the question of whether an interpretive community can be challenged from beyond itself.[59] If "power tends to corrupt," then interpretive communities can corrupt absolutely.[60] Fish's is simply an affirmation of collective authority without accountability so that when he opens up the horizons from the individual to the community, he is left with a communal solipsism that endorses a respectable form of mob rule. Again this was a problem foreseen by Strauss, who observes that, in the absence of natural principles, appeal to some form of community norms was necessary:

---

57. "The verb [πείθω] means 'to convince' [Acts 13:43, 14:19, 17:4, 18:4]. In the passive, 'be convinced' it is close to 'believe' or 'rely on' [11:32; 18:9, 20:6, Acts 5:36–37]. So some manuscripts in this place have 'believe'" (Johnson, *The Gospel of Luke*, 253).

58. This is not a total but a partial identification of the two characters, such as that heard when Jesus declares "what you did not do for the least of these, you did not do for me" (Matt 25:45).

59. Castelli et al., *Postmodern Bible*.

60. See Dalberg, *Essays on Freedom and Power*, 335–36.

> It was evidently impossible to individualise rights in full accordance with the natural diversity of individuals. The only kinds of rights that were neither incompatible with social life nor uniform were "historical" rights: the rights of Englishmen, for example, in contradistinction to the rights of man. Local and temporal variety seemed to supply a safe and solid middle ground between anti-social individualism and unnatural universality.[61]

Thus it may be asked of Fish, what is to prevent one community from being fully justified in annihilating another? The answer lies in the apparently neutral slogan, "might is right."[62] One community is only ever wrong if there exists a more powerful community to overcome it. But Fish remains deliberately and defensively ambiguous over what actually constitutes an interpretive community. What are the boundaries that contain a community, and how are those boundaries shaped and reshaped? Were Moses and the Prophets not part of the wider Jewish community to which the rich man's brothers belonged? There is nothing in Fish's work that might prevent one from presuming that since all humans have humanity in common, humanity as a whole constitutes one enormous interpretive community.[63]

In this case, the notion of community evacuates itself. And what then remains? On the surface it may appear that talk of community de-centres the individual reader, placing her within the wider determinative framework of her historical context. But true to Fish's rhetoric, the term "community" is a flexible rhetorical device. One can belong to the communities of village inhabitants, of fathers, of Volvo-owners, of adulterers, of church-members, of baseball fans, and of the National Socialist Party of America, all at once. In membership of any one of those communities, others will be encountered who belong to a range of different communities. In the end, every individual is a unique combination of community membership.[64] The dynamics of the individuals

---

61. Strauss, *Natural Right and History*, 14.

62. Fish, *Doing What Comes Naturally*, 10.

63. The potential trans-historical nature of a community is an objection raised but not fully capitalised on by Thiselton, *New Horizons*, 42, 592. This may be because it is problematic in itself (with its implied capacity to reduce the ancients to modern puppets) but may nevertheless denote a continuity of human experience that is both unavoidable for and unacceptable to Fish.

64. A parallel difficulty is found with Wittgenstein's "forms of life." How many "forms of life" does one person occupy? Then how can we distinguish language games

within the community are never discussed by Fish. The question of how interaction between communities or community members might look remains beyond the scope of his interest in interpretive communities, even though he writes hundreds upon hundreds of pages repeating the single mantra celebrating their unassailable authority. On the one hand, Fish writes as though community members are shaped by the most convincing rhetoricians (hence the critique above), but on the other as though community members are passive recipients of their conventions and helpless prisoners of their context. Although Fish seemingly refuses to define community, he cannot avoid referring to specific communities throughout this writings. For instance, two different university classes constitute two different communities,[65] as do two different schools of criticism,[66] two different professions,[67] and two opposing nations.[68] Each of these "communities" are inhabited to varying degrees, consciously and decisively by their members. From this perspective, communities refer not simply to one's interpretive context, but also to one's deliberate choices.[69] This suggests that strictly speaking, what Fish often refers to is not a community at all, but an association, requiring critique of a different nature to that offered in 2.2.1 above.

One way of perceiving the difference between community and association is offered by a study that was influential upon Heidegger, Ferdinand Tonnies' 1887 publication, *Community and Society*. Rudiger Safranski notes that it became popular in the 1920s,

> . . . providing conservative critics of the modern mass society with all their principal concepts. Accordingly, community has a higher value than association, or society. Community means a "living organism" and a "lasting and genuine" coexistence. Association is a "mechanical aggregate and artefact," providing

(which are founded in forms of life) since we may be simultaneously bus passengers, evangelists, English men, husbands etc.

65. Fish, *Is there a Text in this Class?*, 322–37.
66. Fish, *Doing What Comes Naturally*, 142.
67. Fish, *Doing What Comes Naturally*, 157.
68. Fish, *Doing What Comes Naturally*, 149.

69. Such deliberate choices, Fish would argue, are themselves predetermined by one's community. But sooner or later Fish is going to run out of determinative communities. Either there will be so many that the notion of community becomes inapplicable, or else it will be reduced to such a general level that it swallows itself whole (e.g., all humans have humanity in common).

only "transitory and superficial" coexistence. In community people are "united despite all division" while in association they are "divided despite all unity."[70]

Membership in the Fishian community devoid of otherness can only reaffirm the individual as a community member. Association rather than community is therefore a better means of describing the Fishian interpretive context. Far from relativising the self in a communal context, the sovereignty of the self is amplified in Fish's programme, so that the individual subjects receive themselves back as reinforced community members. The mutual reinforcement of individuals in a rhetorical world is best described as an association, which gathers on the basis of mutual self-interest.

Some theological interpreters of Fish have regarded the church as the Christian interpretive community,[71] and sought to accommodate his literary theory. Part II of this thesis will argue that hearing any text, including scripture, requires the cultivation of an attentive disposition, and it will be argued in chapter 6 that membership of a community is an essential aspect of this. Fish however, is by no means writing about community in the fullest sense. A brief example will make the point. It is almost obligatory for those writing on the subject of biblical interpretation to genuflect in the direction of "community," and to do so for technologist reasons. That is, to read in a group setting is to be exposed to other perspectives, which in turn yields a richer experience of what the individual is to get out of the text. But such an emphasis remains irrelevant if it does not address the prior question of how members of the community are actually transformed by one another's perspectives. If communal insight remains at the level of extracting interesting information or of unearthing Gnostic gems, then hermeneutics is confined within the Heideggerian categories of curiosity, ambiguity and idle talk.[72] One can imagine how the rich man's brothers may have sat around the meal table, offering alternative readings of Moses and the Prophets, being masochistically micro-challenged by each other's perspectives and grateful that if they had not read together they would never have been so enriched by the text. But this is not to hear Moses and the Prophets—to hear is to be ready for transformation. This is why it is important to

70. Safranski, *Between Good and Evil*, 168.
71. E.g., Saye, "Wild and Crooked Tree."
72. Heidegger, *Being and Time*, 157–64.

consider what it actually means to inhabit a community, because without addressing that question[73] (see chapter 6) one may merely be talking about an association and will be destined to remain content with technologist configurations of the text. Ultimately, Fish is of little use for theologians because for all his talk of community, he has nothing to say about community, only the thinly disguised affirmation of the sovereign self as it acquiesces in the interpretive association.

"Some reader-response critics," Fish complains, "deconstruct the autonomy and self-sufficiency of the text, but in the process end up privileging the autonomous and self-sufficient subject."[74] This may be heard as a comprehensive if unwitting summary of his own work. It was an inevitable outcome, foreseen by Strauss as the natural outworking of the belief that objective principles could be replaced by "principles relative to a particular age or particular nation."[75] Strauss claims that when history was left to its own devices (which is unavoidable when objective status is surreptitiously conferred upon slogans such as "might is right")[76] "the only standards that remained were of a purely subjective character, standards that had no other support than the free choice of the individual."[77] History, like all else, had lost the capacity to stand over against the individual reading subject. It had become technologized.

Fish would argue that history—not history as it is "in-itself," but history as conceived by the community—can resist individual misreadings.[78] The notion of history-in-itself—that is, prior to interpretation, the raw events—would make no sense whatsoever to Fish since to talk about it is already to construct an interpretation. Whatever history is (and here it is used to refer to the historiographical narratives by which we understand the phenomenon of events), it is conceived, approached and quarried in accordance with the antecedent communal conventions that determine in advance what sort of history might be discovered.

---

73. That is, the question of how the community and its members encounter confrontation. Confrontation is not meant necessarily in a negative sense, but rather as the experience of being challenged by that which stands over against oneself, an experience that constitutes a fundamental aspect of transformation. Chapter 6 traces this notion of transformation more fully.

74. Fish, *Doing What Comes Naturally*, 501.

75. Strauss, *Natural Right and History*, 16.

76. Fish, *Doing What Comes Naturally*, 10.

77. Strauss, *Natural Right and History*, 18.

78. E.g., Fish, *There's No Such Thing as Free Speech*, 253.

From the individual's perspective it will naturally remain "history" in an objectified sense, but it will not thereby be history as a timeless force that runs independently of but accessible to historical subjects. In deliberately undermining the power of history, placing it at the mercy of the interpretive community, it may appear that Fish does not quite adhere to historicist convictions. Indeed Fish has gone to great lengths to distance himself from the movement described as "New Historicism" in his essay "The Young and the Restless."[79] New Historicism is a phrase coined by Stephen Greenblatt to describe those who accentuate the sheer textuality of history,[80] with which one may have thought Fish would readily identify himself. Fish's response is predictable. His usual strategy is to divide his targets into two opposing camps—one of them riddled with relativism, the other with foundationalism. In this instance he simply notes the difference between the New Historicists (for whom history is thoroughly conventional) on the one hand, and the materialists (who believe history contains such things as "events") on the other. He will then pronounce a plague on both houses, and proceed to offer an account of how there are always foundations, and though effectively absolute—they remain theoretically relative. Here he notes that the materialists pay insufficient attention to their own historical situatedness, while the New Historicists unwittingly promote their own insights into an a-contextual timeless truth and thereby undermine their own best insights.[81] This latter criticism runs parallel with Strauss's critique of Historicism, which he regards as unwittingly privileging one moment of history above all others, and thereby defeating its own case. That moment is the present one in which an insight about how history works (that is, in accord with the Historicist thesis) is presented as a time-spanning trans-contextual truth:[82]

> Historicism explicitly denies that the end of history has come, but it implicitly asserts the opposite: no possible future change of orientation can legitimately make doubtful the decisive insight into the inescapable dependence of thought on fate, and therewith into the essential character of human life; in this

---

79. Fish, *There's No Such Thing as Free Speech*, 243–56.

80. Greenblatt is a professor of Renaissance literature, whose clearest exposition of New Historicsm is to be found in his essay, "Towards a Poetics of Culture."

81. See esp. Fish, *There's No Such Thing as Free Speech*, 252–53.

82. Marx fell into this problem, Hegel more subtly sought to transcend it.

decisive respect the end of history, that is, of the history of thought, has come.[83]

Fish attempts to sidestep this critique with the predictability of adding that to be truly Newly Historicist one must accept the absence of historical consequence that may emerge as a result of its own insight. One cannot congratulate oneself at having perceived one's historical locatedness, as though one could then move on and become properly historical. Or, to put it slightly differently, "there is no road . . . from the insight that all activities are political to a special or different way of engaging in any particular activity, no politics derives from the truth that everything is politically embedded."[84] Of course, in the narrowest sense Fish is right, especially as he concurs with the common critique that there is little in New Historicism that is new. But, as argued above, the argument for the non-existence of consequences is not without consequences. Ultimately Fish is making claims about how history should be done. History as the phenomenon of sequential events—he implies—is not to be affected by any historical claims that historically embedded subjects might make.[85] And yet Fish does make implicit claims about this history, and these claims have consequences. What is more they are theological claims, propounding not only the alienation of human subjects from historical events, but also the inaccessibility of lived historical context to genuine otherness. History in the widest sense as conceived by Fish, has boundaries that cannot be transgressed by God. The consequence of his view of history is that historical subjects can only conceive of a God who

---

83. Strauss, *Natural Right and History*, 29.

84. Fish, *There's No Such Thing as Free Speech*, 255.

85. In his book, *August 1914*, Aleksandr Solzhenitsyn blames the defeat of the Russian army at Tannenberg on the acceptance by the generals, including Samsonov, of the Tolstoyan thesis that the times create leaders, not leaders the times. According to Solzhenitsyn, the result of this disastrous Tolstoyan outlook was a fatalism amongst the Russian General Staff that meant that when the battlefront crumbled they lost all initiative. General Samsonov committed suicide, but thereby left the whole front to collapse, and a terrible train of events unfold towards the Revolution of 1917. If Samsonov had followed the example of the hero, Vorotyntsev, he would have seized every possible initiative and sought to turn the situation around at every possible point. Solzhenitsyn thought that our views of history have practical consequences on how we behave and thereby how we create our own local history. Further, it is local histories that then create bigger historical terrains. Therefore, Solzhenitsyn suggested, we should take responsibility and seize the hour, and thereby make a contribution to the world before we move on to eternity.

adheres to the community's patterns of acceptability, which finally, is no God at all. Fish's claims then simply echo older theological claims that are by no means inconsequential: his community is predestinately justified in asserting "we will not have this man to rule over us" (Luke 19:14). In deliberately severing history from otherness, Fish retains historicist convictions—even if they are not "new." He is not a positivist historicist (he doesn't believe in there finally being one single irreducible account of history) but he is a pluralist historicist (there are many irreducible accounts of history—one for each interpretive community).

The concept of novelty is the greatest problem for Fish's notion of history, a problem he has in common with radical historicism. History (as concrete human existence) cannot accommodate anything that does not originate from within the confines of history itself. The infusion of otherness—as required by the doctrine of the incarnation—is inconceivable when history is regarded as a closed circuit of cause and effect whose direction is governed by the unidentifiable randomness arising from the power struggles of rhetoricians and warmongers. Fish's emphasis on the determinative nature of historical context delivers historical life and possibilities into the hands of rhetoricians—the consequence of a historicism devoid of external determinants. As Strauss had seen, "Historicism culminated in nihilism. The attempt to make man at home in this world ended in man's becoming absolutely homeless."[86] No overarching context of meaning is provided either by the monolithic assumptions of historicism or by the pluralistic floating islands of interpretation of Fish. The use of such language cannot but call to mind the Heideggerian category of unhomeliness,[87] which in turn casts the shadow of inauthenticity across Fish's neo-pragmatist enterprise.

The rich man's community has its own conventions, and on Fish's logic there is little need for such a community to consider that which lies beyond its own boundaries. But this is precisely where Lazarus is located. Although there is a gateway between them, Lazarus lies beyond the reach of a community that is wholly shaped by its own local rules and conventions. For the rich man and his brothers, to ignore Lazarus is perfectly legitimate; to embrace Lazarus would be an unwelcome disruption to one's entire communal, social and moral structures.

86. Strauss, *Natural Right and History*, 18.
87. Heidegger, *Being and Time*, 176.

CONCLUSIONS: COMMUNAL HETEROPHOBIA

The brand of community heralded by Fish is entirely consistent with the mass mentality Heidegger believed holds sway in a technological age. That is, one that engages with the world in such a way as to diminish otherness, and to safeguard oneself from that otherness by immersion in one's own communal *Gestell*. Chapter 6 will explore more fully how a community in which the presence of the resurrected Christ is incarnate is distinguished from community as Fish has conceived it.

If community is technologically understood, Fish's disturbing insights and claims are absolutely justifiable and true. That is, as descriptions of *some* forms of community, or more precisely "associations," which operate without reference to anything or anyone from beyond the familiarity of their own context. Such claims are certainly true of the Lukan rich man's association, in which as Abraham points out, the rich man's brothers will not hear Moses and the Prophets. On a pragmatist model, of course, they could put words into the mouth of Moses and the Prophets, and thus be able to read them. They may have been most familiar with the Jewish scriptures, and therefore interpreted them in a way that was acceptable within their wealthy association. Their reading strategy was the perfect example of the accuracy with which Fish is able to describe *some* reading associations. However, in a scathing attack upon Fishian rhetoric, Terry Eagleton offers a critique that coheres in substance with what one might imagine the Abraham of the parable to declare:

> With typical American parochialism and self-obsession, Fish . . . is silent about famine, forced migration, revolutionary nationalism, military aggression, the depredations of capital, the inequities of world trade, the disintegration of whole communities. Yet these have been the consequences of the system of which the United States is the linchpin for many perched on the unmetaphysical outside of it. Being unable to leap out of your own cultural skin seems to mean in Fish's case having no grasp of how your country is helping to wreak havoc in that inscrutable place known as abroad. One has the indelible impression that Fish does not think a great deal of abroad, and would be quite happy to see it abolished.[88]

---

88. Eagleton, "The Estate Agent," 5.

Whilst one might nuance Eagleton's apparent anti-Americanism, he is nevertheless acutely aware of the moral implications of Fish's literary theory. In sum, Fish vindicates interpretive communities which operate without external interference. He thereby immunises communities that accept *his description as a prescription* from intrusion by otherness. Communities which accepted his model of themselves would thus become inherently conservative since there would be no mechanism to introduce change from the outside. The parable contains the story of a rich man who could not "hear" Moses and the prophets because he had a self-reinforcing interpretation of the world, one which gave supreme value to himself and none to Lazarus. For such a person not even the resurrection of Christ would make a difference. All that would change his understanding would be the stripping away from him of the supportive structures of his world: his well-defended home, his riches, his homely comforts, the presence around him only of those who agreed with him. When stripped naked of this all too temporary world of security he was horrified to see the true state of things. In this second state of the rich man, the "truth"—which was concealed from him and perhaps even from Lazarus—is eschatologically disclosed. From this perspective, it is little wonder that so many ascetics (including Heidegger) through the ages have recommended the practice of the "remembrance of death" as the way to understand our true state in the here and now. Such an approach to ethics is considered at length by Jacques Derrida, who is the focus of chapter 3.

3

Defacing the Text

DECONSTRUCTION AS AN ATTITUDE

WHO ARE ABRAHAM'S OFFSPRING? This is the central question raised and addressed by the parable of the rich man and Lazarus, as chapter 6 will show. This chapter addresses the question of whether Jacques Derrida carries the Abrahamic gene. Whether this gene is to be found in the bloodline or the faith of Abraham's would-be children, Derrida has a strong case for addressing him as Father. So far it has become clear that neither Bultmann's theology (chapter 1) nor Fish's literary criticism (chapter 2) can break free of the technologist hold identified by Heidegger. However, in the deconstructive concern of Derrida there resides a humility, a faith and a messianic expectation that promise a valiant hermeneutical effort. If the redoubtable force of technologism can neither be demythologized (*à la* Bultmann) nor democratised (*à la* Fish), perhaps it can be deconstructed (enter Derrida). The first part of the present chapter will focus on this possibility, before moving to consider how far the spirit of deconstruction can serve theology.

At the outset it is important to distinguish between deconstruction as a method and as an attitude. If it were nothing more than yet another hermeneutical method, it would require little imagination or insight to demonstrate how it deconstructs itself and defeats its own case. But deconstruction eludes attempts to reduce it to a method, just as it eludes comprehension by those content to interpret it as such.¹ Deconstruction cannot be described as a method any more than water can be described as a tap. Thus, as Stephen Fowl has perceived, deconstruction is an attitude[2]; and as Vanhoozer implies, one that looks very much like humility.[3] It opposes the pride that believes a text can be "mastered" by introducing a profound sense of "otherness." Far from wanting to domesticate a text (as is often supposed) by severing it from its final referent, Derrida is seeking rather to animate the text with the infusion of an otherness that stands over against claims to have mastered it. However, for all the disruption Derrida's form of otherness might entail, this chapter will argue that Derrida has closed in advance the parameters that determine what actually constitutes otherness. In the end, Derrida's apparent humble openness is in practice, thoroughly prescriptive about what the other can and cannot do.

The first part of this chapter analyzes one of Derrida's earlier essays, "Plato's Pharmacy," his reading of Plato's *Phaedrus*. Here Derrida echoes the central concerns of his most celebrated work, *Of Grammatology*, as he questions the privileged status of speech over writing. It is an important piece of work, not only because it highlights the strategy to which, by various means, he has always remained faithful, but also because it brings to light his theory of the technology of language. Attention then shifts to his more recent work, *The Gift of Death*, which is largely a critique of modern technological civilisation as well as a milestone in his interface with religion. Finally, reference is made to another recent work, *Khora*, because it outlines his self-avowed radical openness to that which is *tout autre*. "Khora" is a word drawn from Plato's *Timaeus*, understood to confer both stability and disruption upon the human quest to "make sense" of the world, and is used by Derrida to parry the charge that he is a negative theologian.[4] Analysis of each of these texts will conclude with a brief reflection drawing out their relation to the parable of the rich man and Lazarus (Luke 16:19–31), which is addressed at length in second part of this thesis. Through considering Derrida's stance toward resurrection, his proposed route out of the technological *Gestell*, and his

1. E.g., Vanhoozer, Thiselton.
2. Fowl, *Engaging Scripture*, 40–56.
3. Vanhoozer, *Is There a Meaning in this Text?*, 463–67.
4. Literal translation: place, location, region, country / figurative translation (in Plato): mother, nurse, receptacle, imprint-bearer (Derrida, "Khora," 93).

interest in Messianic readiness, his hermeneutics betray a technologist propensity to reduce divine otherness to down-to-earth familiarity.

"PLATO'S PHARMACY"

"Plato's Pharmacy" is Derrida's attempt to deconstruct the Platonic discourse, *Phaedrus*. During his analysis of "Phaedrus," Derrida's underlying deconstructive approach surfaces clearly enough to reveal his actual concerns and method. In Plato's text,[5] Phaedrus is the conversation partner of Socrates who begins his explicit discussion of the relation between speech and writing by citing an Egyptian myth in which the demi-god Theuth presents to the King/God/Father figure Thamus the gift of writing which is described as a "*pharmakon*."[6] This pivotal word *pharmakon*—that may be variously translated as drug, remedy, poison, medicine, potion, gift—is greatly disturbing to King Thamus, because in creating the mere delusion of wisdom it will prove to be a *poison* rather than a *remedy*. Writing, as a *pharmakon*, will produce "men filled with the conceit of wisdom, not men of wisdom"—because for all their supposed knowledge they will remain incapable of real judgement.[7] "the father [Thamus]," laments Derrida, "is always suspicious and watchful toward writing."[8] Thus begins Derrida's attempt to overthrow the privileged status of speech over writing in the Western metaphysical tradition.

> Even if we did not want to give in here to the easy passage uniting the figures of the king, the god, and the father, it would suffice to pay systematic attention—which to our knowledge has never been done—to the permanence of a Platonic schema that assigns the origin and power of speech, precisely of logos, to the paternal position. Not that this happens especially and exclusively in Plato. Everyone knows this or can easily imagine it. But the fact that "Platonism," which sets up the whole of Western metaphysics in its conceptuality, should not escape the generality of this

---

5. *Phaedrus* 274c.

6. Griswold observes that in all probability, Plato's Socrates has constructed this myth so as to lend plausibility to his own account of language.

7. Derrida, "Plato's Pharmacy," 102 quoting *Phaedrus* 274e–275b.

8. Derrida, "Plato's Pharmacy," 76.

structural constraint, and even illustrates it with incomparable subtlety and force, stands out as all the more significant.⁹

Derrida seeks to unravel the thread of Plato's text and thereby all subsequent metaphysical tradition, by focusing almost exclusively on the rendering of *pharmakon*. This word of such fluid polyvalence, proposes Derrida, is terminally concretised by Plato. In Plato's text, it is argued, Thamus perceives that the *pharmakon* is not only a remedy for the memory but also a poison that deludes its patients into believing that they have attained real knowledge, when their only true acquisition is reported speech, hopelessly bereft of its originary dynamism.¹⁰

Derrida, however, uses the *pharmakon* as a lever to reveal that the supposed binary opposites put in place by Plato are in fact mutually pervasive. The distinction between speech and writing is revealed to be artificial.

> In order for writing to produce, as [Plato] says, the "opposite" effect from what one might expect, in order for this *pharmakon* to show itself, with use, to be injurious, its effectiveness, its power, its *dunamis* must, of course, be ambiguous . . . It is precisely this ambiguity that Plato, through the mouth of the King, attempts to master, to dominate by inserting its definition into simple, clear-cut oppositions: good and evil, inside and outside, true and false, essence and appearance.¹¹

Derrida's relentless contention is that these binary opposites are constructed by Plato in order to arrest the ambiguity, the play that enables words to defy solidification into concrete immutable renderings.¹² Plato has, in Derrida's eyes, drawn up the rules of a power game that has been played by subsequent metaphysicians. Fully aware of the ambiguity of the term *pharmakon*, it is argued, Plato has sought to close the

9. Derrida, "Plato's Pharmacy," 76.

10. Given that some human behaviourists argue that only 7% of communicative efficacy inheres in bare words, one wonders whether Plato was not more observant of human transactions than Derrida (see for instance Hall, *The Silent Language*).

11. Derrida, "Plato's Pharmacy," 103.

12. Clearly derivative from Nietzsche. "Truth and error; no 'truth' at the origin, but 'truths' and 'errors'—neither description more accurate than the other—cast up by the waves of control-preserving interpretations: 'What are man's truths after all? They are man's irrefutable errors.' (NW V.ii 196, GS 219) 'Truth is the kind of error without which a certain species of living being could not live.' (WM II.19, WP 272)" Gayatri C. Spivak, preface to Derrida, *Of Grammatology*, xxviii.

open-ended nature of the word, by setting up the positive and negative renderings as exclusive alternatives. Derrida attempts to show that the foundational disparity of these renderings is unsustainable. In other words, Plato uses writing to warn of the dangers of writing—thus leaving his warning (according to his own analysis) a hostage to likely misunderstandings. The purportedly Platonic separation between the positive and negative alternatives deconstructs itself because these alternatives are mutually pervasive.

Acutely aware of the infinite array of possible renderings for words that are essentially unstable, Derrida's Plato makes his foundational intervention in metaphysics, by introducing order into the chaotic playground of textuality. Plato's binary opposites that impose stability enforce rules that bring the "free-play"[13] of textual meaning to a halt—an illusory and illegitimate move according to Derrida. His usual strategy to resist such closure is to invert the binaries, so that the previously privileged meaning is replaced with its marginalised counterpart. This inversion is no punctiliar moment, but a continuous process. The throne is always hot, because, as the monarch is overthrown by the pretender, their roles reverse—immediately demanding another revolution. In his reading of the *Phaedrus*, Derrida attempts to re-open the play by relentlessly emphasising the inherent ambiguity of the *pharmakon*.

> If the *pharmakon* is "ambiguous" it is because it constitutes the medium in which opposites are opposed, the movement and the play that links them among themselves, reverses them or makes one side cross over into the other (soul/body, good/evil, inside/outside, memory/forgetfulness, speech/writing, etc.). It is on the basis of this play or movement that the opposites or differences are stopped by Plato. The *pharmakon* is the movement, the locus, and the play: (the production of) difference. It is the differance of difference.[14]

Pharmakon is not a word that can be taken in two ways (poison/remedy; drug/antidote), but rather embodies the inevitable instability which in turn gives rise to the open-ended textuality that is then closed by Plato's construction of binaries. Derrida has sought to persuade his readers that this binary structure cannot hold even in Plato's influential dialogues. The elusive nature of *pharmakon* continually evades Platonic

---

13. "Free-play" is a North American rendering of the French *jeu*.
14. Derrida, "Plato's Pharmacy," 127.

arrest, exposing the inability of language to capture and secure stable meaning.[15] This perpetual deferment of meaning is what Derrida means by "Plato's Pharmacy."

Several important elements of Derrida's deconstructive method have thus arisen within this text, and are worth making explicit. Firstly, Derrida's ability to identify binary opposites in the text, where one partner of a dualism enjoys supremacy over the other, is accomplished here by the possible yet contradictory renderings of the word *pharmakon*. Secondly, comes the perception that these supposed opposites actually supervene one another, as demonstrated in the overlap between poison/remedy, drug/antidote, where the difference between dualisms is not absolutely distinct because possible meanings assumed to exclude each other rather spill over into one another. Thirdly, taking up the cause of the marginalised, underprivileged rendering, Derrida seeks to invert the binaries, so that the marginalised becomes privileged and vice versa. Such a strategy is exemplified in this instance in his attempt to overthrow speech's superiority over writing. Finally, however, Derrida is not content with a single successful revolution, but is committed to ensuring that revolution is in constant play as the binaries are perpetually inverted. This guarantees that the finality of so-called meaning remains always elusive.

It is clear from Derrida's seminal *Of Grammatology* that the target of this fourfold textual assault is the monolith of so-called "logocentrism."[16] This slippery term signifies Derrida's diagnosis of Western metaphysics since Plato, and alludes to the sometimes dormant assumption that the written word gains its currency from the presence of an all-pervasive transcendental-signified, a remnant of belief in the Graeco-Christian God, the ultimate point of reference upon which all language depends. This *logos*/supreme being/transcendental-signified/presence is replaced

---

15. Derrida here seems to ignore the nature of many Platonic dialogues, many of which are ironic and inconclusive (see for instance *Phaedo*, 114d–115d, or *Cratylus*). Furthermore, for Plato language is temporal, forms are eternal. This is why the best that can be attempted in language in order to refer to what-is, is to provide a moving image of eternity (*Timaeus* 29b, 38d).

16. Derrida's use of the term logocentrism is clearly outlined by Ward (*Theology and Contemporary Critical Theory*, 23). He offers a more detailed discussion of logocentrisms identified in the work of Cassirer, Heidegger and *Redephilosophie*, in his later comparison of Derrida with Barth (Ward, "Barth, Modernity and Postmodernity," 53–78).

[permanently] with the interminable "play" of meaning, resulting in an elusive open-endedness to all language. Words as signs do not simply find meaning in their difference from one another (Saussure), but meaning is also constantly "deferred" in the leap from one sign to another.

So much for his method, but what of Derrida's attitude? As he enters "Plato's Pharmacy," what Derrida seeks to encapsulate with the phrase "logocentrism" is readily identified. His cannons are zeroed in on what he calls "a metaphysics of presence," in which the over-privileged concepts of speech (the father, the good) stand over against their underprivileged counterparts in writing (the orphaned, the secondary). The inversion of these binaries is intended to liberate language from the mastery imposed by the metaphysics of presence which reduces difference to sameness and otherness to presence.

But has Derrida correctly diagnosed the western tradition as deliberately privileging speech over writing? For example, if the parable of the rich man and Lazarus[17] is read from this perspective, it deconstructs Derrida's perceived polarisations.[18] The rich man assumes the priority of speech over writing, as he appeals for the person of Lazarus to be made present to his five brothers (Luke 16:27–28). Such presence, he believed, would enable them to hear what they were unable to hear from (the texts of) Moses and the prophets. Abraham apparently denies the priority of speech over writing, arguing that if one cannot hear this text, neither will one hear a person—even a resurrected one (Luke 16:31). But both speech and writing are subsumed by another prior entity: the pitiful Lazarus. For the rich man's community, the capacity to hear either living speech or written text is predetermined by one's ethical comportment towards the helpless figure beyond one's gate. But one need not appeal to an eastern parable to question Derrida's diagnosis.

Turning from "Plato's Pharmacy" to Plato's text, it is clear that Plato has been unfairly caricatured. The Abraham of Western Metaphysics does not subscribe to the logocentrism identified by Derrida. For instance in his commentary on the *Phaedrus*, Plato scholar Charles S.

---

17. Although the parable is not of western origin, it has been adopted into the heart of the western literary corpus.

18. The use of Derrida's polarisations is highly questionable in itself, as he crudely applies the Aristotelian law of contradiction (*Metaphysics* IV) to his perceived binaries to Platonic dialogues. Although this would be a fruitful way of critiquing Derrida, the main critique here concerns the motive rather than the method of the deconstructionist project.

Griswold claims that Derrida has failed to take seriously Plato's irony, his use of dialogue as a genre and his urge for self knowledge. The result is, according to Griswold, a gross misreading of Plato by Derrida and the conclusion that, in Plato's eyes, Derrida is Phaedrus.[19] Such a methodological critique is, however, of less relevance to our purposes than a consideration of his attitude, addressing not only "what" Derrida argues but also exploring how and why he is predisposed to read in the way he does. From this perspective the dense but devastating analysis offered by Catherine Pickstock in *After Writing*[20] is of much greater interest.

Pickstock's identifies in "Plato's Pharmacy" a calculated marginalisation of physicality and thereby, one may infer, a diminished tolerance for the historical and the personal. The prime example is the way that Derrida has told the Platonic story in which the enemy comprises the sophists, the battleground is the priority of "Speech" over "Writing," and the *casus belli* is the metaphysics of presence. Pickstock argues that the war is not being waged over this metaphysics, but over the taming of language conducted by the sophists.

> [Plato's] critique of writing and rhetoric does not presuppose a preference for a supra-linguistic philosophical logos, independent of time and place, but, to the contrary, it is precisely such a preference which Socrates associates with a sophistic vision of a purely commercial reality. As heir to this vision, Derrida's insistence on the transcendental writtenness of language is revealed to be, after all, a rationalistic gesture which suppresses embodiment and temporality.[21]

By extracting the Socratic assault upon the priority of writing from the wider struggle against the Sophists, Derrida has identified Socrates himself with the very Socratic manipulation against which he is arguing. Derrida construes Plato as the father of a tradition from which difference is excluded by wielding a metaphysics of presence which diverts the philosopher's gaze from the physical world to the transcendental good. However, as Pickstock shows,

> as well as demonstrating that Plato did not wish to drive a wedge between form and appearance, the strongly positive view of *methexis* (participation) in the *Phaedrus* frees him from the charge

19. Griswold, *Self Knowledge in Plato's* Phaedrus.
20. Pickstock, *After Writing*.
21. Pickstock *After Writing*, 4.

of otherworldliness and total withdrawal from physicality, for the philosophic ascent does not result in a "loss" of love for particular beautiful things, since the particular participates in beauty itself.[22]

Indeed, Pickstock implies that like the sophists, Derrida himself shies away from physicality toward the "atopic"[23] realm of the linguistic. This insight is confirmed by exploring some of Derrida's later, and more explicitly theological essays. It is here that one may appropriate with greater lucidity Pickstock's claim that "Derrida's emphasis on writing is a denial of the living and dying physical *body*."[24]

THE GIFT OF DEATH

The Gift of Death is an essay that addresses our concerns, as Derrida deconstructs such texts as Heidegger's *Being and Time*, Kierkegaard's *Fear and Trembling* and Matthew's Gospel. The essay is an attempt to deconstruct ethics, arguing that the responsibility displayed by the "knights of good conscience" (who have dubbed deconstruction as nihilist, irresponsible, destructive) is ultimately irresponsible because it carries "within itself a nucleus of irresponsibility or absolute unconsciousness."[25] His case is built in conversation with the Czech philosopher Jan Patocka, whose *Heretical Essays on the Philosophy of History*[26] serve as the point of textual departure throughout *The Gift of Death*.

Patocka sets up a tension between the "orgiastic" and "responsibility." By orgiastic is meant "sacrificial violence,"[27] that cult of religion that engulfs individual consciousness with sacred, natural forces which blur the distinction between the animal, the human and the divine. Platonism and Christianity represent Europe's two primary means of overcoming this "orgiastic" with "responsibility"—these two polarities

---

22. Pickstock, *After Writing*, 14.

23. Atopic here meaning "place-less" or "out of place' in *A Greek-English Lexicon of the New Testament and Other Early Christian Literature* (Chicago: University Press), 120.

24. Pickstock, *After Writing*, 19.

25. Derrida, *On the Name*, 20.

26. Patocka, *Heretical Essays*.

27. Patocka, *Heretical Essays*, 101.

providing Derrida's much needed binary opposition. Once he is sitting comfortably with such an opposition, his deconstructive play can begin.

Patocka's history tells the story of the alternative routes out of the orgiastic towards responsibility. On the one hand, the Platonic narrative tells of the soul's quest towards the good generated by rationality. On the other, the Christian narrative is based upon relationship with a personal God, who being incommensurable with humanity ensures the perpetual elusiveness of perfection thereby instilling within humanity a humility absent from the Platonic alternative.[28] Awareness of our exposure before the God who sees in secret and yet cannot be seen—a crucial concept to which Derrida will return—is for Patocka most likely to awaken a sense of personal responsibility.

Unlike Patocka, who sees Christianity and Platonism as alternative (though not altogether inseparable) means of transcending the orgiastic, Derrida sees Christianity as merely incorporating (or perhaps, in Nietzsche's terms, "popularizing") Platonism and thereby unwittingly inheriting the hidden unacknowledged orgiastic that resides therein. A Christianity so construed does not have the means of addressing, critiquing or even being aware of the orgiastic it has unwittingly adopted. However, Derrida forgives Patocka his Christianity because of the latter's emphasis on the structural rather than the particular, as will become clear.

For Derrida, the decadence of modern technological civilisation arises from this repression and denial of the orgiastic. For Patocka this diminishes the structure of personal responsibility by subsuming human responsibility under social roles and allowing the repressed orgiastic to flourish surreptitiously.

> Technological civilisation only produces a heightening or recrudescence of the orgiastic, with the familiar effects of aestheticism and individualism that attend it, to the extent that it also produces boredom, for it "levels" or neutralizes the mysterious or irreplaceable uniqueness of the responsible self. The individualism

---

28. Gregory of Nazianzus criticised Plato for claiming that it is difficult to speak of God. It is impossible to speak of God noted Gregory, and the mischievous implication of saying that it is 'difficult' is that the speaker has attained this knowledge. Nevertheless, there are merits in Plato's work, as Gregory and others noted. Gregory believed that participation in God was required for knowledge of God to be born, but even then it was not a conceptual knowledge but a transformatory encounter. (See the first two of his *Five Theological Orations*.)

of technological civilisation relies precisely on a misunderstanding of the unique self. It is an individualism relating to a role and not a person.[29]

Technological society thus quietly subjects humanity once again to the levelling forces of nature. Unlike Heidegger, however, who seeks to awaken individual responsibility by adopting a being-towards-death, Patocka's Christianity leads him to regard responsibility within the primary context of one's relationship with the wholly other. Since Derrida's polemical artillery is turned upon technological civilisation, Patocka's arguments against sacrificial violence furnish *The Gift of Death* with the perfect anti-violence ammunition.

Patocka's essay is rendered heretical by investing its claims not in the particular aspects and meanings of the Christian faith. "What engenders all these meanings and links them, internally and necessarily," notes Derrida, "is a logic that at bottom . . . has no need of *the event of a revelation or the revelation of an event.*"[30] Patocka's interest lies not in the particular manifestations or doctrines of his own Christian faith, but in the deeper structural possibilities from which such revelation emerges.

> It needs to think the possibility of such an event but not the event itself. This is a major point of difference, permitting such a discourse to be developed without reference to religion as institutional dogma, and proposing a genealogy of thinking concerning the possibility and essence of the religious that doesn't amount to an article of faith. If one takes into account certain differences, the same can be said for many discourses that seek in our day to be religious . . . without putting forth theses or *theologems* that would by their very structure teach something corresponding to the dogmas of a given religion.[31]

It is not only Patocka who is seen in this light, but also a seemingly limitless host of thinkers including Marion, Levinas, and Ricoeur, along with Heidegger and Kierkegaard, Hegel and Kant. All these thinkers "belong to this tradition that consists of proposing a nondogmatic doublet of dogma, a philosophical and metaphysical doublet, in any case a thinking that "repeats" the possibility of religion without religion."[32]

29. Derrida, *On the Name*, 36.
30. Derrida, *After Writing*, 49.
31. Derrida, *After Writing*, 49.
32. Derrida, *After Writing*, 49.

Derrida, one might add, is to be numbered among them, seeking a messianic structure uncluttered by actual manifestations of messianic reality. For Derrida such manifestations represent the sacrificial violence of warring rivalries, as each Abrahamic religion stakes its claim to a piece of the land where the patriarch demonstrated his readiness to sacrifice his descendants.

To summarise *The Gift of Death* at this stage of its argument, one need merely observe that Derrida is carefully preparing the scenery for the performance of Kierkegaard's *Fear and Trembling*. Having drawn out the tension between individual sacrificial responsibility over against European decadence, between an impoverished unthinking Christianity over against its structural possibility, between Heideggerian individual consciousness over against Hegelian totalization, the text positively cries out for Kierkegaard.

Before turning to Kierkegaard, however, a brief outline of Derrida's notion of the gift, as recounted elsewhere,[33] will lend clarity to the unfolding claims of *The Gift of Death*, not least because the essay is fundamentally an argument about economy, the context in which a gift is to be understood. By "economy" Derrida means the circulation of transactions and monetary signs that defines every day human life. This economy by its very nature precludes the possibility of a gift. After all, at the very moment that a free, spontaneous act of grace occurs, its recipient is indebted to the giver. Thus, in order to keep the economy moving, the gift must either be refused or else a gift must be offered in response, thereby relieving the recipient of their debt. Of course, once this occurs, the exchange of so-called gifts is exposed as a mere transaction. A pure gift cannot be accommodated by an economy. Equally, for a gift to be a gift it must be received, and therefore cannot but enter the economy. And yet a gift can be received, though not absorbed into an economy. Rather like counterfeit money, it enters the economy without being assimilated by it, having an effect upon the economy. Whilst on the one hand the economy is necessary, on the other its disruption by the gift keeps alive a tension between itself and that which is not itself. If a gift is in the economy but not of the economy, then the economy is generated from beyond itself by its relation to the an-economical. Behold, the immanence and the transcendence of the gift! Enter Kierkegaard.

---

33. Derrida, *Given Time*.

Kierkegaard's *Fear and Trembling* is a narrative critique of general ethics in its Hegelian form. Through his literary spokesman, Joseph de Silentio, Kierkegaard sought to institute an economic boom. A decadent Europe under the spell of Hegel had, in Kierkegaard's eyes, demoted Christianity to the bargain basement where it had become gratuitously affordable to religious bargain hunters. Like the Dutch merchants who threw their spices into the harbour in order to raise their value,[34] Kierkegaard sought to instigate a religious inflation that would re-value the Christianity long schematized by the mediocrity effected by the Hegelian market crash. Abraham's readiness to sacrifice his son Isaac becomes the focus of de Silentio's economic campaign.

The story of Abraham's willingness to ride roughshod over conventional ethics on the one hand, and over the particular hopes of Sarah, Isaac and even himself on the other, is heard in all of its apparent absurdity. Abraham has been told by God to commit both infanticide—and (one might add) genocide, as he thereby wipes out the entire covenant nation promised to him—and is utterly incapable of giving any account of himself. Only in the very moment of no return does God intervene when having witnessed Abraham's astonishing faith he provides a ram to be slaughtered in Isaac's stead. De Silentio exposes his contemporaries to the fullest counter-conventional extremity of this shocking story.

When Abraham hears the voice of God, it is not mediated through a community but rather severs him from it. He is cut adrift from his *oikos*, drawn out of his economy, into the an-economic moment of the split-second after the decision but before the execution. At the point at which no refund is available, no (re)turn possible, the economy is frozen. In this timeless moment, foundational to all Abrahamic messianisms, "ethics must be sacrificed in the name of duty."[35] His obedience to duty (here described by Derrida in abstract terms though related to God) requires him to transgress ethics that would dub him a murderer.

> Absolute duty demands that one behave in an irresponsible manner (by means of treachery or betrayal), while still recognising, confirming, and reaffirming the very thing that one sacrifices, namely the order of human ethics and responsibility.[36]

---

34. Kierkegaard, *Concluding Unscientific Postscript*, 66.
35. Derrida, *On the Name*, 67.
36. Derrida, *On the Name*, 66–67.

Defacing the Text 89

Highlighting the absurdity, mystery and uniqueness of this event, Derrida draws on the notion of absolute duty to the other and the consequent necessary suspension of ethics to argue for the everyday commonality of the Abraham experience. Since the wholly other is encountered in every other [person], every time I make a decision to fulfil duty to another I thereby suspend the ethical because there are countless other "others" who cannot then receive from me the duty they warrant. And while one is blurring the distinction between the divine and the human why not also the animal, thinks Derrida.[37] Finally, there is little to distinguish Abraham's readiness to sacrifice his only son and with him the entire covenant nation, from Derrida's readiness to feed his cat.[38] (Think of the countless other cats that would each be thereby unable to receive that food.) Derrida's argument for the sheer arbitrariness of responsibility highlighted here is elaborated upon in the final chapter, 'tout Autre Est Tout Autre."

> God, as wholly other, is to be found everywhere there is something of the wholly other. And since each of us, everyone else, each other is infinitely other in its absolute singularity, inaccessible, solitary, transcendent, nonmanifest... then what can be said about Abraham's relation to God can be said about my reaction to every other (one) as every (bit) other [*tout autre comme tout autre*], in particular my relation to my neighbor or my loved ones who are as inaccessible to me, as secret and transcendent as Jahweh.[39]

Since every other person now constitutes the so-called wholly other, there are no criteria by which decisions to favour one *other* against another *other* can be justified. Instead, the shifting ethical assumptions of society, arbitrary though they are, are most likely to determine my individual ethical decisions, which inevitably draws us back to Abraham on Mount Moriah, sacrificing general ethics for the sake of higher individual duty. It is in the timeless moment of absolute singularity somewhere between decision and execution, in that an-economical instant, that Abraham broke free of his *oikos*, his ethical economy, in order to

---

37. Derrida, *On the Name*, 69.
38. Derrida, *On the Name*, 71.
39. Derrida, *On the Name*, 78.

adhere to absolute duty. Then and there God returned Isaac and thus reaffirmed the *oikos* as an economy of investments and rewards.[40]

DERRIDA'S GOSPEL OF MATTHEW

It is at this point that Derrida's characteristic witch-hunt (for the hypocritical) arrives in all its fury at the Gospel according to Matthew. If Christianity claims to transcend ethical economy, or at least reside within the reverberation between economy and gift, economy and aneconomy, the Gospel according to Matthew, in Derrida's view, makes strong but hidden economic demands that collapse the necessary tension once again into a concrete economy. As the purported author of the Gospel, the figure of Matthew represents a promising target with his tax collecting background of checks and balances, investments and rewards, and it should come as little surprise that his market-driven concerns find their way into his version of what constitutes good news. Derrida's genius for exposing hidden hypocrisy spotlights Matthew's promise "your Father who sees in secret will reward you" (Matt 6:4).

For Matthew, secrecy signifies private humility as opposed to a public piety, because long-term, heavenly investments are made by the godly. But they are investments made with the intention of accruing a more rewarding (but well deserved) commutation, nothing whatsoever to do with the gift of grace. This in turn means that the name of God is equated with an invisible subjectivity that in turn means that the Matthean economy is simply a higher form of the very pharisaism against which (on Derrida's view) Matthew's Jesus rails. Externally,

---

40. Buber might serve as an interesting dialogue partner on this issue. Dialogicalism is central to Buber's project, emphasising as he does the significance of that which is located "between" the I-thou encounter. Graham Ward traces a fruitful comparison between Buber and Heidegger. Although there are significant similarities between their work, for Heidegger, encounter with the other is grounded in an ontological otherness that precedes the encounter, whereas for Buber, the I-thou (as opposed to Levinas's later thou-me economy) is ultimately contained within a subjectivism, just as his dialogicalism is contained within a larger monological framework. Heidegger's argument then shies away from prescriptive assertions whereas Buber remains content with them. Ward concludes that "in the end, despite Buber's Kantianism and his desire to overcome the Hegelian hermeneutical consciousness through dialogue, he stumbles into Hegelianism by his very method, and dialogicalism returns to the kind of dialectic it has always spurned" (Ward, "Barth, Modernity and Postmodernity," 135).

Matthew's economy appears to be selfless in renunciation, but internally is driven by the secretively calculating desire for a heavenly return.

For Derrida this secret is 'the clarity of divine lucidity [that] penetrates everything yet keeps within itself the most secret of secrets.'[41] However, being more interested in messianic structure than messianic reality, Derrida re-inscribes the Father with his *Tout Autre*.

> We should stop thinking about God as someone, over there, way up there, transcendent, and, what is more—into the bargain, precisely—capable, more than any satellite orbiting in space, of seeing into the most secret of the most interior places. It is perhaps necessary, if one is to follow the traditional Judeo-Christiano-Islamic injunction, but also at the risk of turning it against that tradition, to think of God and of the name of God without such idolatrous stereotyping or representation. Then one might say: God is the name of the possibility I have of keeping a secret that is visible from the interior but not from the exterior . . . God is in me, he is the absolute "me" or "self." . . . And he is made manifest . . . when there appears the desire and power to render absolutely invisible and to constitute within oneself a witness of that invisibility.[42]

Responsibility thought to arise from encounter with the dreadful otherness of God instead is portrayed as arising from an invisible encounter within the individual. Abraham's sacrifice, as Derrida tells it, is contrasted starkly with the Abrahamic manifestation of Matthew. Whilst the latter seeks to counter an economic problem with an economic solution, thereby compounding the economic problem, the former counters the economic problem with the an-economic solution.

DERRIDIAN ECONOMY

There are two crucial aspects to be considered in Derrida's use of Matthew: one historical, the other economical. Since it is primarily an attitude rather than a methodology that is sought, critique of Derrida is better served by considering how he treats his texts than by analysing his theories of interpretation. There is something of an abyss between

---

41. Derrida, *On the Name*, 108.
42. Derrida, *On the Name*, 109.

Derrida's theory and his practice.[43] This is by no means intended as a negative statement. For instance, on reading Derrida's earlier work it is quite clear that he seems to offer such a radical individualism and incommensurability between individuals, that his enthusiasm for listening to the other sounds like little more than an empty gesture. Equally, however, in his later writings, one cannot but sense a profound level of listening to, or at least curiosity about what the other is saying, in being radically exposed to their otherness. In this sense his practice is better than his preaching.

But Derrida has not listened well to the Sermon on the Mount, for he has misread Matthew just as he has misread Plato. For all of its avowed interest in historicity, *The Gift of Death* is a book that demonstrates little interest in the historical. In his quest for the a-historical Jesus, Derrida has somewhat predictably short circuited the political and historical urgency of his preaching, and extracted instead a collection of timeless moral aphorisms. Such timeless gems are of enormous value in the Derridian economy.

The pragmatic manipulation of the text is demonstrated at the level of the particular. Matthew is regarded as Pharisaic in his condemnation of the Pharisees.[44] Rather than sharing in Abraham's reverberation between economy and gift, Matthew's moral demands gain their cash value from the promise of heavenly reward. In other words—Matthew's report is devoid of grace, simply earning a just reward in a more long-term economy of exchange.

Removing Matthew's Jesus from his historical concerns allows Derrida to exclude other ways of reading the text.[45] Having secured Matthean textuality from the threat of history, his reading is validated in rejecting the particulars of time and space. For instance, Jerusalem, the very site where Abraham offered Isaac, has entered the last generation of Jewish possession. Rather than simply offering a timeless otherworldliness (perhaps another hint here of Derrida reading his version

---

43. Derrida is not alone here. Even for Augustine's, the principles of *De Doctrina Christiana* are not entirely reflected in his *City of God*. Many theologians also identify in Barth's *Church Dogmatics*, the frequent use of sloppy exegesis that does not cohere with his own interpretive theory.

44. Derrida, *On the Name*, 99–100, 107. Although neither for early Christian history nor for Matthew are the Pharisees merely discredited. The Matthaean Jesus exhorts both the crowds and his disciples to obey the Pharisees (Matt 23:2–3).

45. See further below.

of Platonism into Christianity), Matthew is waking his readers up to the fact that Israel as she currently stands does not have a long-term future; the historical violence of AD 70 detonates the under-historical readings of the gospels offered by Derrida and company.[46] This inconvenient account of events, which may be heard without strong appeal to the sources external to the text,[47] overcomes Derrida's anti-historical security measures and suggests a different Matthew altogether. For a theological alternative less likely to be eroded by the demands of the historical one may return to Pickstock via Wright.

For Wright, in Matthew 6 the warnings concerning almsgiving, prayer and fasting "are not . . . directed simply at the difference between outward and inward observance."[48] Just as Derrida had misread Socrates' conflict with the Sophists, so he misreads that of Jesus with the Pharisees. According to Wright, it is the Pharisaic notions of calculating economic returns that is criticised by Matthew. However, the warnings are not about secretive or ostentatious obedience, but about the way that Israel relates to YHWH as Father. In fact, the very facelessness of Derrida's "wholly other" is unwittingly but substantially critiqued by Wright, who continues, "[rebel Israel] claims [YHWH] as [Father], but apparently treats him as a faceless bureaucrat, to be bribed or wheedled into giving her what she wants."[49] The facelessness of Derrida's "other" can be every bit as idolatrous as that of some of Jesus' addressees. Conversely, to treat God [not in a depersonalised way but] as father is

> a matter of worshipping the true God as opposed to worshipping idols: Israel cannot serve the true god and mammon (6.24), and anxiety about the future is a sign that she is trying to do just that (6.25–34). Those who are truly seeking the kingdom need not be

---

46. Understanding Jesus within his historical context, emphasises the historical specificity of the texts that resist the Derridian reading with its premature appropriation of historical statements as timeless truths. See chapter 4 below.

47. As demonstrated in chapter 4. See, for instance, in Matt 7:24–27 the house built upon the rock contrasted with that built upon the sand. There is a clear reference here to the Temple, which—so long as it is regarded as a possession—is destined to fall.

48. Wright, *Jesus and the Victory of God*, 291. There is little room here to expand upon the hints planted by Wright. He notes in these three warnings a reference to key aspects of the Pharisees democratising programme. In the absence of the temple (which apparently unknown to them is imminent) such observances would be enormously important. In addressing those issues it may be that Jesus is offering an alternative programme to that of the Pharisees. See chapter 6 below.

49. Wright, *Jesus and the Victory of God*, 291.

afraid, whereas those whose seeking of the kingdom consists in pursuing a national or personal agenda for the restoration of the land, property or ancestral rights will find that they have been serving a god who cannot give them such things.[50]

After all, Israel were tenants, not owners of the vineyard that was Israel. When the tenants became the owners (Matt 21.33–46), it guaranteed their impending loss, not least as otherness was thereby excluded from their economy. That is, the vineyard was now exclusively in the hands of its tenants—like a true Fishian interpretive community. It is this very issue that is addressed by Pickstock's alternative reading of the gift. In contrast to the presumption underlying Derrida's exposure of Matthew's secret lust for long term economic gain, Pickstock suggests that the very ability to give a gift in the first place itself constitutes a return. "The "giving up" of the gift occurs in trust of a "return" with difference, but this return is not something one can earn, nor is it over against the movement of giving up."[51] Such a return eludes a calculative mentality and does not expect "gratitude."

> In contrast to Derrida, one can speak of a "return" indissociable from the act of giving, simultaneous with it, a condition of its possibility, and yet not reducible to an economic market exchange—not reducible because the return is already receiving in giving. And insofar as one hopes for a continuous return in the future, one is looking to be surprised rather than for the return of a debt of an anticipated amount.[52]

Pickstock here notes that the assumption that giving incorporates loss further assumes that that which was given was previously owned. According to Matthew 6, however, it is precisely when stewardship becomes ownership that the loss occurs. If Derrida claimed that long-term investments are made by the godly, Pickstock's reading suggests that, in accordance with the parable of the pounds, the investors were not investing their own possessions. Such a notion of the gift accords well with Matthew's text, but also once again demonstrates that Derrida's misreading itself exemplifies the very attitude that is more carefully targeted by the text he is deconstructing than his own misreading cares (or dares) to see. Although the text can answer back if listened to, Derrida's

50. Wright, *Jesus and the Victory of God*, 291.
51. Pickstock, *After Writing*, 112.
52. Pickstock, *After Writing*, 112.

de-personalized, de-historicized reading of it guarantees the silence of marginalized but awkward (i.e. historical) renderings.

Relating this critique again to the parable (Luke 16:19-31), it might be noted that Lazarus is an awkward an-economic presence, in Derridian terms, a gift, and one that is rejected by the rich man. He is incommensurable with the rich man's concerns, and remains outside the gates of his economy. However, chapter 5 of this thesis will argue that Lazarus is, in a sense, to be identified with Christ. To exclude Lazarus is to exclude the Messiah (cf. Matt 25:31-46). A Derridian Lazarus,[53] faceless and depersonalised, does not demand ethical action, and negates the possibility of encountering the Messiah in him.[54] Such action would not only be a long-term investment (securing a post-mortem welcome by Abraham), but primarily a present Messianic encounter in which otherness is engaged. Derrida, like many of Jesus' contemporaries, is so busy awaiting a specific Messiah that he fails to recognise the Messiah at his doorstep.[55] Derrida has used his deconstructive tools to manufacture a Messiah whose otherness is technologically pre-inscribed.

KHORA

To portray Derrida as technologist, however, is no easy task because there is so much in his prolific writings that resists such straightforward characterisation. One example is his appeal to the nameless wholly other hinted at by Plato's use of the term *khora*.[56] Derrida follows (and

---

53. I.e., a Derridian construal of the messiah.

54. Crossan's enthusiasm to portray Jesus' parables as "amoral"—by resurrecting "force" and sacrificing "content"—leads to a particular use of historical critical tools. Such tools enable him to chisel the parable (Luke 16:19-31) down to the effigy of the *amoral* historical Jesus he wishes to sculpt. His classification of the parable as one designed to effect reversal (*In Parables*, 75) illustrates his approach. Discarding Luke 16:27-31 as the addition of an early church, it is best, he states, "to take 16:19-26 as an actual parable of Jesus. Its literal point was a strikingly *amoral* description of situational reversal between the rich man and Lazarus" (*In Parables*, 68). See also Crossan, *Raid on the Articulate*, 107.

55. Luke suggests that even John the Baptist ran such a danger (Luke 7:18-23). Cf. also Bockmuehl, *This Jesus*, 48-55.

56. The normal range of meaning for the word *chora* is defined by Liddell and Scott as "the space or room in which a thing is, a place, spot, Lat. *Locus*: the place assigned, the proper place" (Liddell and Scott, *A Greek-English Lexicon*, 9th ed., [Oxford: Clarendon] 830). It is worth remembering that khora has an everyday use that is taken

elaborates) Heidegger in his use of this Platonic term to counter the totalizing claims of technologism. As shown in chapter 1 of this thesis, encountering *aletheia*, i.e., the unfolding and concealment of truth, may be conceived as inhabiting an open space in which revelation occurs. Heidegger himself sometimes uses the word *khora* to allude to this space.[57] Such a fruitful place that constitutes radical exposure to the wholly other who impinges upon our experience is bound to attract Derrida's attention.

Derrida's brilliance surfaces most clearly in his imaginative use of Plato. In fairness to Derrida the dynamic of his open-endedness is generated not as is often supposed by an empty nihilism, but by a curious teleological magnetism. However, the source of this teleological gravity is not the God, the Wholly Other of negative theology. Derrida seeks to escape the insidious positivity of negative theology by appeal to a different, nameless "Wholly Other"—namely the *tout autre* of "*khora*," as Caputo explains.

> If Levinas thinks to find a Greek echo of a very theological *tout autre* in the *epekeina tes ousias*, Derrida seeks out an alternate, outlying, atheological, desert site in *khora*. The otherness of the *khora*—the "barren, radically nonhuman, and atheological character of this "place""—is something "irreducibly other," and in "a certain manner" it is "wholly other." But this *tout autre* does not go under the name of God, is not an event or promise or gift, and has nothing to do with negative theology—although its very barrenness obliges us to speak of it as if it were the Wholly Other that theology calls God, the very same.[58]

In *Timaeus*, *khora* is the raw space upon which the creator's blueprints are imposed in order to forge a world of becoming. *Khora* does not denote "raw material," but perhaps the pre-existent *ex nihilo* from which creation emerged, the dangerous chaos that is a foundationless shadowy cavern in which the ordered world finds its place. *Khora* is the receptacle, the midwife of becoming. Having distinguished between the world of being, and the world of becoming, Plato introduces *khora* as a "third form," a *tritos genos*. It is the blank sheet upon which order is inscribed, a chaotic space in which earth, wind, air and fire are in a

---

up by ancient writers, but is made mysterious by Derrida.

57. Heidegger, *On The Way To Language*, 66.

58. Caputo, *Prayers and Tears*, 37.

constant state of flux. It has no character of its own, but is the smooth surface that bears the imprints of becoming in the image of being.

> We may indeed use the metaphor of birth and compare the *receptacle* to the mother, the model to the father, and what they produce between them to their offspring; and we may notice that, if an imprint is to present a very complex appearance, the material on which it is to be stamped will not have been properly prepared unless it is devoid of all the characters which it is to receive. For if it were like any of the things that enter it, it would badly distort any impression of a contrary or entirely different nature when it received it, as its own features would shine through. So anything that is to receive in itself every kind of character must be devoid of all character.[59]

Before the creation, there existed firstly the eternal world of being upon which secondarily the temporal world of becoming was modelled and which in turn found its home thirdly, in the *tritos genos* in the eternal changeless space that is *khora*. However, as Caputo notes, Derrida introduces *khora* not only as deeply interior to philosophy, but also as an outsider concept, an alternative outlying region beyond the realm of the all-pervasive *logos*, and outside the myth/*logos* binarity.[60] He leaves the word untranslated and is keen to protect it from logocentric attempts at apprehension, quests to "make sense" of it. To name *khora*, or even to make the mistake of saying what it is, is to impose upon it a history of interpretation, to ascribe to it properties that imply that it is sensible or intelligible when in fact it is neither.[61]

Derrida perceives in Plato's *Timaeus* a highly subtle identification of Socrates with *khora*, but the identification is purely for rhetorical purposes, because in truth *khora* cannot be compared with a thing. Later Derrida draws attention not simply to the use of this word in Plato's text, but to the way that it governs the structure of *Timaeus* as a whole. For instance, Socrates refers to a previous political dialogue with a race of poets from beyond the city, who thus have no space of their own—sophists, poets, imitators without access to the *logos*, with no space, and an

---

59. Plato, *Timaeus* 50a–51d.

60. Rather as darkness though parasitic on light helps reveal and enhance light when, light has become over-familiar (consider snow blindness for instance), so the *khora* of the *Timaeus* allows the rationality of reason to emerge into prominence.

61. This is hardly consistent with Plato's use of the term, and at best is to be regarded as a creative misreading.

inability to mimic or imitate that which they see in the city of citizens/philosophers/politicians. Socrates feigns to identify himself with those who have no space, but of course, he is in the city, talking to those with a space.[62] Belonging neither to the people of no place, nor the people with a place, Derrida sees Socrates as presenting himself as a deconstructive "*tritos genos*,"[63] even before the word "khora" has appeared. Socrates is in a position to deconstruct both *genē*, and yet himself inevitably to be deconstructed too. Derrida notes that having cleared the ground in his preamble, Socrates declares himself fully receptive.

> "so here I am, all ready to accept it and full of drive for receiving everything that you will have to offer me" (20c). Once more the question returns, what does *receive* mean? What does *dekhomai* mean? With this question in the form of "what does X mean?" it is not so much a question of meditating on the *sense* of such and such an expression as of remarking the fold of an immense difficulty: the relationship, so ancient, so traditional, so determinant, between the question of sense and the sensible and that of receptivity in general.[64]

Heralding *khora* as a *tritos genos*, present but inassimilable, receptive but unreceivable, Derrida is keen to emphasise here *khora*'s resistance to Hegelian synthesis. He sees in Hegel a rather two-dimensional gesture towards a buxom otherness. That is, an otherness that yields itself readily to the machinations of human progress as otherness is absorbed into familiarity in order that synthesis might be achieved.[65] *Khora* is used by Derrida to open up such a system to the disruptive incoming of the other, as he comments in his essay "Faith and Knowledge":

> Radically heterogeneous to the safe and sound, to the holy and the sacred, it never admits of any indemnification. This cannot even be formulated in the present, for [*khora*] never presents itself as such. It is neither Being, nor the Good, nor God, nor Man, nor History. It will always resist them, will have always been . . .

---

62. Plato, *Timaeus* 19b–21a
63. Plato describes khora as a *"tritos genos,"* (*Timaeus* 48e).
64. Derrida, *On The Name*, 110.
65. That Derrida has fairly represented Hegel here is debatable, since Hegel's encounter with otherness had the intention of transcending rather than underwriting the self.

the very place of an infinite resistance, of an infinitely impassable persistence . . . an utterly faceless other.[66]

In de-facing otherness so explicitly, Derrida has clearly parted company with Heidegger. If technologism depersonalises humanity, then of necessity deconstructionism in like manner depersonalises the *tout autre*. Caputo's colourful commentary on Derrida highlights this distance between Derrida and Heidegger. He perceives that Derrida exhorts us

> to avoid saying of her/it that *es gibt*, that she/it gives, that *khora* gives. For that Heideggerianism sounds all too beneficent and theological, like God giving. Unlike God, *khora* cannot rise to the level of a command or promise of a determinate giver; and unlike *Ereignis* there is nothing proper or properly giving about *khora*.[67]

Thus it seems that Derrida is all too determined in his search for de-terminate faith. Despite his avowal of radical openness, many of his questions have already arrived at their terminus and stand as antecedent conclusions about what actually constitutes otherness. For all the disturbance and disruption promised by the vulnerability of exposure to this nameless wholly other heralded by deconstruction, it also manages surreptitiously to pacify and tranquillise expectations against the wrong sort of otherness.[68] A personal, historical, messianic expression of otherness is not welcome to the professedly all-embracing Derridian hospitality. This raises questions not only about the wrong sort of otherness but also about what in Derrida's eyes is the right sort. Just how other is other?

66. Derrida, "Faith and Knowledge," 58–59.
67. Caputo, *Prayers and Tears*, 36.
68. Derrida himself carries the pharisaic torch in his religious compulsion to "build a hedge around *khora*." (Derrida's vigorous desire to shield *khora* from eisegesis is witnessed clearly in "Khora," *On the Name*, 98–99). In fact if, as is widely supposed, the appellation "Pharisee" is derived from *Pharash* (to separate), then Derrida's own pharisaic tendencies are revealed by reading an under-privileged rendering of *khora*'s verbal derivative, namely *khorizo*, (to separate). E.g., Mark 10:9 "What . . . God has joined together let no man *put asunder (khorizeto)*." Derrida is at his most extreme separatist/*khora*-ite/pharisaical in his drive to maintain the otherness of otherness. Compared with the Abrahamic humility of the voiceless and passive Lazarus (who is thrown at the gate, licked by the dogs, carried by the angels and helped by God), Derrida's audacious defence of *khora* is merely the source of the hyper-humility (and therefore a pseudo-humility) with which many Pharisees are cast by the Gospels. Furthermore, like many of the Pharisees, Derrida knows exactly what sort of Messiah (or "Christ") around which to center his reading.

Derrida's playful portrayal of the *tout autre* is still effectively an exercise in underwriting one's own preconceived expectations. Of what other "other" can he conceive once he has buried his religious concerns below the surface of history? Derrida's religious convictions do require a divinity but are compelled to reject a personal God. There is therefore little option for Derrida but to nod his head toward *khora*, the only divinity on hand willing to meet the demands of deep structural religion. The *tout autre* is divine, all too divine. Since it is necessary to defend such a nameless divinity from the offence of history, Derrida builds his protective fence around *khora*.

Applying these insights to the parable (Luke 16:19–31) one notes that the word "*khora*" is present in the parable, at least in a more original form.[69] However, the "chasm" here is not the location of divine otherness. Rather it is the barrier between Hades and Abraham's bosom, that is, between those who are in the kingdom and those who are excluded from it (Luke 16:26). An ethical/social chasm might also be identified stretching out between the rich man's community and Lazarus, but here there is a gate between them.[70] After death, the gate is barred. In short, the parable might be heard as an urgent insistence to enter through the gate, and deal face to face with this "khora."[71] That is precisely not what Derrida intends, with his desire to maintain an exclusion zone around *khora*. According to the parable *khora* has a gateway called Lazarus—to encounter Lazarus is to encounter the otherness of khora. However, on Derrida's advice, the rich man would

---

69. The Greek χώρα is ultimately derived from the word χάσμα that Luke uses to describe the 'chasm' in Luke 16: 26.

70. The presumption that Abraham's lap is "up" and that Hades is "down" is, according to Grobel, derived from the Semitism of lifting up one's eyes to look (Luke 16:23). It "no more involves a spatial lifting that '*sursum corda*' refers to a cardiac displacement" (Grobel, "Whose Name was Neves," 379). The chasm might be thought of then as a horizontal distance, rather than the gap between a heavenly upstairs and a subterranean hell.

71. Such an interpretation may be found in B. B. Scott's sociological reading of the parable. Scott makes good use of historical critical tools, but imposes modern categories upon the supposed experience of those who first heard the parable: 'The gate is not just an entrance to the house but the passageway to the other . . . In any given interpersonal or social relationship there is a gate that discloses the ultimate depths of human existence. Those who miss that gate may, like the rich man, find themselves crying in vain for a drop of cooling water' (Scott, *Hear Then, the Parables*, 159). S. I. Wright appreciates this reading, but highlights its historical unlikelihood (Wright, *The Voice of Jesus*, 168).

remain every bit as incapacitated as Lazarus, respecting the barrier that separates him. Nevertheless by the end of the parable, *khora* itself has become the exclusion zone (Luke 16:26).

THEOLOGICAL IMPLICATIONS

Whether Derrida is regarded as ingenious in subtlety or tedious in predictability, his religion without religion is still religion, just as his a-theological demands are still theological. Those who have negotiated the terrain of his prolific writings may find their theological reading enriched, as Isolde Andrews has attempted to show with a Derridian reading of Barth.[72] It is possible that his claims may provoke readings that might not otherwise have been encountered, for instance in the reading of Matthew's economy outlined above.

But Derrida has no intention of being positive. All Abrahamic—i.e., "determinable"—faiths, are inherently dangerous because they claim to know (even if such knowledge parades itself in apophatic clothes) the object of their messianic expectation. They know what they are waiting for, and thus betray an audacity from which it is supposed that a more indeterminate faith is immune. It is this very messianic readiness to embrace that which is entirely unknown, the *tout autre*, a readiness far exceeding the pre-determinate, concretised formulae of Abrahamic expectation, that is the pulsing heart of deconstruction. Hence, deconstruction claims to furnish Abrahamic religion with a vulnerability that can too easily be sacrificed in the quest for secure foundations and certainties. It claims to serve religion, not by strengthening but by weakening religious certainty. Danger and not safety, exposure and not security, vulnerability and not certainty are Derrida's offerings.

At the level of method, there may even be hints that the Gospels portray Jesus as something of a deconstructor. As a subversive storyteller in the prophetic tradition, Jesus certainly adopted an attitude of deconstruction, primarily deconstruction of the reader/hearer. Some of deconstruction's key methodological steps can be clearly seen in his prophetic ministry: If deconstruction begins with the call to recognise centres of concretized stability and draw attention to marginal cases, Luke's Jesus appears deconstructive: He highlights the marginal case when he

---

72. Andrews, *Deconstructing Barth*.

asks the Pharisees whether it was good to destroy life on the Sabbath (Luke 6:9); when he accuses the scribes "you have hindered those who were entering" (Luke 11:52); when he reveals that the synagogue leader held the life of a donkey more important than the life of a woman (Luke 13:15–16); when he warns his disciples not to cause "one of these little ones to sin" (Luke 17:2); when he healed the blind beggar who was being rebuked (Luke 18:35–43). The response is invariably either to praise God (and de-centre the self) or to plot opposition (redoubling self-assurance). Secondly, Jesus frequently inverts opposites, when he declares that "the first will be last and the last first" (Luke 13:30), when he announces "whoever saves his life will lose it and whoever loses his life for me will find it" (Luke 9:24), and most explicitly in the Lukan beatitudes where Jesus' Blessings and Woes contravene his contemporaries' construct of common sense (Luke 6:20–26). The Deconstructive Jesus finally affirms that only those who place their selves perpetually under erasure can be His disciples: "If anyone would come after me, he must deny himself, take up his cross daily and follow me" (Luke 9:23).

Despite this convergence between Derrida and the textually mediated Jesus, there are also significant divergences. Deconstruction is for Jesus necessarily inseparable from the advent of the Kingdom of God, and its implied transformation. This regenerative work is not so much an antecedent possession of the church that would serve to consolidate self-assuredness, as an eschatological hope based on faith in the risen Christ, without whom Abrahamic faith is in vain (1 Cor 15:14). The final reversal of deconstruction is a grace-initiated reversal best described as Resurrection. Jesus did not simply come to tear down but to rebuild ("Destroy this temple . . . ") But as Wright has argued, Jesus came not *to build* but *to be* a new temple. Jesus promises a presence for which there is no room in the deconstructive enterprise.[73]

How then can Derrida call Abraham "father"? If Abraham had been ready to commit infanticide, Derrida's humility compels him to commit parricide. Derrida seeks to resist being identified with determinable, "Abrahamic" faiths because of the violence they have engendered. It is

73. The promise, 'where two or three gather together in my name, I am there in their midst'(Matt 18:20), is best understood alongside the rabbinical saying, 'if two sit together and words of the Law are spoken between them, the Divine Presence rests between them.' (*Pirque Aboth* 3.3) Jesus is not simply replacing the temple, but replacing Torah and embodying Shekinah. He promises a *parousia* that is an affront to the spirit of deconstruction just as it is to the Pharisees.

rather the notion of Messianic expectation that interests Derrida. His concern with deferral is closely related to the messianic consciousness that seems to enliven history with the expectation of an immanent irruption of otherness. Such messianism casts the shadow of provisionality over human life, and is clearly akin to Derrida's concern for incessant humility in the light of otherness. However, the historical messianisms do have the unpleasant by-product of belief in the actual arrival of the Messiah/Other. Such an arrival would be disaster for Derrida. Whilst he happily declares *"viens, oui, oui, . . . "* (*Parages* 25), if the Messiah had the ineptitude actually to turn up, Derrida would have to parody John the Baptist and announce, "If you are he who is to come, we will wait for another."[74] Thus he betrays his antecedent circumscriptions upon the *tout autre*. Finally in Derrida's case, where the *tout autre* is forbidden personality and historical expression, *tout autre n'est pas tout autre*.

This is why, anticipating chapter 5 below, we must say that the advent of Christ displaces our presuppositions. This is very different from the Derridian (and to some extent, the Bultmannian) desire to clear away our presuppositions in order that messianic otherness might subsequently be encountered in the space *we have created*. Such otherness would be severely circumscribed before it was ever encountered. The otherness of Christ, as outlined in the Introduction to this thesis, is content-full.[75] The explicit presupposition of chapters 5–7 below is that in Christ the other has arrived and is arriving. This is borne out by the brief reflections this chapter has offered on the parable (Luke 16:19–31) in relation to deconstruction. In each instance it was implied that serious engagement with the other as encountered in Lazarus is forbidden by deconstruction. This coheres with Vanhoozer's sharp critique of deconstructionist otherness: "If the other is *so* other that nothing can be said (or done) about it, then it can make no concrete difference to our lives . . . The postmodern rhetoric in favour of the other apparently leads to the postmodern ethic of indifference to the other."[76] For the sake of respecting the deconstructionist otherness, Lazarus is left to suffer. Since chapter 5 will argue that, according to the parable, the suffering of

---

74. 'Were the Messiah ever to show up, that indiscretion would ruin the whole idea of the messianic' (Caputo, *Prayers and Tears*, 78).

75. See pages 5–6 above.

76. Vanhoozer, *Is There a Meaning in this Text?*, 404.

Lazarus is inseparable from the suffering of Christ,[77] one may venture the claim that homage to the *tout autre* requires indifference towards the already-arrived Christ as presently encountered in Lazarus.[78]

DERRIDA THE TECHNOLOGIST

It is Derrida's blueprint for the *tout autre* which, despite his celebration of paradoxology, finally betrays his technologist attitude. Just how paradoxological is Derrida? Whilst there is something enigmatic in his religion without religion, one that both serves and offends religion, this is no paradox. It may appear to be so, as it both relies upon and disaffirms the importance of the messianic, preferring a passive messianic structure to an active messianic expression. This affirms the messianic by seeking its hidden, underlying, originary dynamism, even as it recoils from actual historical messianicity. But there is neither paradox nor doxology here; only the patient reassertion of technological manipulation. A text with otherness is defused of its capacity to answer back, because it has been deconstructively recycled into something ready to hand, something useful, a convenient tool. Mining for the deep structure of the text enables the deconstructor to make use of a text without the inconvenience of historical complications.[79]

We have argued that Derrida's technologism has two main features. The first is a denial of history, such that his theological claims can only amount to eschatology without parousia and deity without incarnation. Derrida is rightly concerned about the misuse of history, an abuse which Caputo has brilliantly described: "We cannot simply slip out of the back door of the text and steal away to some transcendental signified and

---

77. See pages 173–75. Cf. Matt 25:31–46.

78. Such a criticism is made with caution, especially considering Derrida's own background. Being of Algerian Jewish descent, not moving to France until the age of 22, Derrida has good claim to "outsider" status. Furthermore, he was politically active, speaking out on behalf of other Algerian immigrants in France, supporting the rights of the Czech Charter 77 dissidents, and opposing apartheid. By Matthean logic he may unwittingly have encountered Christ through such struggles (Matt 25:31–46).

79. In his superb critique of postmodern philosophy in general, and Derrida's progenitor, Nietzsche, in particular, David Bently Hart provides a summary statement that aptly identifies postmodernity's impatience with inconvenient details, when he notes that "surfaces are always more complicated than 'depths'" (Hart, *The Beauty of the Infinite*, 113).

then triumphantly march back in the front door with the Secret Key to the story."[80] History can always be created to provide justification for the wayward interpreter. History however can also bring otherness to the text. There is therefore no reason to repel historicity as such because to do so, following Caputo's analogy, is to bolt the door of the text. Such security measures necessarily exclude aspects of otherness and therefore otherness itself.

This hidden closure predisposes one's repulse toward the actual arrival of a messiah, as Caputo has pointed out.[81] Thus one may align Derrida's deep structural Messianism with those of whom Barth writes in his discussion of human receptivity to revelation. Commenting on the phrase "thy Kingdom come, Thy will be done *on earth* as in heaven," he observes that

> ... this *kai epi ges* was the self-unveiling, the form of God which Israel found attested in its Holy Scripture on every page and which now stood fulfilled before it, it denied again and again just as the fathers in the desert had murmured against Moses and later the prophets had been stoned, not out of irreligion, but in the protest of the most refined and most ponderable religion against revelation, which will not leave even or especially the righteous man alone but confronts him with God. Thus the revelation of Jesus ends with his crucifixion by the most pious men of their time, who even though they had Immanuel daily on their lips and in their hearts did not want this Immanuel in its unconditionally enacted fulfilment.[82]

This leads inexorably to a second major feature of Derrida's technologism, namely the de-facing of the text, the de-personalisation of the other, such that his theological humility amounts to a cross without resurrection.[83] The wholly other cannot be allowed to make unwelcome intrusions into history, which leads deconstruction not only in perpetual deferment, but in perpetual docetic retreat from the Kingdom of God. Derrida depersonalises God by regarding Yahweh as one who merely occupies the space opened up by the *tout autre*. Despite its subtle inge-

---

80. Caputo, *Prayers and Tears*, 177.
81. Caputo, *Prayers and Tears*, 190.
82. Barth, *Church Dogmatics* I.1, 319.
83. This paragraph anticipates the main argument that is to follow in the next chapter, i.e., on what resurrection actually is.

nuity, Derrida's entire project demands rather brutal religious reforms in a drive to stamp out textual idolatry, de-facing the text with an almost Cromwellian iconoclasm.

Finally, Derrida's advanced knowledge of the *tout autre* serves as evidence of a technologist faith. If the future is pregnant with limitless otherness and unbounded possibility, humanity is in the privileged position of being able to create *ex nihilo*.[84] To adopt such a position is to yield to the temptation that allured Adam (and the builders of Babel) in his quest to "be like God" (Gen 3:4; 11:6). To conceive of a universe pregnant with infinite possibility, under human construction and as yet undetermined even in the identity of its governing deities, opens the way for human pride to rejoice at its own potential. In Derrida one sees this alternative to an attitude of worship intensified through relentless interpretive re-creation *ex nihilo*.

CONCLUSIONS: "TOUT AUTRE N'EST PAS TOUT AUTRE"

Having viewed deconstruction as an attitude, it becomes difficult to endorse the seemingly obligatory partial affirmations of Derrida's work, dutifully honouring his contribution with politeness by promising to adopt his spirit into the pantheon of hermeneutics. To do so is hardly fair to Derrida for whom deconstruction is all or nothing. One cannot simply reduce it to a method in order to absorb it into a wealth of interpretive wisdom. Deconstruction is an attitude; and as such will not fit into a methodological toolbox. It denotes the adoption of an all-encompassing disposition towards God, the world and the text, and as argued above rejoices in the overwhelming infinitude of novelty, thereby renouncing humble receptivity even as it accords with technologist convictions. That is why one cannot simply "apply" this attitude to certain types of text or wield it to dethrone certain ideologies. To do so may once again be to employ technologist patterns of hermeneutics, and to turn deconstruction into a convenient tool it was never intended to be. What is more, if one is to reduce deconstruction to its methodological components, then

---

84. This is far from Derrida's intent, but there is little in Derrida to resist such a construal.

it has nothing to offer that has not already been articulated with greater clarity and theological acumen—not least by the early Barth.[85]

The later Barth, however, perceived problems with the construal of God as "wholly other." For this later Barth, such a conception is yet another idolatrous attempt to fashion God into humanity's dislocated image, a thoroughly pagan and (as argued here) technologist move.[86] Whilst one may see in Derrida's text an incessant openness and reshaping by the other who disrupts our economy, this chapter has suggested that the source of this otherness is simply a technologically conceived divine resource, which by Derridian logic is just another human resource. Arresting every possibility of otherness before it comes to fruition, Derridian reading prohibits the reader from responding to the otherness of a text, such as that represented by the parabolic figure of Lazarus.

---

85. The major methodological steps identified in Derrida are clearly witnessed in Barth's *Epistle to the Romans*. Firstly, the Derridian deconstructionist will seek the under-privileged partner of a dualism, and attempt to effect a reversal so that the marginal case becomes central and vice versa. This idea of mutual supervention between privileged and marginal finds expression in Barth's interaction with Platonic dualisms (*Romans* 358–61). Barth is discussing double predestination, and the 'childish' question of how God can be both angry and merciful, why "Jacob He has loved and Esau He has hated." Barth it seems, is drawing attention to the unity of God that underlies human duality. "For in God is no 'and', nor any duality. In Him the first is dissolved by the second. He is One . . . But our thought cannot escape from dualism. We know that we are unable to comprehend otherwise than by means of a dialectical dualism, in which one must become two in order that it may veritably be one" (358). This leads naturally to a second feature of deconstructionism: "mutual supervention" between binaries. "All the visible distinctions that emerge, and must emerge, among men, are subjected to an invisible dissolution . . . Then what is without becomes within . . . And then it is, when Israel rejoices in its assured security, that Isaiah—*crieth* . . . He cries that the Jew is not as such the servant of God. When it is God that loves and elects and shows mercy, who that is within can be certain that he is not without?" (360). Thirdly, Barth is deeply aware that the prophetic denunciation must not simply establish an alternative but equally over-privileged authoritarian regime: "The prophet will adopt no particular point of view without the secret intention of abandoning it as soon as he has gained a merely tactical advantage; for there is no question but that his point of view will be shown to be finally inadequate. He will never build up without at the same time making preparations to demolish what he has built; and he will always guard against any stability of his which would militate against the freedom of God" (366).

86. See Watson, *Text, Church and World*, 244; and Barth, *Church Dogmatics* IV.1, 186.

4

Resurrection as the Chiasmus of History and Biblical Interpretation

INTRODUCTION: RESURRECTION AS TRANSFORMATION

THE GOD OF ABRAHAM, Isaac, and Jacob does not know how to behave in public. Interpretive theories, especially those considered earlier, often propose structures of engaging with the text that happily accommodate a "God of the gaps" divinity, while (sometimes unwittingly) barricading themselves against the intrusions of a God whose presence might prove disruptive. Given such a context, this chapter may be read as a plea for biblical hermeneutics to heed the Psalmist:

> Lift up your heads, O you gates;
> lift them up, you ancient doors,
> that the King of glory may come in.
> Who is he, this King of glory?
> The Lord Almighty –
> he is the King of Glory.[1]

Interpretative theory must rest on a radical readiness for the coming of God in all of his historical superabundance. Taking account of this, salvation history itself is structured around the central event of God's explicit and decisive action in the world: the resurrection of his Messiah.

---

1. Ps 24:9–10. This psalm was in the ancient church, and still is in the Orthodox Church, read Christologically in relation to Christ's resurrection.

Resurrection as the Chiasmus of History and Biblical Interpretation 109

If biblical interpretation is to remain faithful to scripture, it has to take its bearings from this central event, not only as a springboard into hermeneutic theory but also remains perpetually, consciously and actively oriented around it, as we follow the divine life into the cosmos, creating renewal. This chapter forms a bridge between the two parts of this thesis, as the emphasis shifts from a deconstructive to a reconstructive one.[2] In so doing, it regards the resurrection as the basis for all interpretive endeavors and examines in more detail the parable of the rich man and Lazarus which will provide the textual focus for the second part of this thesis.

The argument thus far has focused on negative critique, and before offering more constructive alternatives it will be helpful to retrace some steps. In the first instance, borrowed from Heidegger is the insight that a technological worldview fashions the mode in which individuals encounter the world. Given this *Gestell* or "enframing,"[3] the manner in which texts are treated by readers is predetermined by a disposition to make use of that which is "ready to hand."[4] If earth's resources are perceived as a neutral depositary of raw potential, then the text may equally be treated as a resource to be made useful by a humanity that seeks to impose order upon it by means of methodology.[5] The earth's capacity to answer back, highlighted on Heidegger's account by art, is permanently bracketed out by the technologism he identified in the twentieth century.[6] If Heidegger's insight is applied to the way that readers engage texts, then readers within the *Gestell* will be unable to allow the text to confront them with a destabilizing otherness. In the light of Heidegger's insights, three hermeneutical methods were critiqued, which in different ways seek their own exodus from such technologist dominance.

First to be considered was the work of Heidegger's Marburg companion, Bultmann. Bultmann's attempt to demythologize the New Testament supposes that encoded within scriptural text stands an

---

2. Reconstructive is used here not in the sense of recapturing historical experiences or punctiliar conversion experiences. By reconstructive we mean a perpetually fruitful and generative disposition towards the world in general and therefore the text in particular.
3. Heidegger, *The Question Concerning Technology*.
4. An important phrase for early Heidegger (e.g., *Being and Time*, 65).
5. A crucial step in Heidegger's analysis of technology (1953).
6. Heidegger, *The Question Concerning Technology*.

essential *kerygma*. Given the right method, this essential *kerygma* can be unearthed and contemporaries may be exposed again to its disturbing force. However, despite Bultmann's best intentions, it was argued that he unwittingly sought a technological solution that only served to exacerbate the technological problem. Bultmann believed that the essential meaning of scripture lay buried beneath the sedimentary layers of interpretive tradition, but that its timeless truth could be unearthed using historical-critical tools.[7]

Secondly, attention turned to Fish, who positively delights in the dominance of interpretive tradition. While he has not consciously written about Heidegger or technology, his work stands as evidence supporting Heidegger's diagnosis of metaphysics. For Fish the authority of the interpretive community is absolute, even if it retains a theoretical relativity to alternative patterns of interpretation. Alternatives, however, remain wholly other, and thereby incomprehensible until they have been assimilated into the familiarity of one's own communal interpretive conventions. Fish has thus sought to relocate so called meaning[8] from the text to the reading community. The consequence—if Fish can allow a thing so opposed to descriptive theory—of this application is an association of readers with no compulsion for attentiveness to that whose origin lies beyond familiarity. With both text and readers deprived of otherness the technological *Gestell* remains absolute in shaping how scripture is encountered.

Thirdly and finally, attention turned to Derrida who heralds a radical exposure to the "other" in his insatiable open-endedness. His conscious attempt to break free from the modern preoccupation with "meaning" led him to retain a ceaseless sense of play in interpretation. Constant openness to that which is wholly other prevents one from ever securing meaning from a text. Such interminable deferment of meaning is akin to some Jewish strands of interpretation, and has been likened to a form of messianic readiness.[9] There is much to be said for this approach, but it comes at a price. Derrida is finally so prescriptive about

---

7. This is certainly not Bultmann's intent (see Thiselton, *The Two Horizons*, 183), but in practice his readings of the Gospels fail to parry such a criticism.

8. Stephen Fowl critiques the notion of meaning as a textual property that can be unearthed given the correct interpretive method in his discussion of determinate meaning (Fowl, *Engaging Scripture*, 33–40).

9. Not least by Derrida himself, but also by his commentators. E.g., Caputo, *Prayers and Tears*.

the non-identity of the "other" that the otherness he espouses is insidiously domesticated. His passion for timelessness has led him to ignore the disruptive otherness that history can bring. Ultimately, even Derrida treats the text as a resource to be manipulated rather than as a means to engage otherness.

HISTORICISM

With varying degrees of consciousness each of these models retains the underlying assumptions of historicism. Bultmann, Fish, and Derrida have each been described as representatives of historicism in an incisive treatment on the subject by Paul Hamilton.[10] Following the discussion in chapter 2, a further though brief outline of the historicism that determines much contemporary hermeneutics will help to clarify the argument presented in this chapter. Although historicism is a notoriously indefinable term, its history may be loosely traced through a variety of thinkers spanning from Kant, through Hegel, and diversifying into a spectrum of views which nevertheless share some basic characteristics.[11] As it relates to hermeneutics, it is best considered in the light of such figures as Giambattista Vico (1668–1744), Johan Gottfried Herder (1744–1803) and Leopold von Ranke (1795–1886).

Vico represented the view that the study of nature is to be distinguished from that of history in that the former is not created by humanity in the way that the latter is.[12] This means that the unchangeable principles thought to govern nature lead to misguided assumptions and findings when applied to historical narrative, which must be considered in terms of a developmental rather than a static model. This early view of historicism was articulated more clearly by Herder,[13] who critiqued a simple linear development as a model for describing civilizations,[14] bringing instead a stronger emphasis upon the importance of cultural

---

10. Hamilton 1996: 37–38 (Demythologization); 169, 205–206 (Fish); 5, 144–150 (Derrida).

11. Hamilton, *Historicism*, 30–50.

12. Vico's *Scienza Nuova* (The New Science) 1725.

13. *Auch eine Philosophieder Geschichte* (Also a Philosophy of History), 1774.

14. Hegel's view of history for instance, though seeking to embrace a perpetual clash of alien views, is ultimately vulnerable to this historicist critique as the views embraced are finally subsumed in a single end.

particularity.[15] This in turn necessitates that historical research embrace a diversity of developmental models. The supposedly eternal principles represented by religion, philosophy, science and art are seen as the interpretive products of particular cultures[16], and cannot therefore offer any means of access to alien cultures without distorting the way those cultures are understood. Such principles must therefore be abandoned, in order that historical objects may be understood in their own terms. Ranke similarly argued that one's own pre-understanding must not obstruct the historian's immersion into a factual re-animation of the past as it was lived.

Only such a view of history, rather than any timeless moral or religious principles, can yield worthy resources for questions of human existence. For Ranke, this was a radical attempt to respect what Thiselton describes as the "pastness of the past,"[17] a concern that it not be subsumed by the overwhelming principles that might impose the modern upon the ancient. Rationality therefore, no longer governed historical understanding but vice versa. There is some convergence here with the thought of Hegel, insofar as Hegel argued for a developmental historical understanding. What distinguishes this historicism from Hegel's was that for Hegel such development was itself rationality. For Hegel, although history follows the developmental pattern in which otherness is perpetually embraced and born anew, this does not render history "timelessly unchangeable,"[18] because it has an end. As such it is sharply distinguished from the more radical anti-Enlightenment historicism. As Hamilton concludes,

---

15. This was not merely a thesis about how to understand history, but had important political implications. Strauss for instance, using the example of the French Revolution, points out that the "recognition of universal principles thus tends to prevent men from wholeheartedly identifying themselves with, or accepting, the social order that fate has allotted to them. It tends to alienate them from their place on the earth. It tends to make them strangers, even strangers on the earth" (Strauss, *Natural Right and History*, 13–14).

16. This rests upon Herder's belief that language is the fruit rather the root of human communication. To understand an ancient language therefore, is still a long way from understanding the ancient culture from which it is derived. See Hamilton, *Historicism*, 38–39.

17. Thiselton, *The Two Horizons*, 53.

18. Pannenberg, *Basic Questions*, 181.

Hegel's absolute resting-place recreates an Enlightenment universal at a higher level; or so it seemed to the emergent hermeneutic tradition, which pictured all transactions of human understanding as historical negotiations between present and past, not their cessation.[19]

Leo Straus (see chapter 2 above), who produced an insightful critique of historicism,[20] majored upon this notion of a genuine intercourse between past and present, rejecting the impossibility of such a discourse. Strauss was defending the notion of "natural right," that is, the existence of the eternally valid principles upon which the champions of the historicist tradition turn their guns. He outlines how the need for a natural right that would enable the individual to find liberation, without thereby negating the apparently man-made convention of one's own wider society, led eventually to the practice of identifying temporal, local, historical rights with natural principles rooted in eternity. "As a consequence, what claimed to be universal appeared eventually as derivative from something locally and temporally confined, as the local and temporal *in statu evanescendi.*"[21]

In his 1965 essay, "Hermeneutics and Historicism,"[22] Gadamer responds to Strauss's criticisms by objecting that only a naïve historicism would wholly privilege the present over the whole of the past and, one may infer, the local over the eternal. A more dignified historical approach would be to concede that there is no such thing as the present. Instead, there are only the constantly shifting horizons of past and future, rendering it unthinkable for any tradition's perspective to regard itself as finally correct. "'Historical' understanding, whether today's or tomorrow's, has no special privilege. It is itself embraced by the changing horizons and moved within them."[23]

The historicist tradition outlined here has the positive intent of respecting historical cultures and characters on their own terms, rather than subjecting them to the presuppositions of the present inquirer. From a theological perspective however, the tradition also has a major

---

19. Hamilton, *Historicism*, 50.
20. Strauss, *Natural Right and History.*
21. Strauss, *Natural Right and History*, 15.
22. Published as "supplement I" in Gadamer, *Truth and Method,* 505–41. Although Gadamer regards himself as more of a critic than a supporter of historicism.
23. Gadamer, *Truth and Method*, 535.

negative component. Historicism pens a history according to the flesh,[24] that is, without reference to God. It is a means of plotting humanity's place in time and space, and one that remains impenetrable to external causality in general, and to divine purpose in particular. Instead it suggests a closed nexus of cause and event, each moment of history giving way to the next within the two-dimensional unfolding of time. This is not to say that each moment loses its capacity to exert its influence over subsequent events. Francis Watson's helpful distinction between historical and historic events elucidates the point. A historical event is one that happens in history, whereas a historic event changes the course of history. Historicism certainly has room for historic events, events of sufficient magnitude to reach beyond their historical location and generate their own future.[25] For the historicist, however, such events do not have the privilege of overpowering history itself (i.e., history as a sealed unit secure against unwelcome intrusion from an otherness whose origins lie beyond the reach of historically attributable causes) so as to transform it.

Oliver O'Donovan undertakes his fine account of ethics in relation to the Resurrection fully cognisant of its importance for historical thinking. His description of historicism frames Gadamer as a conservative representative occupied with bridging the chasm of historical distance.[26] Gadamer's sense of historical distance provides what he regards as a necessary tension over against the horizon of the interpreter, and is not to be overcome so much as relied upon for the so called "fusion" of horizons. However, the necessity of such a fusion rests upon a certain historicism,[27] which O'Donovan holds in contrast with eschatology. From a historicist perspective, events such as the creation and the eschaton are historical (rather than fully historic) moments like any other, devoid of external causality. The contrast with salvation-history could hardly be sharper; the canon which recounts biblical history is itself set within the proclamation of God's sovereignty both "in the beginning" (Gen 1:1) and "in the end" (Rev 22:12). Indeed history for O'Donovan is characterised by a tension between that to which one looks back (creation) and that for which—with creation—one waits (the final restoration of the cosmos).

---

24. Note the convergence here with Bultmann's view that the quest for the historical Jesus was a quest to know Jesus according to the flesh (Cf. 2 Cor 5:16).

25. Watson, *Text and Truth*, 51.

26. O'Donovan, *Resurrection and Moral Order*, 162.

27. Against Gadamer, *Truth and Method*, 312–24.

At "the center of time" stands the climactic Christ-event.[28] The resurrection of Jesus is not a resurrection *from* creation, but sets off a chain reaction that is the resurrection *of* creation and thereby involves every part of the created order.[29]

Far from conceiving of humanity as ethically oriented towards the empty space of an undetermined future (i.e., one that is still under human construction), in taking creation seriously O'Donovan adopts the position of the psalmist who rejoices that "the world is firmly established; it shall never be moved" (Ps 96:10).[30] Human action finds its place in a universe of created order; and, though that order is in need of transformation and redemption, it remains a given order. It is this order that generates history, in contrast to the historicism that regards history as a process. On the process view of history, the resurrection of Christ can only be regarded as a historical phenomenon. It is thus deposed from its God-given place on the throne of history, and demoted to the status of a subject, like any other moment in history.

Given this historicist framework, the passing of time opens up an alienating distance between figures of different historical settings. The possibility of the twenty-first century reader being able to hear and respond to a first century writer is rendered impossible. The "pastness of the past"[31] becomes the paramount issue to be addressed by those who attempt to engage with ancient texts on historicist terms. If the voice of the ancients might indeed be capable of addressing contemporary readers, all that the ancients might say is that " . . . between you and us a great chasm has been fixed, so that those who might want to pass from here to you cannot do so, and no one can cross from there to us." (Luke 16:26). Historicism fixes a great chasm between ancient writers and modern readers, a chasm that none from either side may cross. Enter Hermes.

---

28. *Die Mitte Der Zeit*, as Conzelmann's insightful account of Luke's historical scheme was entitled prior to its unfortunate translation as *The Theology of Saint Luke*.

29. The "God of the gaps" theory runs aground here. God the Creator is also God the Sustainer, because nothing can exist without him (cf., John 1:3). God the Sustainer of all things is also the Guide of all things. If God is the Guide of all things, he is also the Purpose (the *telos* or end) of all things. The natural sciences are descriptive of the means by which the God-sustained, guided and purposive universe is governed.

30. O'Donovan, *Resurrection*, 61.

31. Thiselton, *Two Horizons*, 53.

HERMENEUTICS

Hermeneutics is all too often described as the project to bridge the chasm that has been quarried by historicism.[32] Hermes, as messenger of the gods, and at times, messenger of the dead, is the divine go-between whose bridge-building activity is the subject of hermeneutics.[33] If historicism as described above, is founded on the conviction that history is devoid of external causality, it follows that events are sealed within an inescapable cause and event nexus, which in turn opens up the unbridgeable gulf of unintelligibility between events and characters separated by centuries. Hermes is called upon to address these issues, but how much can he be expected to achieve?

The three thinkers considered in part one of this thesis, though in different ways offering assent to historicist principles, seem to represent a loss of faith in Hermes to bridge the perceived chasm of history. In chapter 1 it was demonstrated that for Bultmann the contemporary experience of the reader takes precedence over the inaccessible historical life and work of the Jewish Messiah. Any attempt to gain access to the person, Jesus of Nazareth, demonstrates a desire to know Jesus κατὰ σάρκα.[34] Bultmann's concern here displays his belief that the alienating distance of centuries cannot be bridged, and his hermeneutics are invested instead in the believer's existential encounter. Similarly, for Fish, the notion of access to historical circumstances is utterly misleading.

> The distinction between a "found" history and an "invented" one is finally nothing more than a distinction between a persuasive interpretation and one that has failed to convince. One man's "found" history will be another man's invented history, but neither will ever be, because it could not be, either purely found or purely invented.[35]

Again, Hermes cannot negotiate the chasm of history, and in Fish's program is left instead to try his hand at rhetoric. Finally, Derrida's deconstructive attitude exhibits a historicist bent in its desire on the one hand to maintain an exclusion zone around historical

---

32. E.g., Hamilton, *Historicism*, 20, 44; Thiselton, *Two Horizons*, 51–84; Gadamer, *Truth and Method*, 505–40.

33. Most writers on the subject of hermeneutics will point out that its name is derived from Hermes.

34. See Robinson, *A New Quest of the Historical Jesus*.

35. Fish, *Doing What Comes Naturally*, 95.

existence that protects it from the unwelcome interference of actual Messianic otherness,[36] and on the other to reduce such transcendent otherness to the imminent otherness encountered in one's neighbor.[37] The Deconstructionists' Hermes is thus allotted the task of unmasking pseudo otherness.[38] Each thinker has been of interest in recognizing that Hermes cannot cope with the gap traditionally assigned to him, that is, that between ancient text and modern reader. Whilst remaining within the parameters of the historicist tradition, each has reconceived of the hermeneutical task, re-commissioning Hermes to address existential, rhetorical or deconstructive concerns.

Having so comprehensively reinterpreted the hermeneutical task, it can appear to many that these figures are no longer respecting the "pastness of the past," a critique that is not unwarranted. But the "pastness of the past" is a problem that can be idolized, which leads to historicist hermeneutics being understood as "the science of interpretation," rather than a single (if necessary) facet of interpretation. Once hermeneutics is understood exclusively as attending to the problems identified by historicism, that is, problems based upon a world from which God is excluded, the theological legitimacy of the entire enterprise is jeopardized. The historicist predicament is summarized well by Paul, who instructed the Ephesian church, "remember that you were . . . apart from Christ [a problem addressed in chapter 5 below], separated from the commonwealth of Israel and aliens in regard to the covenants of promise [the subject of chapter 6], having no hope [the eschatological focus of chapter 7] and without God in the world" (Eph 2:12).[39] The historicist foundation for hermeneutics leaves interpreters operating within the

---

36. As argued in chapter 3 above.

37. E.g., *"tout autre est tout autre,"* in *On the Name*, 68.

38. Conversely Hermes may be construed as the subversive character who disrupts interpretive norms. Such a Hermes is of much greater interest to Derrida. Hamilton's description of this Hermes accords with objections made by Thiselton and Vanhoozer in their critiques of Derrida, as they complain that deconstruction destroys the foundations on which hermeneutics is based. As Hamilton states, Hermes, ". . . this supernatural patron of hermeneutics is sometimes only recognizable in the character of trickery and deceit in which he frequently appears. Mischievous, obstreperous rebellion against current norms of interpretation problematizes the tradition and continuity often thought to be hermeneutics" exclusive inheritance from religious thinking. Hermeneutics, that is to say, can perversely require us to reinterpret the very notions of tradition and continuity on which it is based" (Hamilton, *Historicism*, 52–53).

39. Translation by Lincoln, *Ephesians*, 123.

parameters of a world without God, and in this light the basic thrust of the first part of this thesis may be summarized in a simple claim: "the wages of sin is hermeneutics" (cf. Rom 6:23).

This is by no means to deny the legitimacy of historical distance, but rather to demote it from its status as the primary interpretive problem. Historical distance casts the shadow of humility across all attempts to heed ancient texts, but historicist hermeneutics promotes this problem above its proper status, and relativizes other crucial problems. When historicist hermeneutics becomes synonymous with interpretation it should hardly be surprising that the major obstacle to understanding a text should be perceived as one that forces one back onto the interpretive technical genius of contemporary methodologists. In the face of the pastness of the past, technologist designs upon texts can masquerade undetected in the apparel of interpretive humility. However, to proponents of historicist hermeneutics, Aquinas might have said, "you have not yet considered the exceeding gravity of sin."[40] As the second part of this thesis will show, the most important obstacle to understanding the biblical text is the human propensity for rebellious pride, an ethical reluctance to be reformed by the text as it confronts the reader across the centuries.[41] It is crucial for biblical interpretation to attend to this critical issue. It is a problem that is addressed most sharply in the parable of the rich man and Lazarus, and is one that Hermes cannot solve. In sum, it will be shown that biblical interpretation conceived in terms of historicist hermeneutics is a stark alternative to taking seriously the resurrection of Israel's Messiah in its full historicity.

RESURRECTION IN SALVATION HISTORY

A common strand of the three hermeneutical models critiqued in Part I is that their contemporary application of the text bypasses the historical specificity of the events that are absolutely central to Christian belief: namely, the death and resurrection of the Jewish Messiah. Despite the various professions concerning the importance of historicity, each model quietly assumes its own privileged access to a timeless sphere

---

40. Quoted in Chesterton, *Saint Thomas Aquinas*, 140.

41. A problem Augustine recognized as clouding his own ability to engage scripture on its own terms (*Confessions* III.5).

in which true meaning is located. Were such models to accommodate Christianity, it would thereby be a Christianity shorn of its incarnational givenness. It would follow that the death and resurrection of Jesus of Nazareth need not have been the death and resurrection of the Messiah, because that event could happen (or could have happened) at any point on the flat plane of history with the death of any member of any community. But scripture offers a different story: one in which the Messiah was a representative of a particular people charged with a divine purpose. If one is to seek a scriptural means of hearing scripture, this narrative forms the structural framework for the attentive disposition.

The claim that Jesus was Israel's Messiah carries with it the implication that the purposes of God are invested in *this one man*. Despite the breadth of applications in the ancient world—and even within Judaism itself in the tradition that Israel is God's son (Ex 4:22, Deut 14:1; Isa 43:6; Jer 31:9; Hos 1:10; 11:1)—for the phrase "son of God,"[42] one may nevertheless hear the divine affirmation at the baptism and the transfiguration as the vulnerable investment of the divine purpose: "*This one man* is my son."[43] The promises made to Israel and the hope she carried all have devolved upon this single figure, Jesus of Nazareth. Thus, when the Messiah is crucified the purposes of God for Israel, for the nations and for the entire created order appear to be utterly defeated.[44] Furthermore, this defeat is no tragic accident, arising from the misfortune that the Son of God happened upon a place and time that were unjust or irreligious.

The Jewish religious system and the Roman legal system were both extremely sophisticated.[45] What is witnessed in the crucifixion,

---

42. E.g., see Dunn, *Christology in the Making*, 12–64. Absent from Dunn's discussion is the question of whether the phrase "son of God" was used in the Synoptics. Instead, the affirmation of Jesus as the Son of God comes not from human acclamation but out of the mouth of God himself. As such we may infer from Isa 55:10–11 that he will accomplish the purpose for which he was sent.

43. This claim will be addressed more fully in the next chapter on reading Christologically. The use of the word οὗτος can hardly have been intended to convey the weight it is given here, but we have given it this weight in order to highlight the fact that the one man in question was the bearer of fate for all humanity.

44. There is an implicit echo here of the covenant with Abraham (see chapter 6 below), an observation made by Tomson. As the voice from heaven refers to the son, the beloved (Mark 9:7), so Abraham had referred to Isaac, who—like Jesus himself—embodied Israel in a substantive sense (Tomson, "Jesus and His Judiasm," 28, 39).

45. Raymond Brown's detailed study of both the Jewish and Roman trials demonstrates that, despite various ambiguities, local particularities and individual failings,

therefore, is not simply a fragment of immoral behavior that has splintered off from the otherwise ethical goodness basic to humanity. Rather, as Luke reads Psalm 2, it is by conscious decision that "the kings of the earth [gentiles] took their stand, and the rulers have gathered together against the Lord and against his Messiah" (Acts 4:25-26). Golgotha is the fusion of Jewish and Roman horizons. As the representative of Israel and, since Israel was called to be a light to the nations, a herald for all the world, Jesus of Nazareth was the figurehead of humanity. For *"this one man"* to be put to death by as efficient and sophisticated a religious and legal system as humanity could offer, is of enormous significance. It is the very climax of human initiative. If Jesus of Nazareth was God's Messiah, then the resounding communal speech-act "Crucify him" is the ultimate enacted interpretation of the Kingdom of God.

As Luke himself recounts the scene (Luke 24:13-35), the desolation encountered by the followers of this Messiah was unspeakable in its hopelessness. This was not simply attributable to the tragic loss of a friend, nor even to the destruction of a hope in which they had invested their lives. The death of the Messiah simply meant that God had lost control of his creation. His divine purposes had been thwarted by the machinations of human sophistication. If *"this one man"* upon whom God's spirit and favor rested had been executed and left to rot in a tomb, then God was no longer God. Neither was the world a place of stability, coherence or hope. Such was the apparent state of creation on the Sabbath before Easter.

Before moving from a consideration of the cross, it is worth reconsidering the theological implications of many well-meaning brands of hermeneutic enquiry, and asking at which point in the sequence of the Christ event they make their home. For those who have consciously disavowed the possibility of a historical, bodily resurrection they are contentedly located at this stage of the theological narrative, failing to take seriously enough the resurrection of Christ. Equally, however, Christian hermeneutics with strong convictions about the bodily resurrection of God's son may well find themselves hopelessly lodged at this stage of salvation-history. Examples of both groups are not difficult to find.

---

both systems were highly developed and efficient. See Brown, *The Death of the Messiah*, 1:331-71, 676-722.

Marianne Sawicki's exciting survey, *Seeing the Lord*,[46] constructs a highly creative, deeply imaginative and utterly provocative conception of how resurrection affects the way a reader encounters a text. She offers a superb defense of the necessity for resurrection to be appropriated in the lives contemporary readers today, and argues that if they are to be exposed to its transformative capacity it must be viewed through their theology, their liturgy and their solidarity with the poor. Resurrection as a bodily, political, social reality is unpacked in all of its disturbing force and portrayed as an explicitly all-embracing energy that perpetually invokes crises and challenges. The scope of resurrection life that is portrayed is extremely colorful and wide ranging, and lacks only one ingredient: its origin in a historical event.

Sawicki suggests that the gospels are merely the early church's preferred means of preserving the body of the dead Jesus and because he now lives on in the text we may rejoice that he is alive today.[47] The Jesus of history is thus displaced by the Jesus of textuality. The post-crucifixion Jesus is bodily available only because he is textually available, affording readers the ability to resist the self-imposing schematic blueprints of race, class, and gender.[48] "Can a person be a text?" she asks. Not surprisingly, she finds support in the Johannine prologue, even if she has quietly inverted its order—a move that reveals one of her dominant characteristics. The author of the fourth gospel certainly did not write that "the flesh became word"; but, true to her deconstructionist faith, Sawicki has little interest in the word that became flesh. Accordingly, historical questions are frequently bypassed in order to bring one into a timeless sphere.

For instance, her reading of the parable of the rich man and Lazarus buttresses her call for solidarity with the poor and with women. At times her exegesis is curious; this is demonstrated in her comparison of the parable with the Johannine raising of Lazarus on the basis of surviving the grave, the featuring of a dining room, and "oral contact with someone hairy: a dog or a dog-like woman with undone hair!"[49] She is on surer ground as she compares this parable with the parable of the prodigal son. "The implication seems to be that the possibility of understanding

---

46. Sawicki, *Seeing the Lord*.
47. Sawicki, *Seeing the Lord*, 285.
48. Sawicki, *Seeing the Lord*, 286–92.
49. Sawicki, *Seeing the Lord*, 155–56.

resurrection comes through hunger."[50] One can hardly complain at such an insight, but the historical setting of the passage remains unheard. Instead, one sees the implicit portrayal of a Jesus of Nazareth plucking timeless truths out of heaven and depositing them into some textual account from which those with the requisite literary competence may withdraw at any point in history.

We may take these moves as evidence of her commitment to the flat historicism that dictates the direction of hermeneutical endeavor. Indeed, the Risen Lord, "*cannot be both past and risen*, for to be past means not to be active and available now."[51] This prescriptive confinement of Jesus to textuality, even with the proviso that contemporary readers can resurrect him by playing with the text, suggests that God is limited in his ability to control his universe.

Sawicki reaches the pinnacle of Christian interpretive genius required by those who are nonchalant about a historical resurrection. In tempering her thesis with the hope that her readers will disagree with her,[52] she demonstrates the obligatory modesty incumbent upon all such expressions of hermeneutical *hubris*. This modesty is no voluntarist virtue but a methodological necessity, because, once the subject has deliberately amputated itself from its object, its ventures into new hermeneutical territory are destined to move *towards* (but never to arrive *at*) its object. That this is the fate of all supra-subjective hermeneutical endeavours one can only affirm. But such adventures are destined to be fundamentally tentative, and the modesty that attends them is an expression of the insidious pride endemic with the technologist enterprise. To state one's readiness to be superseded by those who share one's hermeneutical dream is nothing other than a statement of hubristic faith. It remains a persistent refusal to allow for the breaking in of the kingdom and the catastrophe of resurrection, preferring to be unhindered in its hermeneutical exploits by the slightest hint of objectivity. Translated into Gospel language, this modesty gives voice to the cry, "We do not want this man to rule over us" (Luke 19:14).[53]

Vanhoozer's invaluable contribution to the questions of contemporary biblical interpretation is presented as "a hermeneutics of the

---

50. Sawicki, *Seeing the Lord*, 90.
51. Sawicki, *Seeing the Lord*, 334 (emphasis original).
52. Sawicki, *Seeing the Lord*, ix.
53. After all, "We have no king but [Caesar]" (Jn 19:15).

cross."[54] There is much to be said for Vanhoozer's work, and although as will become clear, it stops short of making some crucial points, it does not hit a dead end in the manner Sawicki's proposal does. Nevertheless, it is our contention that Vanhoozer has paid insufficient attention to the resurrection. His magnificent repository of interpretive insight, *Is There a Meaning in this Text*,[55] is clearly presented within a resurrection-shaped structure. The first part critiques post-modern hermeneutics, focussing especially on Fish and Derrida, whom he describes as "undoing interpretation." In the second part, his more constructive claims surface by "redoing interpretation." But the assessment of how to "resurrect the author," "reform the reader" and "redeem the text"[56] make no significant reference to the resurrection of Christ, either in the general thrust of his thesis or in the contents by which it is generated.

Vanhoozer is very well informed about the dangers of historicism and the need for biblical interpretation to offer an alternative to the skepticism of Lord Acton's unhappy phrase, "the beginning of wisdom in history is doubt."[57] However, his constructive chapters are all simply hermeneutical theories about dealing responsibly with the void quarried by historicism. Here O'Donovan's discussion of ethics and Resurrection returns to the foreground. O'Donovan draws attention to the distinction between the objective law as it is out there, and the internal appropriation of that law in the believer's life, enabled by the Christly action of the Holy Spirit. Arguing that whether it is Torah or some pagan conception, it remains a law in the flesh that stands over against the individual, O'Donovan insists that the resurrection overcomes this binarity.[58] It is the same binarity Vanhoozer seeks to overcome with a hermeneutic theory of the Spirit.

For this reason, Vanhoozer is compelled to argue that reading is a moral exercise. However, the moral action required by Vanhoozer is exclusively restricted to hearing the meaning of the text. For all his claims about perlocutionary effects, despite his emphasis on mission and discipleship, and although he tips his hat to Hauerwas's call for action in the

---

54. This is the title of the closing chapter of his critique of post-modern hermeneutics, *Is There a Meaning in This Text?*

55. Vanhoozer, *Is There a Meaning in This Text*.

56. The titles of his three constructive chapters.

57. Quoted by Vanhoozer, *Is There a Meaning in this Text*, 24.

58. As will be demonstrated below.

Christian interpretive community, ethical reading for Vanhoozer first and foremost means respecting the author and acting morally towards the text as though it were a person.[59] But the divide between the meaning of the text, and faithfully appropriating its significance leaves Vanhoozer with a monumentally truncated conception of reading as ethical action. In this sense, Derrida's claim that "there is nothing outside of the text,"[60] which was so comprehensively thrown out by Vanhoozer, returns like a boomerang to strike his own work. In seeking to address the problem of the "pastness of the past,"[61] hermeneutics often neglects what might be called the problem of "the textuality of the text," that is, the sheer separability of the written word from lived life. The appeal to speech act theory[62] is insufficient to bridge such a gap, because it supposes—in true Kantian fashion—that one must firstly understand a text and then secondly go and apply it. Whilst this is sometimes a valid means of appropriating a text, it is by no means the only way. The direction of arriving at the historical specificity of a text may often be reversed, not least by the notion of "faith seeking understanding,"[63] upon which Vanhoozer himself is happy to ground his work. One may think for instance of a grieving widow, struck by words of comfort, who then goes in search of the true "meaning" of the text only after its "significance" has been fully appreciated. Vanhoozer's conception of living in accordance with scriptural revelation rests so thoroughly upon dichotomies, upon extracting—albeit with careful humility—the true meaning from the text, that

---

59. Although this thesis affirms that the way the reader relates to a text is inseparable from the way she relates to a person, Vanhoozer never discusses how ethically responsible personal relationships might look.

60. Derrida, *Of Grammatology*, 158.

61. Thiselton, *Two Horizons*, 53.

62. Speech-act theory as developed by J. L. Austin and J. R. Searle is invaluable in its description of how words gain traction in lived context, over against deconstructionist tendencies to perceive words as hopelessly wheel-spinning in groundless intertextuality. Vanhoozer however becomes over reliant on its categories. See Vanhoozer, *Is There a Meaning in this Text*, 209–214.

63. Vanhoozer, *Is There a Meaning in this Text*, 15. *Fides Quaerens Intellectum* (faith seeking understanding) was a principle of Anselm which Barth examined in some detail (Barth, *Anselm*,) as he contended that such faith is neither the idolatry nor the sacrifice of the intellect. For Barth, theology is based upon the Word of God (who gives himself to be known objectively through Christ). When this Word is (subjectively) approached through faith, theology is a necessity.

serious engagement with life outside the text is a thoroughly secondary issue. Resurrection will not tolerate such dichotomies.

RESURRECTION OVERCOMING DICHOTOMIES

"We had hoped that *he* was the one to redeem Israel" (Luke 24:21), laments a dejected Cleopas, who has not yet fathomed the report of Luke's angels: "*He* is not here, but has risen" (Luke 24:5). This "he," while referring to Jesus of Nazareth, is a "he" that carries with it the entire hope of God's promises to Israel. Far from being a mere proof of the atonement for the sins of humanity, of life beyond the grave or that the death barrier has been supernaturally broken, the resurrection is the ground of history.[64] God has not lost control of the universe he created, nor have his purposes for creation through his chosen people been thwarted. The resurrection is the divine response to the ultimate human initiative. In short, the resurrection of Jesus of Nazareth is God's interpretation of the world. This divine interpretation is neither the imparting of correct information, nor the pronouncement of doctrinal truth, but is fundamentally the climactic, decisive action in human history wrought by the God of Abraham, Isaac, and Jacob.

If biblical interpretation is to take seriously God's resurrection of *this one man*, then its implications for history must be taken into account. The resurrection invalidates the dichotomies that inhere within radical historicism. While these dichotomies take various forms (e.g., fact and interpretation, event and meaning, meaning, and significance etc.) they arise from and depend upon the existence of the great "ugly ditch."[65] Biblical historicism perceives a breach between what God has said when he inspired authors and what modern readers hear when they strain their ears to listen to ancient texts. In order to offer an alternative framework of interpretation, the present argument will proceed by focusing upon the time and place in human history which towers above all others, in which resurrection is revealed. Wright's analysis of the historical situation provides the basis of this thesis, and his reading

---

64. That is insofar as resurrection denotes explicitly divine activity in human history, an affront to historicist conceptions of the world.

65. Lessing, *Lessing's Theological Writings*, 55.

of the parable of the rich man and Lazarus offers a lens through which to perceive the wider historical framework arising from the resurrection of Christ.

Wright's work is important for this thesis because of the manner in which it integrates careful consideration of its historical and literary context, with a sophisticated narrative hermeneutic. In parable interpretation the Julicher-Jeremias tradition[66] has produced studies of the parables that are invaluable for those considering their historical context, but went little further in considering their nature as "language events."[67] Conversely, those who have considered the literary structure of parables have often under-emphasized the historical setting of such parables.[68] The advent of the "Third Quest" for the historical Jesus however, has emphasized the political nature of the Kingdom of God, depicting Jesus in relation to national hopes for a restored or reconstituted Israel.[69] Wright's work offers a fine example of how the political specificity of Jesus' actions is put into effect through the telling of parables. This approach to the subversive nature of Jesus' storytelling makes room for fruitful readings (offered in chapters 5 and 6 below) of the parable of the rich man and Lazarus that would have been unconvincing given the criteria of the so-called New Quest.

Wright regards Luke 16:19–31 as "a parable that stresses repentance."[70] In contrast to Sanders's understanding of repentance, which focused primarily on the individual and only secondarily upon the community,[71] Wright maintains that repentance is primarily a

---

66. E.g., Dodd (*Parables of the Kingdom*) who echoes Julicher's assertion that parables have a single meaning (18). Jeremias (*Parables*) built on the work of Dodd to offer readings that took their historical setting most seriously. Unfortunately the Jeremias-Julicher tradition's own interpretive environment tended towards de-historicising Jesus from his Jewish context, a tendency that is reflected in the parable interpretation it produced.

67. A phrase coined by Ernst Fuchs.

68. For instance, Jones (*The Art and Truth of Parables,*) dislocates the parables from their historical setting; Perrin (*Jesus and the Language of the Kingdom,*) regards them as content-less messages, devoid of a meaning; Via (*The Parables,*) is prone to imposing Western criteria upon Eastern literary form (See Bailey, *Poet and Peasant*, 25).

69. Representatives of the Third Quest locate Jesus firmly within the complex and pluriform Judaisms of his day. For a detailed analysis of the Third Quest see Witherington, *The Jesus Quest*.

70. Wright, *Jesus and the Victory of God*, 255.

71. Sanders, *The Historical Figure of Jesus*, 234.

communal matter, inverting Sanders's emphasis. Why did Jesus then call the community of Israel to repentance? Though Israel was to be an agent of God's mercy and grace to the world, Wright's Jesus perceived in the nation a deeply ingrained sense of nationalistic pride that issued in a condemnatory attitude towards foreigners and outsiders. Israel had in essence come to regard herself no longer as an agent of grace but of judgment and had thereby adopted a satanic role; hence the call to return to her true scriptural character. Wright's Jesus is announcing that Israel must undergo a total reconfiguration of identity, suggesting that Jesus would have been understood as saying:

> Give up your way of being Israel, your following of particular national and political aims and goals, and trust me for mine instead. And he was heard to be investing that call for repentance with a significance . . . which had Deuteronomy, Jeremiah and other classic texts resonating in the background: this is the repentance which will constitute you as the returned-from-exile people, the renewed and reconstituted Israel.[72]

According to Wright, Israel, though having long since returned from geographical captivity in Babylon, remained acutely aware of a present experience of exile.[73] Wright then regards the parable of the rich man and Lazarus as echoing that of the prodigal son in sounding as its key note resurrection as the return-from-exile, which is "happening all around, and the pharisees cannot see it."[74]

Israel is a rich man, the "wealthy" beneficiary of God's covenant promise and the scriptures, who yet remained content to squander this wealth on himself. Meanwhile, the outcasts are located safely outside the gate with the dogs licking their sores. For Wright, the repulsive figure of

---

72. Wright, *Jesus and the Victory of God*, 254.

73. Wright, *The New Testament and the People of God*, 268–72; *Jesus and the Victory of God*, 126–29. This is a point that has been critiqued in various reviews of Wright's work. See Newmann, *Jesus and the Restoration of Israel*. Markus Bockmuehl has penned a sympathetic but rigorous critique of Wright's volume on Resurrection (Wright, *The Resurrection of the Son of God*), comprised of three main points. Firstly, he asks whether Wright had explored fully enough the interpretive patterns of first century Judaisms and how they conceived of individual resurrections; secondly he asks whether Wright has displayed the interpretive humility proposed in his own earlier work (Wright, *The New Testament and the People of God*); thirdly he expresses his concern about Wright's apparent rejection of traditional belief in going to heaven after death (Bockmuehl, *This Jesus*).

74. Wright, *Jesus and the Victory of God*, 255.

a filthy, blemished, diseased Lazarus is a powerfully dramatic representation of Israel's outcasts as Israel's "in crowd" (especially the Pharisees) were happy to perceive and to leave them. However, the ministry of a Messiah who "welcomes sinners and eats with them" (Luke 15:1) is an utter reversal of such contempt for the outsider, and conversely a vindication for those regarded as outcast.

The final destinies of the rich man and Lazarus constitute not only a reversal of their plight in life, but for some interpreters of the parable, a reversal of expectation in the hearers. However, some interpreters of the parable believe that the existence of parallel traditions and stories in the Ancient Near East,[75] which also reverse the fate of rich and poor after death, means that this aspect of Jesus' story comes as little surprise. For Richard Bauckham, whose careful analysis of this parable features more fully in chapter 7, the point at which the distinctiveness of Jesus' new story protrudes most sharply, and the section of the parable that warrants the closest attention, emerges at this point. When the rich man asks for Lazarus to be sent to his five brothers to warn them of their impending catastrophe, contrary to popular expectation Abraham says, "No." Bauckham has considered at length a wealth of parallel literature in the Ancient Near East in which glimpses of the after-world are offered by messengers from the dead.[76] The basis for this unexpected refusal to allow Lazarus to return from the dead is that the five brothers already have the means of hearing what Lazarus would tell them, namely Moses and the Prophets. It is from these scriptures that the brothers should be able to hear that God's riches are for the outcasts. The resounding note of the prophets echoes the warning, that if Israel is prodigal with the riches at her disposal, and uses them merely for self-interest, then the forthcoming day of the Lord will be a curse rather than a blessing, a catastrophe rather than a vindication. This is a recurrent theme in "Moses and the Prophets," most notably Amos, as the rich man in possession of the scriptures should have known. He remains unperturbed however, as he persists, "No Father Abraham, but if someone went to them from the dead, they would repent" (v. 30). Abraham's response serves as a tragic comment on the Jewish opponents of Jesus, "If they don''t listen to Moses and the Prophets, neither would they be convinced even if someone did

---

75. These parallels and their significance are dealt with fully in subsequent chapters.

76. Considered in more detail in chapter 7 below (and see Griffith, *Stories of the High Priest of Memphis*).

rise from the dead" (v. 31). In this closing comment, Wright takes Jesus to be stating subversively that resurrection is a present characteristic of his ministry here and now, and the Pharisees are refusing to see it.[77]

> Jesus' welcome of the poor and outcast was a sign that the real return from exile, the new age, the "resurrection," was coming into being; and if the new age was dawning, those who wanted to belong to it would (as in Deuteronomy and Jeremiah) have to repent. The story points up the true significance of what Jesus was doing, and the urgent need of those who were at present grumbling to recognise this significance. The five brothers at home correspond quite closely to the older brother in the prodigal son. "Resurrection" is happening, but they cannot see it.[78]

Wright's point is that this resurrection of Jesus is fore-present in the ministry of Jesus to the outcasts, sinners, prostitutes and tax collectors: in short, the exiles. As these exiles respond to Jesus' call to follow him, resurrection is witnessed by and for those whose eyes are open. Wright's favorite example of such mini-resurrection is found in the story of Zacchaeus. As Jesus enters his house, one would expect him to become infected with impurity, whereas it is Zacchaeus who is infected with Jesus' purity. As he enters the house, Jesus' status as the Messiah is questioned, and as he leaves the house Zacchaeus the outcast walks into the light of day as a child of Abraham, an ironic demonstration of Jesus' true messiahship. In like fashion, in the parable, Abraham's descendant is thought to be the prodigal rich man; and expectations are reversed as it is Lazarus, the outcast, the exile outside the gate, who is truly revealed to be a child of Abraham. Today, he says, salvation has come to this house. Conversely, the rich man's status as an ethnic descendant is revealed to be worthless, as across the abyss Abraham acknowledges that status (and yet implies its irrelevance) as he addresses the rich man as "son." Ultimately, the community of God's people is defined not by social, ethical or ethnic status, but by faith.

The Zacchaeus story is, therefore, no divergence from the subject of resurrection. Wright has correctly perceived that Luke's telling of the Gospel story is itself a story about resurrection.[79] The resurrection of

---

77. For the significance of *seeing* in relation to the Kingdom of God in the Gospel of Luke, see Stephen D. Moore, *Mark and Luke in Poststructuralist Perspective*, 129-44.

78. Wright, *Jesus and the Victory of God*, 255-56.

79. Wright's observations here are discussed in more detail in chapter 7, which of-

Jesus informs the entire sequence of events in the ministry of Jesus as Luke tells it—a sequence of events that demonstrates the microcosmic presence of resurrection. The resurrection did not come as a surprise to Luke as he neared the end of his first publication. Rather, both the form and content of the Gospel were generated by the belief in the resurrection of Jesus, which Luke saw not as a totally unexpected turn of events but in strong continuity with the character of the covenant God.[80]

This insight in itself requires further elucidation. It would be foolish to suppose that every faithful Jewish follower of Jesus knew exactly what to expect when their Messiah was crucified. Sanders and Wright have gone to great length to show that while Jesus had prepared his disciples for a forthcoming monumental event, it took them totally by surprise when it actually happened, despite the frequency of explicit forewarning that the gospels report. Only with retrospect could the resurrection be understood within the framework of God's redemptive purposes for the Christ and therefore for Israel and in turn for the world. Such a reading reveals three aspects of resurrection that are of key importance to our thesis.

Firstly, if Second Temple Judaisms assented to a general belief in resurrection it was perceived as something that would mark the climax of the age, when evil is overcome and harmony obtains between God and his people. Though this belief is not a clearly defined doctrine and remained fluid in character, it may be said to comprise two strands of expectation, which, though mutually distinct, were not separable. On the one hand, it referred metaphorically to the socio-political restoration of Israel in fulfillment of covenant promise. On the other, it referred quite simply to the raising of the dead, the actual reconstitution of physical bodies that had died. This second sense finds its place within wider Jewish beliefs about life after death, but is thereby inseparable from the political fate of God's covenant people. "Both senses" according to Wright, "generated and sustained nationalist revolution. The hope that YHWH would restore Israel provided the goal; the hope that he would restore human bodies . . . removed the fear that might have undermined

fers an eschatological reading of the parable.

80. A parallel observation is made by Schillebeeckx, who sees the disciples of Jesus conceiving the shape and purpose of the ministry of Jesus in the light of their Resurrection experience. Interestingly, Bultmann moves in precisely the opposite direction, arguing that the early church conceived of the Easter events out of the starting point of the historical mission of the Jesus they had known.

zeal."[81] When resurrection happened it would constitute a transition to a new era, instigating "the age to come."

Secondly, against such a background Jesus of Nazareth was raised from the dead, and the early church believed this event somehow to be the fulfillment of wider expectations about resurrection. The resurrection of Jesus did not, however, put an end to suffering and death and therefore did not completely fulfill all aspects of resurrection belief. Believers still died and were not raised again. The "present age" was not quite as finished as one might have hoped, nor was the age to come as fully present as may have been expected. Whilst the struggle of early Christians to come to terms with this tension is a fascinating and important story,[82] of greater immediate importance to this survey is how the resurrection of Jesus shaped perceptions of him.

Within this overlap of the ages, Jesus was raised from the dead. Luke has Peter declare, "God has made him both Lord and Messiah" (Acts 2:36). For Wright, the former designation arose out of the latter. With the advent of the resurrection, the Jewish concept of Messiah was developed by Christians in accordance with its roots in the Psalms, most notably in the belief that the Messiah of Israel was the true Lord of all the world. However, there were certain other developments that were not contained in Jewish categories. Firstly, the role of the Messiah was no longer restricted to benefiting the Jews. Secondly, the Messianic battlefront was redrawn so as no longer to confront militaristic threat, but evil itself. Thirdly, the reconstituted temple was not to be constructed out of bricks and mortar, but would be a household in which the presence of God would dwell. Finally,

> the justice, peace and salvation which the Messiah would bring to the world would not be a Jewish version of the imperial dream of Rome, but would be God's *dikaiosune*, God's *eirene*, God's *soteria*, poured out upon the world through the renewal of the whole creation.[83]

Contrary to Bultmann, to move from this view to the acknowledgement of Jesus as Lord of all the earth is not a departure from but an

---

81. Wright, *The Resurrection of the Son of God*, 204.

82. Neville Clarke addresses such questions with startling and convincing clarity in his book, *Interpreting the Resurrection*, 62–80.

83. Wright, *The Resurrection of the Son of God*, 563.

expression of traditional Jewish belief about the Messiah.[84] Citing Royal Psalms (2; 72; 89), Daniel 7, and Isaiah (11:1, 4, 10; 42:1, 6; 49:1–6), Wright seeks to emphasize their expectation of a king who would be both over Israel in the first instance, and in the second over the whole world. Noting that these are passages used by New Testament authors, he argues that their conception of Jesus after the resurrection was that Jesus of Nazareth had become not only the Messiah of Israel but the Lord of the nations. The extraordinary event of the final resurrection had happened to Jesus, reversing the Roman and Jewish verdicts of his trial and vindicating him as the Jewish Messiah and in turn as *kurios*.

Thirdly, these first two aspects of an end-time resurrection and of a present experience of that resurrection in God's vindication of his Messiah suggest that, although the flashpoint of resurrection is highly localised and specific, the category of resurrection cannot remain hermetically contained in this specific time and place. As Luke was clearly aware, resurrection was a defining characteristic of Jesus' ministry and as such in accord with the redemptive activity of the covenant God.

The upshot of all this for biblical interpretation must now be explored. To presume that an unbridgeable chasm of two thousand years stretches out beyond the twenty-first century reader, as she gazes upon first century resurrection, is a total falsification of history. Even within the gospels themselves, the resurrection will not remain confined to that corner of land and history that belonged to Joseph of Arimathea. It not only casts its light upon, but makes its presence felt, both throughout the preceding ministry of the Messiah, and through the subsequent action of the Messianic body, the church.

RESURRECTION AS INTERPRETIVE MASTER CONCEPT

If biblical interpreters are to affirm the resurrection of Jesus a historical event, then their conception of history itself must be transformable. The stone that the builders of the historicist framework have effectively rejected must become the chief cornerstone of history. From here three crucial aspects of biblical interpretation unfold, each of which corresponds in turn with the constructive chapters in the second part: firstly, historical criticism finds its basis not in historicist frameworks of

---

84. Wright, *The Resurrection of the Son of God*, 563–83.

thought, but in resurrection; secondly, to hear scripture is to belong to a people characterized by repentance; and thirdly, to en-counter scripture is to recognize its capacity to stand over against the reader. These three aspects will be considered in turn.

To begin with, Thomas Torrance points in the right direction:

> Regarded in the penetrating light of the resurrection, "the observational facts" about Jesus now assume a conceptual organization in accordance with their own intrinsic significance and are found to be interpreting themselves in terms of a natural vectorial coherence of their own. Thus, an astonishing thing about the resurrection is that, instead of cutting Jesus off from his historical and earthly existence before the cross, it takes it all up and confirms its concrete factuality by allowing it to be integrated on its own controlling ground, and thereby enables it to be understood in its own objective meaning . . . It is the resurrection that really discovers and gives access to the historical Jesus, for it enables one to understand him in terms of his own intrinsic *logos*, and appreciate him in the light of his own true nature as he really was—and is and ever will be.[85]

There is an important implication in Torrance's perceptions. It is that resurrection rather than history provides the means by which the facts of resurrection may be apprehended. Torrance adopts a very Barthian logic as he claims that historical criticism can become quite unhistorical. The Gospel texts arise from a dynamic relationship between the risen Lord and his followers—a relationship which shapes the form and content of what may be deemed as a textual artefact. To suppose that history can get behind this relationship to unpack deeper truths or "raw facts" can only result in the discovery of fragmentary truths and facts that have little or nothing to do with the Gospel that is claimed as the object of its inquiry. Neither can one embark upon a historical study with theological convictions temporarily suspended because to do so is immediately to place one's faith in history itself. There is a subtle but important distinction to be made between this approach, and one in which theological convictions are consciously exposed to the challenges of history and vice versa. According to Torrance, it is faith in the risen Christ, with all the personal involvement that resurrection embraces, that provides historical access to the Jesus of history.

85. Torrance, *Space, Time and Resurrection*, 165–66.

> While the resurrection . . . took place within a definite span of space and time . . . it is possessed of a finality and universality whereby it transcends all mere localization or temporal transience, yet in such a way that far from infringing the space-time reality of Jesus Christ it establishes it forever. As such the resurrection constitutes in all times and places the one avenue of real access to the historical Jesus Christ . . .[86]

There is no intention here to deny the necessity of historical critical work, but neither can it simply be said that biblical interpretation requires *more than* historical criticism can offer. Rather such analyses must be configured in terms of resurrection rather than in terms of historicism. Historical criticism must be called out of historicist categories just as the historical Jesus was called out of the tomb that would not contain him. In failing to do so it is destined to remain *less than* historical. Moreover, if this is true for historical criticism, then it is also crucially important for interpretive frameworks that assume historicist categories.

From here one may derive a second aspect of resurrection that impinges upon biblical interpretation. It is the notion of reversal, or more precisely, of catastrophe.[87] As Moltmann perceived, "Jewish messianism is by origin and nature—and this cannot be too much stressed—a theory about catastrophe. This theory stresses the revolutionary, subversive, element in the transition from every historical present to the messianic future."[88] At the centre of history, in the particular case of the Messiah, the resurrection constitutes God's reversal of the verdict that humanity had passed on his son. The generation that rejected God's anointed one was destined to be the last to inhabit the holy city, and catastrophe was therefore inevitably to befall Jerusalem in the form of the Roman military machine. Furthermore, if one's bearings are taken from salvation history, there is a sense in which the course of history changed direction on Easter Sunday. The era of prophetic expectation moves into the era of remembrance. Resurrection, which had served as metaphor for the

---

86. Torrance, *Space, Time and Resurrection*, 172.

87. "strephein means to move; a strophe is what the chorus sings as it moves from right to left across the stage; hence, a kata-strophe means a reversal of movement, to get the chorus moving in the opposite direction, to sing a new song and strike up a change of tone" (Caputo, *Prayers and Tears*, 92).

88. Quoted by Moltmann, *The Way of Jesus Christ*, 22.

Exodus and for every little exodus of history, now became the reality for which the experience and idea of Exodus became the metaphor.[89]

Broadening out from there, Jesus' call to repentance was in essence a call for a reversal of direction, as he summoned the nation to abandon its headlong drive into political disaster and become Israel in a new, reconstituted sense. Deconstructionists like Crossan have rightly perceived and majored upon this structural aspect of the ministry of Jesus in general and on his parables in particular.[90] The parable of rich man and Lazarus is explicitly described by Crossan as a parable of reversal.[91] Crossan here is in accord with Wright who, as noted above, has stressed repentance as a characteristic of this parable. The implication is that repentance is not merely the boundary into some promised land that one may pass and forever leave behind; rather, it is a perpetual characteristic of the people of God. According to the parable, if Moses and the Prophets cannot be heard (by those unwilling to embrace reversal/repentance/revolution), then the absence of such a disposition predestines the brothers to adopt an unbelieving attitude towards one risen from the dead. It is noteworthy at this point that Luke's Jesus expects what historicist hermeneutics deems impossible—namely, that Moses and the Prophets (despite the apparently unbridgeable gulf of centuries) can and should be heard. Those who cannot hear the voices of the ancients are precisely those resistant to resurrection. Such hearing also implies an element of moral action, though, it must be added, not simply as a secondary application of what the text is telling the listener to go away and do. Moses and the Prophets are cited not as merely pronouncing ethical instructions with which all subsequent listeners must then comply. The

---

89. See, for instance, Wright's comments on the parable in *Jesus and the Victory of God*, 255–57.

90. Crossan categorises the parable of the rich man and Lazarus as one of reversal (Crossan, *In Parables*, 75). Central to Crossan's program is the notion that the historical Jesus effected a stunning reversal of his hearer's world, a reversal so unpalatable to the early church that the evangelists diluted the shocking essence of these parables with their own editorial water. Crossan's colourful arguments certainly place a question mark against models of interpretation that have become encrusted with over-familiarity, and heralds with freshness the ability of this parable to achieve reversal and defy closure. However, Crossan's enthusiasm to portray Jesus" parables as "amoral" by resurrecting "force" and sacrificing "content," leads to a particular use of historical critical tools. Such tools enable him to chisel the tradition down to the effigy of the *amoral* historical Jesus he wishes to sculpt—an un/ethical move in itself.

91. Crossan, *In Parables*, 75.

rich man and his brothers are hardly having their wrists slapped for not giving more to charity. Rather, they must be heard as propounding what it truly means to be the people of God. This means not to be a people wallowing in ethnic or covenant privilege whilst remaining content to leave the outsiders outside. Such an attitude is a radical misconception of the covenant. That is why, as discussed in chapters 6 and 7, the parable of the rich man and Lazarus serves the purpose of redefining who is to be regarded as "inside and outside." To be among those who hear scripture is to belong to a people not simply ready to repent of this or that particular sin, but to be characterized by the readiness to repent, conceiving of repentance and its attendant humility as the capacity for transformation in all its moral, social and religious fullness.

The third interpretive implication of resurrection is that to hear scripture is to encounter the text, which is to regard the text itself as something that stands over against readers and calls them to engage it. There are two aspects to this engagement. Interpretation is the reverberation between exegesis and eisegesis, between making and being remade. To focus exclusively on either one of these aspects is to adopt another dichotomous stance over against the resurrection. Examples of both are always ready to hand.

"Can the first-century churches have intended to show us how to make Jesus?" asks Sawicki, "Yes—exactly," she answers, "It is the recipe of the Kingdom of God."[92] The Gospels are perceived as yielding all that is required to construct a home made deconstructive Jesus, one who is ready to reach beyond the text to destabilize oppressive social, religious and political structures. In this case, there is no sense of a final resurrection that determines the shape of eschatological conviction in the present. This is a natural symptom of historicism, homogenizing every piece of unfolding time as it suffers the stamp of human making. Appeal to otherness is made to legitimize rather than criticize (which after all is the true function of eschatology) one's own political structures. This in turn means that the given order (e.g., of marriage) offered in an ancient text like Scripture, is rendered untranslatable by the alienating distance opened up by a humanity that advances through the increasingly sophisticated passage of history.[93] Human making which marches into the void of the future, unconstrained by the givenness of the created order,

---

92. Sawicki, *Seeing the Lord*, 282.

93. O'Donovan, *The Desire of the Nations*, 72–73.

is sure to produce strategies for reading scripture that belittle the importance of exegesis.

Conversely, the supposition that exegesis is a one-way street that carries meaning from author to reader is equally mistaken. One need simply return to Vanhoozer to hear this claim. "The goal of interpretation" he claims, "is to recover the original meaning of the text."[94] This goal is pursued by Vanhoozer in a highly sophisticated way; but, although he is well aware of the pitfalls of hermeneutics in general and helpfully issues some interpretive safety guidelines, his entire framework for interpretation finally struggles to allow for serious participation of the reader without thereby construing her as the master of meaning. For instance, it is difficult to imagine how Vanhoozer might account for the interpretive morality of John, as he implies that Caiaphas spoke truer than he knew when he prophesied that one man should die on behalf of the people (John 18:14). At times the interpreter can consciously impose meaning onto the intent of an author and reframe it. In fact Jesus does exactly this to Pilate! "Are you the king of the Jews?" he asks. "You speak (*su legei*) [the truth]," is Jesus' response (Matt 27:11; Mark 15:2), violating Pilate's question by turning it into a statement.[95]

The first part of this thesis has critiqued at length the hermeneutical models that embody technologist categories as they create meaning out of the text with little room for the God to answer back through the text. Equally manipulative is a phenomenon as yet not discussed but nevertheless worthy of mention: that is, the desire to be mastered by the text. To seek a total subservience to the text can be every bit a technologist attempt to master it by turning into precisely the sort of authoritative entity that is useful to our enterprises. Within such a strategy even the desire for the text to stand over against the reader comes within a definitively circumscribed capacity to challenge. While Vanhoozer certainly does not follow this line, it is one that can be readily accommodated by the hermeneutic structure he presents. Readers are not merely passive recipients who are told what in humility they should do and then put their bibles down to make scripture come alive by going away and doing

---

94. Vanhoozer, *Is There a Meaning in this Text?*, 46.

95. Against the possible objection that this is an instance of reported speech encounter (between speaker and hearer), and therefore fundamentally different from the reading encounter (between reader and text), one need simply appeal to Schleiermacher: the interpretation of a text, "has no other goal than we have in listening to any piece of everyday speech" (Schleiermacher, *Hermeneutics and Criticism*, 21).

what it says. Whilst there is much to be said for such a pattern, it is by no means guaranteed that this is a genuine expression of humility.[96] A technologist reading can follow this precise pattern, without allowing its own wider interpretive framework to be threatened. For instance, one might rejoice in loving one's neighbors without every having one's understanding of what constitutes a neighborly otherness serious challenged (cf. Luke 10:25–37).

Nevertheless, despite our extended critique of human making, there is a proper place for technological reading: one that engages with the text as it engages the world, with the dual intent of embracing it as a cooperative support whilst respecting its excess, its ability to resist. There must be an element of human action, because reading scripture is not simply the passive reception of God's word. Since language is fallen, then, just as Adam and Eve had to sweat and toil to make the earth yield its fruit, so such work must be involved in reading scripture. That is why to read scripture is to struggle, not with the text in itself, but to wrestle with it as Jacob wrestled with an angel—and, in so doing, wrestled with God himself. Scripture is the place where readers are grappled by God, or his messenger, and in so doing recreate and are recreated by the text (cf. Gen 32:22–32).

CONCLUSIONS: THE REDUNDANCY OF HERMES

However virtuous its intentions, a historicist hermeneutic constrains us to peer down the wrong end of a telescope to see a distant figure who in reality is not so far away. If the parable compels one to hear "Moses and the Prophets," then in the light of historicism one would do well to pay serious attention to Moses' own reflections on Torah:

> This commandment is not in heaven, that you should say, "Who will go up to heaven for us, and get it for us so that we may hear it and observe it?" Neither is it beyond the sea, that you should say, "Who should cross to the other side of the sea for us, and get it for us so that we may hear it and observe it?" No, the word is very near to you; it is in your mouth and in your heart for you to observe.[97]

---

96. Humility is defined below as the capacity to be transformed by encounter with otherness.

97. Deut 30:12–14.

Critics of historicism have often claimed that the mere fact of sharing a common humanity itself offers sufficient common ground for communication with ancient authors.[98] This is not the promise of Moses, nor is it the precise claim of our thesis. Our argument is rather that it is God's action in history, in which salvation history rejoices, that enables us to hear Moses and the Prophets. This means that belonging to the covenant people of God locates readers in a relation to the text that is anathema to historicist hermeneutics. This passage from Deuteronomy is also cited in Rom 10:6–13, where it is applied to Christ, and his resurrection. For Paul, the one who obeys the righteous precepts of the law, "will live by them" (Rom 10:5). The presence of resurrected Christ in the active life of the believer renders redundant requests for an intermediary.[99]

According to historicism, the void that separates horizons requires the services of a Hermes, because as the later Heidegger used to remark, "only a God can save us."[100] Interpretive faith is better placed in the Holy Spirit than in the figure of Hermes. In the parable Lazarus is not permitted to play the role of Hermes[101]—not because of Abraham's lack of mercy, but because when resurrection is a reality no such role is necessary. The resurrection of Jesus is the redundancy of Hermes. This has not prevented post-Enlightenment biblical hermeneutics from appealing to Hermes to as the bearer of a message from the divine. Such technologist attempts to invoke historic or divine presence are destined to confuse what they discover with what they create. Conversely, *resurrection displaces technologist reading categories that seek to make use of scripture, with the cultivation of an attentive disposition which enables the reader to be transformed by the God encountered in scripture.*

Chapters 5–7 below will now explore how the cultivation of this disposition relates to a reading of the parable of the rich man and Lazarus, and how the technologist reading strategies laid out in chapters 1–3 are contrasted by interpretive approaches which arise from and remain attentive to the resurrection of Jesus of Nazareth.

---

98. E.g., see Thiselton, *Two Horizons*, 53.

99. Paul himself knew only too well about Hermes, having once been mistaken for and worshipped as him (Acts 14:8–20).

100. Heidegger, "Only God Can Save Us."

101. Hermes is the messenger from the dead, delivering souls to Hades. (See Diogenes Laertius: *Lives and Opinions of Eminent Philosophers* VIII [Pythagoras]).

5

Christological Reading as Humility

INTRODUCTION: "WHO IS THIS MAN?"

THROUGHOUT THE GOSPELS THE presence of Jesus constantly evokes the question, "Who is this man?" Whether it is uttered with Pharisaic contempt (Luke 5:21), Herodian unease (Luke 9:9) or fearful astonishment (Luke 8:25), it is a question by which Luke's readers are frequently confronted.[1] This is no question of disengaged curiosity, posed by Luke in order to reveal correct truths about the identity of Jesus. Heard in its first century context it was a question densely packed with religious, political and social significance. In an atmosphere that was highly charged with messianic beliefs and programs it was not a safe question to answer. It is a question this chapter is intended to raise.

As with each of the constructive chapters in this second part of the thesis, this chapter will be comprised of two sections: the first will highlight the manner in which a text is encountered while the second will reconsider the claims of that first section in light of a reading of the parable of the rich man and Lazarus. Chapter 3 considered the messianic structure of Derridian thought, recognizing its desire to be radically open to the transformative challenge of the so-called "other." Given that there is a predisposition dormant within the deconstructionist attitude that all-too-prescriptively determines how the "other"

---

1. For assessments of Luke's overall aims in writing the Gospel that cohere with the recurrence of the "who?" question, see Marshall, "Luke and His Gospel," 289–308; and Strauss, *The Davidic Messiah in Luke-Acts*, 344–49.

Christological Reading as Humility 141

may or may not behave, it was concluded that even the notion of *différance* could insidiously endorse the claims to violent power to which it supposes itself a foil. Scandalized by the notion of messianic particularity, Derrida is happy to retain messianic structures of thought but utterly rejects any concrete expression of that thought.[2] Seeking to expose the technologist reading strategy identified by chapter 3 in Derrida, this chapter seeks to view deconstructive thought through the concept of resurrection outlined in chapter 4 and offer a Christological way of encountering the text.

PART I: CHRISTOLOGY AND INTERPRETATION

The questions of Christology often centre on the supposed conundrum of whether and more importantly *how* the second person of the Trinity can be both fully human and fully divine. To begin with these questions however, is to suppose that one already knows what it means to be God and indeed, what it means to be human. A Christology which takes full account of messianic expectation begins not with the question of *how* but of *who*, namely who Christ is in relation to those who inquire, because after such a question has been adequately addressed the presupposed categories of humanity and divinity may be drastically reconfigured. Dietrich Bonhoeffer sought to locate this *who* at the centre of Christology, and the apocalyptic collection of his Christological writings forms the basis of our attempt to situate biblical interpretation within its proper Messianological coordinates.[3] From Bonhoeffer one may draw upon several key Christological themes of major import for this thesis.

Using the Johannine conception of the Logos, Bonhoeffer sees in Christology an assault upon the human "Logos," an assault that lies juxtaposed with Derrida's critique of logocentrism.[4] For Bonhoeffer, the human Logos describes a presupposed order of existence that enables one to know *how* to classify that which is encountered as novel. Christology

---

2. Derrida, *On the Name*, 166–67. Herein lies the distinction between Messianology and Christology. The latter is a based upon an actual, historical, personal manifestation of the former.

3. Bonhoeffer, *Christology*. This is a reconstruction of Bonhoeffer's thoughts compiled from the lecture notes and recollections of his students.

4. Derrida, *Writing and Difference*, 10–14.

is a spanner in the works of such structural presupposition. Bonhoeffer's entire Christological discussion is based upon this question.

> What if somewhere the claim is raised that this human Logos is superseded, judged, dead? What happens if an Anti-Logos appears which refuses to be classified? A Logos which annihilates the first? What if the proclamation goes out that the old order has been dissolved, that it is out of date, and that the counterpart of a new world has already begun?[5]

An Enlightenment response to such interrogation might be for the human Logos to reconstitute itself in order to accommodate the Anti-Logos, in the manner of Hegelian dialectic. In so doing of course, the Anti-Logos is eventually domesticated and once again systematically subjugated to the totalizing authority of the human Logos. But the Anti-Logos is not only an idea to be considered but a person to be confronted. Appearing in history as the Anti-Logos his presence finally compels only one question: "who are you?" This is no expression of passive curiosity but a question that deconstructs the entire interpretive framework of the inquirer.[6] It is the end of the human logos, and only at this point – the point of faith – does the Anti-Logos disclose himself. "Christ gives an answer to the question "who?""[7]

The question, "*How* are you possible?" is regarded as a godless irrelevance to the identity of Christ. But the *who* question is one that takes seriously the otherness of the other, the strangeness of the one encountered, in such a way as to call into question one's own present existence. However, even the *who* question can, and is most likely to be asked in terms of the *how* question. By such politely veiled means, the human Logos reasserts itself. After all, according to Bonhoeffer,

> . . . the Logos cannot endure the Anti-Logos. It knows that one of them must die. So it kills the person of whom it has asked. Because the human Logos does not want to die, the Logos of

---

5. Bonhoeffer, *Christology*, 29.

6. There is some clear convergence here with the early Barth, who was a major influence upon Bonhoeffer's thought. Barth's famous essay "The Strange New World Within the Bible" (Barth, *The Word of God and the Word of Man*, 28–50) opens by claiming that for scripture to be heard, the reader must be deconstructed: "The question, What is within the Bible? has a mortifying way of converting itself into the opposing question, Well, what are you looking for, and who are you, pray, who make bold to look?" (Barth, *The Word of God and the Word of Man*, 32).

7. Bonhoeffer, *Christology*, 30.

God, who would be the death of it, must die so that it can live on with its unanswered questions of existence and transcendence. The Logos of God incarnate must be crucified by man's Logos.[8]

Nevertheless if the Anti-Logos cannot be so readily annihilated, if he returns from the dead and confronts his murderers, then the *who* question reasserts itself upon those who would be rid of it, as they become not only the subject but the object of that question. The Christological *who?* is only truly asked once the motives of the inquirer have been reshaped around this reverse question, i.e., *who* is the inquirer. Since God alone can confront humanity in this sense, then the only human response to this reversed question is the basic foundational question, "Who are you?" The supposedly Christological questions of "how" and "whether" two natures coexist evaporate in the intensity of personal confrontation.

Only in the light of God's revelation may humanity grasp what it means to be human, and what it means to encounter the divine. Christology then cannot be addressed in abstract terms, because this would be to trust human logology to produce a means of comprehending the Anti-logos. Christology therefore is an event in which the knowledge sought is in a sense already known. It does not ask *what* is possible, or *how* the Anti-Logos can be understood. To pursue Christology is an act of self-sacrifice, as the human Logos is reconfigured by its nemesis.[9]

If in their critique of naïve logocentrism, there is some convergence between Bonhoeffer's Christology and Derrida's Messianology,[10] it leads to a divergence of their respective concerns. For Bonhoeffer the personal presence of Christ, encountered both temporally and spatially, is a prior assumption that sets the context in which Christological questions are properly asked. There is no room in Bonhoeffer for a depersonalized Messianology because this subjects the person of Christ to the power of history.[11] When Messianology is perceived as a free floating principle

---

8. Bonhoeffer, *Christology*, 34.

9. Bonhoeffer, *Christology*, 31–32.

10. As discussed in chapter 3 above, Derrida is happy to live in expectation of a Messiah, but if such hope is ever materialised it is therefore extinguished. The arrival of a Messiah is not good news for Derrida. See also Caputo, *Prayers and Tears*, 190.

11. In accord with radical historicism as outlined in chapter 4, Christ would be perceived as a phenomenon of history, subject to prior causes and categories rather than as a source of genuine otherness. Bonhoeffer challenges historicist assumptions not, like Derrida, by expecting a form of "messianic" otherness devoid of concrete content,

of history that may or may not be activated or expressed by the actual arrival of Messiahs, the category of the person (not to be confused with the abstract category of personality) is violently decentered.[12] The person of Christ is thereby disenfranchised by the effects of his supposed *dunamis* within history, and quietly but comprehensively excluded from historical consideration. Thus historicism sacrifices Christology (and its threatening particularity) for the security of Messianology (and its safer generality).[13] Even so, in the light of the resurrection the category of the person is not so easily dismissed. Bonhoeffer perceives this as the first problem of Christology:

> If Christ is present not only as power, but in his person, how are we to conceive of this presence so that it does not violate the wholeness of his person? To be present means to be in the same place at the same time. Even as the Risen One, Jesus Christ remains the man Jesus in space and time. Only because Jesus Christ is man is he present in time and place. Only because Jesus Christ is God is he eternally present everywhere.[14]

The presence of Christ that may be claimed by those who read scripture is not simply a presence that endorses and upholds my reading of scripture, a mystical hidden proof that yields private assurances of certainty that must subsequently be concealed behind the modest veil of humility. Such a presence is rightly critiqued by Derrida.[15] It has always been at odds with theological interpretation because the presence of Christ, as Bonhoeffer has rightly perceived it, is one that stands over

---

but by depicting Christ as embodying a content-full otherness that demands concrete response.

12. See for instance Schillebeeckx (*Jesus*, 660–68) who offers a superb summary of the concept of the person specifically relating its troubled philosophical and theological history to the specific gospel Christologies. A person was traditionally understood as a person-in-relationship. The more modern notion of personality, a person's individual self-consciousness without reference to others, is thus sharply distinguished from Christ's person. Christ cannot be understood when abstracted out of his relationship to others, including those who consider his personhood.

13. The so-called "scandal of particularity" is visited upon the reader in full force, not simply as an idea about a particular Christ, but in being addressed by this inescapably particular Christ.

14. Bonhoeffer, *Christology*, 45.

15. See ch. 3 above. The scope of deconstructive influence may be largely attributable to this untheological conception of presence that continues to find a home in the church of Christ, an issue addressed in our next chapter.

against the interpreter. Nevertheless, it is at this point that Bonhoeffer may be overstating his case.

The political situation in which his theology was forged and the urgency of the theological challenge that he issued led to a strong emphasis on Christ as a counter-conventional presence at the expense of Christ as a supportive presence for the church.[16] The presence of Christ is one that may confirm as well as confront the reader of scripture.[17] The Gospel portrays a Messiah who came not only to tear down the constructive housing for the presence of God, but also to rebuild it around his own presence (cf. John 2:19). Bonhoeffer's most pressing concern is that the presence of Christ remains absolutely central to Christology. To consider Christ is by no means to consider him in the abstract and then to go in search of his effects in history as though they were a manifestation of some prior essence. Neither can one consider Christ in isolation from who he is in relation to me. Christ is ontologically *pro me*.

> The question may not run: "How can the man Jesus, or how can the God Christ be contemporaneous here?" There is no question about the fact of his presence. The question must run: "By virtue of what personal structure is Christ present to the Church?"[18]

Here Bonhoeffer reaches the climax of his argument. Christ cannot be considered as a thing-in-himself, in isolation from his relation to the one who inquires. To meditate on Christ as he is in himself rather than who he is in relation to me is, for Bonhoeffer, a godless pursuit.

> Christ is Christ not as Christ in himself, but in relation to me. His being Christ is his being *pro me*. This being *pro me* is in turn not meant to be understood . . . as an accident; it is meant to be understood as the essence, as the being of the person himself . . . Christ can never be thought of in his being in himself, but only in his relationship to me. That in turn means that Christ can only be conceived of existentially, viz. in the community.[19]

---

16. For instance, one might note the practical dangers of leading a confessing congregation in Nazi Germany (Bethge, *Dietrich Bonhoeffer*, 408–9, 481–82. See also 363–66).

17. This objection cannot be pressed too forcefully, however, partly because his Christological writings are unfinished, and partly because the supportive role of Christ is latent within the more controversial portrait he produces.

18. Bonhoeffer, *Christology*, 47.

19. Bonhoeffer, Christology, 47–48.

The individual inquirer can no more be abstracted out of the question of Christ than the Christ of faith can be abstracted away from the Jesus of history, which brings us to a third aspect of Bonhoeffer's Christology.

To suppose that there is no demonstrable continuity between the Jesus of history and the Christ of faith is not only counter to the New Testament witness,[20] but in Bonhoeffer's view, to impose an artificial barrier. A Christ who is present *pro me* transcends the methodological reach of historical investigation. His presence in the church means that the historical facticity of the Christ event is not past but present, and "what is historical is contemporaneous."[21] This statement is possible only where "what is historical, what is hidden has made itself contemporaneous and open, i.e., faith in the miracle of God in the resurrection of Jesus Christ."[22]

> There is no absolute ground of faith in history. But from where does faith receive its sufficient ground to know, when history is uncertain? There is only the witness of the Risen One to himself, through which the church bears witness to him as the Historical One. By the miracle of his presence in the church he bears witness to himself here and now as the one who was historical then.[23]

Historical means of access to the so-called historical Jesus has little purchase on faith, because, after all, in reading any historical figures one can claim a certain presence in their company. Nor may one retreat to the inner, private sphere in order to establish some means of access to the historical Jesus. Only by the resurrected Jesus who awakens faith and orients one to the Christ event does one have access to the historical Jesus. "In faith, history is known in the light of eternity. That is the direct

---

20. To talk of "the New Testament witness," and one that is "demonstrable" may sound over ambitious but here we rely upon James D. G. Dunn's analysis, *Unity and Diversity in the New Testament*, in which it is argued convincingly that the only common element traceable through all New Testament literature is the assumption that there is continuity between the earthly and heavenly Jesus. "I think it can justly be said that we have discovered a fairly clear and consistent unifying strand which from the first both marked out Christianity as something distinctive and different and provided the integrating centre for the diverse expressions of Christianity. That unifying element was the unity between the historical Jesus and the exalted Christ . . . " 369.

21. Bonhoeffer, *Christology*, 74.

22. Bonhoeffer, *Christology*, 74–75.

23. Bonhoeffer, *Christology*, 75.

access of faith to history."²⁴ Bonhoeffer is aware of the dangers to which such a profession may lead, but points out that the self-attestation of Christ is mediated by means of scripture. Where scripture is regarded as a secular book "just like any other," one must employ every exegetical tool available. However, because such endeavor is based upon very uncertain grounds, he proposes that scripture be read in the light of scripture, through the kaleidoscopic shift of inter-textuality.

For Bonhoeffer exegesis is not utilized in order to establish a fixed, stable and singular meaning in which one can anchor one's interpretation and subsequent ethics. It is rather an untameable witness through human words that becomes active in a divinely enabled event. This rests quite firmly upon Barth's understanding of revelation, which is encountered always as an event,²⁵ although God may not necessarily grant such revelatory events.²⁶ Despite Bonhoeffer's respect for Barth, he differed significantly on this issue: "God is not free *of* man but *for* man. Christ is the Word of his freedom. God is *there*, which is to say: not in eternal non-objectivity but "haveable," graspable in his Word within the Church."²⁷ Bonhoeffer's reading of Barth suggests that Barth's God is somehow detached from the lives of believers, whereas Bonhoeffer was at pains to emphasise that in Christ, God exists as Community.²⁸

If historical distance from Christ is regarded as an obstacle, his presence within the contemporary church suggests that it is one that is not to be overcome solely nor even primarily by historical method. The Christ of the church is also the Christ enthroned at the centre of history. Bonhoeffer, like Barth and indeed like Oscar Cullmann, rejects the opinion that regarding Christ as the centre of history can be philosophically justified. However, unlike Cullmann, Bonhoeffer does not fall into the trap of thinking that this disavowal of itself thereby divests oneself of a philosophical position.²⁹ Bonhoeffer's view is rather that the desire

---

24. Bonhoeffer, *Christology*, 75.

25. See particularly Barth, *Church Dogmatics*, I.1, 193–98.

26. This is to avoid the temptation to "discover" divine legitimation for human endeavors.

27. Bonhoeffer, *Act and Being*, 90. Barth's notion of the freedom of God permeates the first volume of his *Church Dogmatics* (see especially pp. 301, 321).

28. For Bonhoeffer, the concreteness of Christ's existence is derived from his existence in the community. See Rumscheidt, "The Formation of Bonhoeffer's Theology," 50–70, esp. 64–65.

29. E.g., In *Christ and Time* he states, "If we wish to grasp the Primitive Christian

for philosophical justification for regarding Christ as the centre of history may unwittingly but effectively dethrone Christ from this position by making philosophy into a "kingmaker" and thereby relativizing the Messianic centrality. "Were Christ demonstrably shown to be the climax of all religions, that would still not prove that he is the centre."[30] One cannot sneak behind the Cosmocrator to establish some independent necessity that would justify the centrality of Christ. The conviction that Christ is the centre of history must be conceived of and described from a different perspective altogether.

Following Bonhoeffer, Moltmann believes that history is not concerned solely with the past, but relies on a tension between promise and fulfillment, as may be seen in the case of Abraham. Abraham followed the call to leave his own land, and lived by faith in God's promise.[31] Moltmann regards the tension between the Abrahamic experience and expectation, between the promise and the fulfillment of divine promise, as the framework of Israel's history.

> What was imagined in individual terms with Abraham was Israel's collective experience in the exodus from Egypt, an experience which was told from generation to generation. Exodus means leaving an old reality which was endured as an imprisonment and seeking the land of promise. It we transfer this to the experience of time, exodus means leaving what is behind and reaching out to what lies ahead (Phil. 3.13). Past and future become distinguishable in the transition of the present.[32]

The radical historicism engendered by deconstructionists is based upon messianic expectation, and, as already noted, it is one that perpetually eludes fulfillment.[33] History is adorned with an awesome capacity for newness, carrying within itself the messianic resources to decenter the old age of logocentric oppression and enter the liberation of a playful new one. By contrast, from a Christological perspective, history is as

---

idea of eternity, we must strive above all to think in as unphilosophical a manner as possible" (62).

30. Bonhoeffer, *Christology*, 63.

31. As will be seen in our next chapter, the parable of the rich man and Lazarus addresses directly how that particular promise finds fulfillment within the purposes of God.

32. Moltmann, *The Way of Jesus Christ*, 237.

33. P. 95–97 above.

fallen as its tenants. As Bonhoeffer argued, it cannot fulfill its Messianic promise any more than humanity can fulfil the Law. However, Israel is the one place where Messianic promise is fulfilled, not by means of history's own omnipotence but rather as the hidden action of God. Like Moses, history can only take the people of God so far. It points them where it cannot lead them: not beyond its horizon but beyond itself. To remain content with the witness of history is to ignore it. To see history as an end in itself is to idolize it. The only way to respect history is to address the *who* question as it is posed both of me, and of the one who stands at its centre. Only in Christ can history become what it is. Hence Bonhoeffer's conclusion: "Christ stands where history as a whole should stand. He is the *pro me* even for history. He is even the mediator of history."[34]

To acknowledge the incarnate Christ as the fulfillment of history is to discard the incessant open-endedness heralded by deconstruction. To move from a general Messianological to a specific Christological reading is to sacrifice one's interpretive freedom, because hermeneutical "free play" is precluded by the reader who seeks to de-liberate. As Bultmann saw, and as will be clarified in chapter 7, existential interpretation is always the result of de-liberation. Clearly, this runs contrary to the spirit of deconstruction, which in some quasi-pious quest for liberation is prevented from actually making final decisions. As Bonhoeffer has revealed, to read Christologically is unavoidably to commit to final decision in that it sacrifices human logology, and it is much more likely that the Anti-Logos itself will be sacrificed. This is precisely what is seen in deconstructionist Messianology. The cry for liberation, "Hosanna," is constantly on the lips of the disciples of deconstructionism. But on the arrival of an actual person, the Messiah, the cry *Hosanna* must give way to one of two alternatives. On the one hand it might emanate in the cry *Hallelujah* at the presence of the Messiah and the experience of liberation. Deconstruction rightly understands that this liberation is not total, but is simply a regime change in which individuals do not become masters of their own destinies, but are rather the subjects of a new master, and will therefore seek to be liberated from the Messiah. For this reason they are compelled to adopt the counter position, the alternative outcome of the cry *Hosanna*: when there arrives a Person

---

34. Bonhoeffer, *Christology*, 65.

who is Messiah, who (as Anti-Logos) radically reshapes the aspirations of his subjects, the natural response is to cry "Crucify him."

There is a deeply rooted irony here that is missed altogether by Derrida's anti-historical pronouncements: that is, that concrete Messianisms can take radically different forms. Derrida's assumption that all Messianisms are essentially violent is one that led to the crucifixion of Jesus of Nazareth. Pilate himself recognized that this Messiah was actually no warmonger, and it was this very lack of military action that led to his rejection by the people.[35] But to defeat the forces of evil did not simply mean overthrowing the Gentile overlords, even if this was the focus of many Jews' designs for their Messiah.[36] It was this very demand that arose from the spirit that rendered Israel unfaithful to their divine purpose as the people of God. Derrida's assumptions that Messianic expression leads inevitably to violence arise from the very notion of the Kingdom of God that Jesus' entire prophetic ministry was designed to challenge.[37] The Messianic fault-line between the old age and the new ruptured over opposing hopes for the Kingdom of God: Barabbas the revolutionary activist or Jesus the (un)expected Christ? This crisis is perpetually re-ignited by a Messiah who is Anti-Logos, personally present and historically contemporaneous.

Christological Crisis inexorably reasserts itself upon contemporary readings of scripture, disturbing presumed patterns of anthropocentric logology and ensuring the elusiveness of a so-called final meaning. But with this recognition of perpetual crisis, does one not fall back into Derridian open-endedness, the readiness to greet the incessant *differance* of the other? Is the faithful Christian life really an inescapable cycle of crisis and despair? If one takes Christocentrism (as one should take deconstruction) primarily as an attitude, then it constitutes a worldview saturated with humility. Our next two chapters will explore in more

---

35. Theissen and Merz identify Jesus' non-resistance to the occupying power as a radically distinctive aspect of Jesus' prophetic activity (*The Historical Jesus*, 146). Sanders believes that Pilate did not perceive Jesus as a violent threat (*Jesus and Judaism*, 294–97; *The Historical Figure of Jesus*, 273–74). Conversely, S. G. F. Brandon, followed by a more cautious R. Horsley, contends that Jesus' revolutionary activity rendered him a violent threat to the Roman authorities (See Witherington, *The Jesus Quest*, 145–52).

36. See again Witherington, *The Jesus Quest*, 145–52, 213–14; Bockmuehl, *This Jesus*, 50–59; Wright, *Jesus and the Victory of God*, 481–86.

37. See Caputo, *Prayers and Tears*, 190.

detail how such an attitude is learned both communally and existentially.[38] Personal transformation in the midst of everyday life need not be regarded as constant upheaval and crisis, because it is generated by a personal presence rather than an impersonal force. The ultimate event of dis-closure is neither concretized law nor abstract principle, as Derrida seems to imply, but the active presence of a life-giving Spirit.

The Spirit of Revelation

It has been our contention that both technological method and historical criticism are indispensable but insufficient to awaken the crucial attentive disposition of humility amongst those who would hear scripture. Tom Smail has insisted as much in his insight: "The techniques of biblical scholarship can certainly bring us to a more accurate appreciation of what the biblical writers are saying; but, to bring us to a conviction of the truth of the gospel and relationship with the God of whom it speaks is the prerogative of the Holy Spirit alone."[39] As *didaskalos*, the Spirit of Truth (John 14:17) is not only a Spirit of correctness, graciously bestowing exegetical precision upon the prayerful scholar. The Spirit of *aletheia* leads the individual to an unveiling that is not simply the unveiling of correct information about the world, but is an eventful exposure of the individual to the world. Thus the world is encountered not merely as 'standing reserve,'[40] but a world in which Christ is encountered. Heidegger believed that from the technologist *Gestell*—in which our capacity to encounter either human or divine otherness is radically diminished—"only a god can save us."[41] Within this *Gestell*, humanity cannot create its own space for the Spirit subsequently to fill. Part of the Spirit's role as *didaskalos* is to lead believers into *aletheia* (John 16:13), that is, to encounter the genuine content-full otherness of Christ.

---

38. Glancing forward to chapter 7 on eschatology, one may simply state that Sabbath is the quiet place where personal transformation takes place. Moltmann's Christology points in this direction: "Beside the noisy messianism of the apocalyptic of catastrophe, and the wild messianism of revolutionary utopianism, the Sabbath is a still but steady, and thus lasting, messianism. It comes in everyday life, and brings the dream of redemption into the unnoticeable ordinariness of life as it is lived" (Moltmann, *The Way of Jesus Christ*, 27).

39. Smail, *The Giving Gift*, 94.

40. Heidegger, "The Question Concerning Technology," 322.

41. Heidegger, "Only God Can Save Us."

The "age of the spirit" inheres between the resurrection of Christ in the past and the anticipated resurrection of the dead at the last day. It has been argued that history hangs upon the tension between these two poles. The past resurrection of Christ is not alien, neither is the future resurrection otherworldly because the presence of the risen Christ is encountered as life-giving Spirit. Here Moltmann's insight resurfaces, as he sees that the resurrection cuts across a two-dimensional historicism.

> The positivist, materialist reduction of history to the level of past facts and times that have gone suppresses the future of the past. This kind of historicism was in its trend and effect anti-historical. Rather than the experience of history, it meant a farewell to history.[42]

Moltmann hears Saint Paul integrate three different tenses of resurrection with the presence of the spirit abiding in the life of believers. "If the Spirit of him who has raised Jesus from the dead dwells in you, he who has raised Christ Jesus from the dead will give life to your mortal bodies also through his Spirit which dwells in you" (Rom 8:11). The perfect tense of Christ's resurrection is connected with the present tense of the Spirit's indwelling in the believer, and in turn orients hope towards the future tense of the final resurrection of the dead. The past event of Christ, the ontic reality of the Christ event and the future reality disclosed through that event are presently encountered noetically through the animation wrought by the life-giving Spirit. Christ is present in the Spirit. Furthermore, just as the Messiah instigates the era of freedom, so in the lives of believers in whom the Spirit dwells, liberation is actually encountered. Paul has emphasized as much by referring to the present reality of resurrection not as the private infusion of otherworldliness that directs one's hope away from real life, but as the life conferred upon mortal bodies, a this-worldly experience of resurrection effected by the Spirit.

> In the Spirit resurrection is not merely expected; it is already experienced. Resurrection happens every day. In love we experience many resurrections. We experience resurrection by being born again to a living hope through love, in which we already, here and now, wake from death to life, and through liberation: "Where the Spirit of the Lord is, there is freedom" (2 Cor 3.17).[43]

---

42. Moltmann, *The Way of Jesus Christ*, 240.
43. Moltmann, *The Way of Jesus Chris*, 242.

The notion of the Spirit's indwelling in the believer resonates with the notion of the shekinah presence in the temple. The Spirit's departure from the temple is signified at the moment of Jesus' death. If stones could cry out, then the cry of dereliction might well have been uttered by the temple: "My God, My God, why have you forsaken me"(Matt 27:46). In a sense, this is the very cry that was articulated by the temple in an inverted speech act, as its curtain was torn down the middle (Luke 23:45). It is thoroughly mistaken to regard this primarily as God breaking out of the holy of holies and becoming immediately accessible to all.[44] Instead, it is an incident that signifies the redundancy of the temple.

Biblical interpretation can all too easily presume that there is no longer any substantive role for the temple. The temple signified a special presence of YHWH, even despite the fact that he was in no means distant from his creation. After the temple is rendered redundant, one is not left with a universally immediate access to the Holy God; rather we are left with the Holy Spirit. Even the citation of Joel's prophecy that the Spirit is to be poured out upon all flesh (Acts 2:17–21; Joel 2:28–32) does not mean that every individual has automatic unrestricted access to the holy of holies. The era of salvation history described as the "Age of the Spirit" is by no means dispossessed of the temple because the category of the "holy" has not been abandoned. In contrast to the Christology outlined by Bonhoeffer, to blur the distinction between the Spirit of Christ and the human Spirit flattens out the notion of presence and endorses every individualistic attempt to invoke it. The conception of the torn temple curtain as the legitimization of individualistic religion and consequent biblical interpretation is alien to both Christology and Temple Theology. As Bonhoeffer's Christology affirmed, the presence of Christ is not to be taken lightly.

Matthew's Jesus offers a presence that is an affront to the spirit of deconstruction. Part of the effect of the exile was to make the people of Israel into a people of the book, because in the absence of the Promised Land and the Solomonic temple, the Torah became the focus of presence and hope. It was a strand of tradition seized upon by the Pharisees, who with little official religio-political influence had little leverage over

---

44. Raymond Brown's detailed study of the temple's torn veil concludes that despite the positive interpretation suggested by the letter to the Hebrews (6:19–20; 10:19–20), as far as the synoptics were concerned it was an event symbolising divine wrath. See Brown, *The Death of the Messiah*, 1097–1118.

the conduct of temple worship and therefore relocated temple worship in the study of Torah.[45] The rabbinical saying of Pirque Aboth captures this strategy perfectly: "where two or three gather to study Torah, the Shekinah rests upon them."[46] The Torah was thus perceived as a substitute, although prior to AD 70 by no means a total one, for the temple that housed the glory of YHWH. It is highly likely that this rabbinical saying provides the context in which the Matthean saying (Matt 18:19–20) is to be heard: "If two or three of you agree on earth about anything you ask, it will be done for you by my Father in heaven. For where two or three are gathered in my name, I am there among them." In short, both the Torah and the Shekinah as the meeting point between heaven and earth have been displaced by the personal presence of Jesus. Far from discarding the temple, the Messiah has now taken up its function. Whilst our next chapter will discuss in more detail the manner in which that function is embodied in Christ, our aim in this chapter is to show that his embodied presence is to be taken seriously by those who would hear scripture. This is best discussed within the context of the ambiguous relationship between so-called general and special hermeneutics.

The distinction between the general and the special has taken a variety of forms, which need to be acknowledged. First, is the distinction between the hermeneutics of the text in particular as over against the hermeneutics of the world in general; secondly between the biblical, sacred text and literature in general; thirdly a Christian approach to scripture/text as opposed to a secular approach. The first two of these sets of distinctions will be addressed by a focus on the third.

The relationship between general and special hermeneutics is not solely an issue of subject matter. It is rather a question in the first instance of the appropriation of that subject matter: pagan and Christian alike can study Holy Scripture with a total disregard for the holiness such reading requires. But if the disposition of the reader distinguishes

---

45. The purity laws propounded by Pharisees were inseparable from their political interests. In sight of Roman and Hellenistic influences, purity laws could hardly be conceived as apolitical (Saldarini, *Pharisees, Scribes and Saducees*, 132–33, 281–82). Having little influence either in the Temple or in civil law, the purity laws developed by the Pharisees—according to Saldarini—largely regarding food, sex and marriage, 'set out an agenda of holiness for the land and people which was a fitting response for a powerless people dominated by the Romans . . . " (Saldarini, "Pharisees," 291).

46. *Pirque Aboth* 3.3.

general from special hermeneutics, has not so called "reader response"[47] hermeneutics become determinative? This would be a facile if alluring conclusion. To accentuate the importance of reader holiness is by no means theologically to cut the reader adrift from the text, nor is it to promote the reader to master of the text. Just as worship in the temple is inseparable from wider moral attitudes and practices (e.g., Jer 7:9–11), so too is the Christian reading of scripture. The implication of Jeremiah's polemic is that life outside the temple (wholly but not solely) determined worship in the temple: "Will you steal, murder, commit adultery, swear falsely, make offerings to Baal, and go after other gods that you have not known, and then come and stand before me in this house . . . " (Jer 7:9–10). Furthermore, to enter the temple and reduce its holiness to personal moral endorsement, ("we are safe . . . to do all these detestable things . . .), is to treat the temple like any other place and effectively if unwittingly to reject its holiness and thereby its very essence. Hence Jeremiah's indictment, which is powerfully echoed by Jesus, "Has this house, which bears my Name, become a den of robbers to you?"(v. 11). This is no pagan desecration of the temple. Such deliberate desecration follows only after its unwitting desecration by those who worshipped there. By way of analogy, for the Christian reader of scripture to respect its holiness requires not so much a tenacious adherence to doctrines about its divine authority, as a moral disposition that effects all of life, without which the bible is effectively treated like any other book. General hermeneutics can thus determine avowedly biblical hermeneutics just as pagan religious practices in Jeremiah's day determined temple worship.

To buttress these claims one may turn to Vanhoozer's insight that Christians ought not merely read the bible like any other book, but to read any other book as though one were reading scripture. For Vanhoozer, "*the best general hermeneutics is a Trinitarian hermeneutics.*"[48] Although one might want to nuance Vanhoozer's call to allow the [biblical and in

---

47. The designation "reader response" is a highly misleading one. In effect it generally refers to the meaning that readers or reading communities make out of the text in true technologist fashion. To speak properly of "reader response" presupposes the primacy of the text because it is this that exerts its influence over against the reader forcing her into "response." This conception has little to do with theories that tend to be categorized as reader response, in which readers or reading communities are the primary determinants of textual encounter.

48. Vanhoozer, *Is There a Meaning in this Text*, 456.

turn, any] text to "do what it intends,"[49] to follow Ingraffia's alternative—a hermeneutics of suspicion—would be a mistake. When Vanhoozer's call for trust in the text is heard within the wider context of his theological approach, it is not a blind trust that needs to be tempered with suspicion. To trust requires a framework of critical reflection rather than blind obedience. Conversely to begin reading from a position of distrust may promote a predisposition toward technologist security measures against the otherness of the text. Although Ingraffia approves of Vanhoozer's intentions, he is uneasy about the claim that only through the Holy Spirit can communicative action take place, because "surely non-Christians understand communicative actions all the time, without the aid of the Holy Spirit."[50] This raises the question of what actually constitutes communication, an issue that has been perceptively analyzed by ethicist Bernd Wannenwetsch in his essay, "Communication as Transformation: Worship and the Media."[51]

Wannenwetsch's Christological account of communication rests on the notion of Holy Communion. He identifies three separate but interrelated levels of communication: technical, interactive and transformative. The first is simply the technical imparting of a piece of information from a sender to a receiver. The second is basic everyday exchanges between people. The third is existential, where communion results in the transformation of those involved. Whilst the first and third categories are not to overspill into one another, the second overspills into both of them, and cannot be considered as a pure form in itself.

Wannenwetsch argues that communication is not simply a binary affair between communicants but a triadic affair in which the fear of God is invoked. The technological conception tends to dominate communication, providing the framework in which the other two levels are heard. This means that sender-message-receiver is regarded as the primary aspect of communication. On such a scheme it can appear that the communicants are constants, but Luther's emphasis on communion questions the validity of such a view. "The theological notion of *communicatio idiomatum* . . . is originally a christological concept,"[52]

---

49. Vanhoozer, *Is There a Meaning in this Text*, 379, quoted by Ingraffia and Pickett, "Reviving the Power of Biblical Language," 244.

50. Ingraffia and Pickett, "Reviving the Power of Biblical Language," 245.

51. Wannenwetsch, "Communication as Transformation."

52. Wannenwetsch, "Communication as Transformation," 96.

in which relations between believers and God also embraces relations with other believers: "We are mutually transformed into one another and brought to communion through love, without which no transformation is possible."[53] Communication is not an event that is external to the communicants. Communication does not simply denote the impartation of a message from one person to another, but rather "it is actually the *communicators*, who might seem to be the constant factors, that are transformed in the unfolding of true communication."[54]

If communicants are prepared to be transformed by communicative encounter, it requires a humble readiness to listen based not on the notion of flat equality between speaker and listener, but one in which the speaker is privileged. This "primary receptiveness of the communicators contradicts a technological understanding and handling of communication—as though it were 'manageable' and not dependent on the '*ubi et quando visum Deo*' of the Augsburg Confession."[55] Theologically the relation between sender and receiver is not equal, but asymmetrical. To give priority to what the other seeks to say articulates more clearly Vanhoozer's concern to treat every text with the readiness to let it have its way. Ingraffia's objection to such a claim however is inapplicable to Wannenwetsch's notion of a hierarchy between listener and speaker. As Wannenwetsch makes quite clear, to acknowledge the primacy of the other is not to divest oneself of critical filters. "Under certain circumstances, the way I shall receive myself from communication with another person makes us part company. But even in this case it is still a matter of the other's power to transform me in the course of our communication."[56] In contrast to technologist conceptions of communication, in which the technical level provides the context in which the others are encountered, Wannenwetsch concludes that while each of the three levels of communication he has identified are important in their own right, the third aspect of transformative communication provides the wider context in which the first two levels are to be properly located.

---

53. Luther, quoted by Wannenwetsch, "Communication as Transformation," 97. "Das is die rechte Gemeinschaft und die wahre Bedeutung dieses Sakraments: So warden wir ineinander verwandelt und zur Gemeinschaft gebracht durch die Liebe, ohne die kein Wandel eintreten kann."

54. Wannenwetsch, "Communication as Transformation," 99.

55. Wannenwetsch, "Communication as Transformation," 99, Article V: "when and where it pleases God."

56. Wannenwetsch, "Communication as Transformation," 100.

Ingraffia's objection to Vanhoozer, that communication happens all the time without the Holy Spirit, is thus thoroughly relativized if communication is conceived as a complex of levels founded upon the primary level of transformation. However, whilst it may be an exaggeration to insist that communication happens "all the time," it may indeed appear to occur without the explicit action of the Holy Spirit. But whilst such communicative action *can* occasionally take place, it does not necessarily follow that it *does*. In accord with both Wannenwetsch and Vanhoozer, transformative communication is a "triadic" event. The self-communicating God does not necessarily yield a divine presence that can be casually invoked by humans wishing to communicate with one another. God's communicative action is by no means restricted to the conscious wager on transcendence,[57] just as his presence was not restricted to the temple. But if God can speak through a dead dog,[58] then gathering around canine corpses is no way to cultivate the attentive disposition. Over against technologist programs to wrench self-disclosure out of the other, we may follow Barth in stating that whilst God is by no means restricted as to when and where he speaks, human listening is limited by divine command.[59] The church and its members become a temple in which God lives by his Spirit, not in the manner of a Solomonic house built for God by human endeavour, but rather by the special presence of the Holy Risen Christ. To hear the God who speaks "when and where it pleases him," the Christian is consciously attentive to the presence of the Christ who is never absent from transformative communication.

To recall the three means of distinguishing between special and general hermeneutics it may be noted that they are parallel to that between the Temple and the Earth. It was argued above that the primary distinction to be drawn is that between the Christ-centered and the secular approach. A radical attentiveness to the risen Christ, enabled by the risen Christ becomes the "temple" inhabited by the Holy Spirit and is to be sharply distinguished from the notion of a secular world in

---

57. A phrase Wannenwetch appears to have borrowed from George Steiner (*Real Presences*, 214) whose own work is consulted below.

58. Barth, *Church Dogmatics* I.1, 55.

59. As Barth states, "While God is as little bound to the Church as to the Synagogue, the recipients of His revelation are. They are what they are because the Church is what it is . . . " (Barth, *Church Dogmatics*, I.2, 211).

which general communication constantly and naturally happens. This is not thereby to exclude the Holy Spirit from the world in general, just as believing God was somehow present in the temple did not thereby mean that he was confined within the temple. Furthermore the second distinction between the text in particular and the world in general is equally informed by Jeremiah's critique of temple practices. While temple and world remain distinct neither are they unrelated, and neither are text-free. Textual obedience is closely intertwined with temple worship (Jer 7:5–8), so to restrict the text to the sphere of temple worship without allowing it to spill over into the world outside both temple and text, is to abuse the grace of God's living presence. If the attentive disposition is located in the reader, far from being a set of methodological principles that are activated the moment written language is encountered, it will be a singular and humble propensity to listen to the other, regardless of whether the other is mediated through text, person or world. The same may thus be said of the third distinction, between the biblical text in particular and other texts in general. Whilst one may retain the belief in the fact that the bible is different from other literature, this does not mean that one's interpretive stance can be entirely changed when one addresses scripture. At a secondary level of course, the attentive reader will take genre recognition seriously, but to locate the core of the hermeneutical task in the type of material under consideration is to subvert grace. First and foremost, the attentive disposition is graciously formed in the life of the reader as an act of transformation accomplished by the Holy Spirit. The capacity to be transformed is not primarily a methodological endeavor but as a total disposition of the affections and will, it cannot be activated and deactivated according to the type of text being read. Such Christ-centered readiness to be transformed by the Spirit is the essential meaning of humility. It is not merely an exclusively external modest means of expressing passionate convictions and certainties, but is rather a way of life adopted by those whose convictions are exposed to the potentially transforming presence of Otherness. Christ-centered humility—which in order to be humility at all presupposes active confrontation—is the critical difference between special and general hermeneutics.

Summary

From the Christological perspective the claim was advanced that God's self-revelation cannot be neatly packaged into a technical transaction. This would be the technologization of truth, and theological hermeneutics would have to conform by describing Trinitarian revelation within some mechanical scheme. For instance, the Father is perceived to wrap his Word in scriptural packaging and uses the Spirit as a delivery service to ensure that the package arrives safely with its subsequent recipients.[60] Trinitarian patterns of interpretation cannot be so polarized because communication is not something that is restricted to conscious acts of interaction between one person and another, but rather is rooted in the entire life of communicants. At the heart of the doctrine of the Trinity is not a triadic formula that enables us to trace *how* he acts in the world, but to borrow J. B. Torrance's phrase, when God is revealed as Trinity he is thereby revealed as one who "has his being in loving communion." One cannot therefore engage in any form of Trinitarian interpretation without thereby being exposed to the full force of the awful *who* question.

We have proposed that to hear scripture is to be confronted with the Christological *who* question as it reaches beyond the text into the moral identity of the reader. Encountered as Anti-Logos, the resurrected Christ has the capacity to deconstruct the technological *Gestell* described in chapter 1 above. This *Gestell*, thought Heidegger, embraces the entire life of those subjects, so the exodus from it does not lie via correct hermeneutical methodologies, but by a total ethical reorientation of the reader. For biblical interpretation in particular, the greatest obstacle to understanding is neither methodological nor historical but ethical, because when one is confronted by the Anti-Logos a most likely response is not one of welcome, as discussed in our Christological reading of the parable below. Historical methodology simply does not have the capacity to overcome the textuality of the text. Indeed, any text on the subject of hermeneutics carries the implicit statement that the text itself is an insufficient guarantee of interpreting the text itself. As long as it remains possible to misread a text, or perhaps more perniciously to understand it correctly, discussion of hermeneutics must wrestle with a world outside the text. A Christological reading of the parable will now bring this necessity into focus.

---

60. Vanhoozer, *Is there a Meaning in this Text?*, 456–57.

PART II: CHRISTOLOGICAL READING OF LUKE 16:16–31

The Parable's Preface

The parable of the rich man and Lazarus is usually understood to begin at Luke 16:19, and there is good reason for this, given that the introductory phrase, "there was a certain rich man" is highly conventional.[61] However, if the parable is considered in its literary context, verses 16–18 can create an atmosphere in which the parable is to be heard and should not be regarded as an unrelated tradition.[62] These verses may appear "awkwardly placed,"[63] but when set against a Christological reading of the parable might well provide the crucial framework in which Luke the historian intends his readers to interpret. The historical importance of John the Baptist in relation to a violent response to annunciations of kingship (Luke 16:16), the denunciation of divorce and remarriage (Luke 16:18), and indeed, the need to emphasise the indispensability of the law (Luke 16:17), combine to produce a subtle but noticeable allusion to a single historical character, namely Herod Antipas. The translation of these verses takes various forms among historical critical commentators, according to the (largely unacknowledged) historical schemes by which they are operating. From the outset, the scheme with which our translation will operate is that the primary referent of this apparently disjointed tradition is Antipas. When understood in this way an obvious and cohesive unity emerges from these three verses, without straining the language.

Agreement concerning the most fitting translation for verse 16 is impossible on the basis of linguistic concerns alone, as the statement itself remains frustratingly plurivalent.[64] If one is to hear these utterances as timeless aphorisms, then the debates concerning their interpretation

---

61. See Jeremias, *Parables of Jesus*, 100.

62. Hanson ("A note on Lk xvi-14-3," 221–22) links the parable with verses 16–18, drawing out the common theme of Moses/the Law and the prophets.

63. Fitzmyer, *Luke*, 1125.

64. For instance, Perrin follows Kümmel in taking the *biazetai* as passive, so that oppressive powers act violently towards the kingdom (Perrin, *Jesus and the Language of the Kingdom*, 171–74). Similarly Ellis sees demonic powers oppressing against it (e.g. Ellis 1966, 203). Conversely Morris takes *biazetai* as active, so that believers have to force their way into it (Morris, *Luke*, 274) and Geldenhuys suggests that disciples require "spiritual violence" to gain access (Geldenhuys, *Luke*, 345). Leaney however, maintains that the entire passage (16–18 – or possibly as much as 13–18) might be a veiled condemnation of Antipas (Leaney, *The Gospel According to St Luke*, 223–25).

become complex and inconclusive. If however, they are anchored to a historical situation, the debate concerning their proper interpretation is relocated and the focus of translation considerably sharpened. Each verse will be considered in turn.

Verse 16 is notoriously difficult to translate, partly because *biazetai* can be taken as passive or middle, and partly because of the divergence in meaning from the Matthean parallel (11:12–13). An appropriate paraphrase might be to retain the ambiguity of *biazetai* thus: "The law and the prophets were until John; since then [the arrival of] God's Kingship is announced as good news, but everyone [is destined to respond] violently."[65] The *pas* here, is not a universal "everyone," but rather embraces the understood "everyone" for instance in the parable of the tenants (Luke 20:9–19) who unanimously rejected the true heir of the vineyard that was Israel. In verse 16, *euangelizetai* is to be understood not as preaching a sermon on the subject of the kingdom of God whose content might be described as "good news." On the contrary, John the Baptist was proclaiming the imminent arrival of the Messiah, and the violent response is made towards both the kingship and the heralds of its arrival, as the death of John the Baptist, the response to the parable of the tenants and the eventual crucifixion all bear out. *Euangelizetai* is the annunciation of the King's imminent arrival which one would have assumed to be "good news."[66] The whole of the Gospel is concerned with the violent response made to such a claim, and who is more likely to respond violently than the Herod whose own kingly authority would be displaced? Throughout Luke's Gospel Jesus remains acutely aware of the inevitable rejection and suffering his kingship must undergo,[67] and whether *biazetai* is taken as a middle or a passive, implicit in the annunciation of the kingdom's arrival is its violent rejection by those

---

65. There is warrant for such a translation from Black *An Aramaic Approach to the Gospels and Acts*, who takes *biazetai* as a transitive and *eis* as a barely noticeable trace of an underlying Aramaic preposition, thus "everyone oppresses against it." See Leaney, *The Gospel According to St Luke*, 223.

66. Perrin (*Jesus and the Language of the Kingdom*, 174) regards the second part of v16 as a possible (but by no means certain) reference back to the Baptist, as does Leaney (*The Gospel According to St Luke*, 224).

67. E.g., Simeon's song predicts conflict and rejection (2:34–35), the Nazareth manifesto resulted in a violent response (4:16–30). Jesus is depicted as a prophet (4:24; 7:16, 39; 24:19) and as such is destined to be rejected (4:24; 6:23; 11:47–51; 13:33–34).

who ought to have entered it joyfully.[68] As noted above, the imperative "Hosanna" gives way to the imperative "Crucify him." Regardless of which side of the new era John himself is located,[69] Antipas epitomizes the violent response to the Kingdom, as he executed the Baptist and apparently intended to do the same to Jesus (Luke 13:31–33). Read in this way the Matthean parallel actually seems parallel.

Verse 17 follows on naturally from the claim that the era of the law and the prophets has been superseded. Not before heaven and earth themselves have been superseded will the law and the prophets become void. From a messianic perspective, this is a pertinent issue. Any legitimate claim to messiahship assumed the intensification of Torah. As Harold Hoehner states in his study of Herod Antipas,

> it seems that anyone who claimed to be the Messiah must conform to the Torah. According to the synoptics, however, Jesus did not conform to the rabbinic understanding of the Law. He broke the written Torah by working and healing on the Sabbath . . . He also broke the oral Torah by not conforming to the traditions of the elders . . . The Pharisees . . . would have concluded that, since he had broken both the written and the oral Law, he could not legitimately be the Messiah.[70]

Jesus himself of course, claimed that the Pharisees had missed the point of the law, and in Luke 24 reveals to the disciples on the Emmaus Road that Moses and the Prophets point towards the Messianic ministry he had enacted.[71] However, the model of Kingship pursued by the Herodian dynasty apparently attached little significance to Torah. As Wright notes, "royal movements (such as Herod's) went ahead without, so far as we know, the need to appeal to Scripture."[72] Lack of respect

---

68. Note that the ambiguity surrounding the violent response to the kingdom is retained in Luke 20 as violence reasserts itself on those who have rejected the "capstone." "Everyone who falls on that stone will be broken to pieces, and it will crush anyone on whom it falls" (20:18).

69. Matt 11:12–13 (like Luke 16:16) suggests that the ministry of the Baptist belongs to the new era when the Kingdom is announced, but Matt 11:11 may be read as excluding John from the Kingdom.

70. Hoehner, *Herod Antipas*, 205.

71. A passage discussed in more detail in chapter 6.

72. Wright, *Jesus and the Victory of God*, 483. Wright notes, "according to Mt. 2.4–6, the aged Herod had to ask the chief priests and scribes 'where the messiah was to be born.'" Chilton goes further in representing the view that not only was Antipas

for the law negated the legitimacy of Herodian pretensions to kingship, a lack which was not only a textual theory, but one that was carried through into the world beyond the text, as verse 18 demonstrates.

Here the implicit reference to the violent end of the Baptist is restated, drawing the coherence of these three verses into a clear pointer towards the parable that follows. John had been imprisoned by Antipas for denouncing the dismissal of his first wife *and* marrying the wife of his half-brother, Philip. In verse 18 is a twofold denunciation in which Antipas is incriminated on both counts. This was no empty condemnation unrelated to the political realities of Herodian rule, still less was it a timeless truth destined to evaporate into the thin air from which it was drawn. Hoehner accentuates the sharp, deliberate messianic thrust of such a condemnation for the Baptist:

> John was urging the people to repent and be baptized because Messiah's kingdom was at hand. He counseled the crowds, tax collectors, and those in the army to prepare themselves morally and spiritually for the coming One. But he also made a scathing denunciation on their ruler for violating the commandments of God. Such a denunciation is significant, for at the climax of Messianic expectation the laws of God are heightened, and believers far less tolerant towards those who oppose the law.[73]

Antipas' execution of the Baptist may thus be seen as an important political move, even if it failed to prevent the retribution (which according to Josephus was divine) exacted upon him at the hands of his divorced wife's insulted father, Aretas.[74] In sum, this apparently disparate and oddly placed tradition, when read Christologically, may be heard as an implicit clue to the identity of the rich man in the parable that follows. Indeed, moving from this tradition immediately to the words, "there was a rich man who was dressed in purple . . . " it may have been impossible for Luke's earliest readers not to picture Herod Antipas. Given that there are three main characters in the parable only one of whom remains provocatively unnamed, Luke may well be expecting his readers to fill in the blanks. That the narrative persistently demands an identity for the rich man is attested by various texts that insert a name for him, Dives

---

indifferent to the Torah but deliberately flouted its requirements (Chilton, "Friends and Enemies," 73).

73. Hoehner, *Herod Antipas*, 142.

74. Josephus, *Antiquities*, XVIII, V, 2.

(Latin for "rich man"), Ninevah (Sahidic), Neves (P75) and others.[75] But instead of seeking to supply an artificial name to balance the text,[76] it may be more faithful to the intention of an able crafter of subversive stories simply to allow the alert listener to infer the rich man's identity, i.e., to "let the reader understand."

Herod and the Rich Man

The claim that Herod can be identified with the rich man is impossible to make with any degree of certainty. But if such an allusion were deliberate, then the most that one can expect to find in the text is circumstantial evidence.[77] Given that in Luke's Gospel the parable was uttered en route from Galilee where Antipas had jurisdiction, it may be that messianic pronouncements were uttered with more polemic subtlety by Jesus than by his late cousin, whose infamous lack of subtlety resulted in the cessation of his ministry.[78]

Although such royal allusions do not mean that the parable is solely concerned with Antipas (or Archelaus), they may provide an important interpretive stepping stone. As John A. Darr argues in his analysis of Antipas' place in the third Gospel, "Luke utilizes Herod as a negative paradigm of recognition and response. That is, Herod is an example of hearing but not understanding and seeing but not recognising."[79] Particular characters types are thus used to compel the reader to certain responses. A major problem with this "Herodian" interpretation is the fact that strictly speaking Antipas was not of pure Jewish descent. Nevertheless, as a character type, and unofficial king of the Jews, he does represent the Jewish nation. To picture Herod as the rich man is neither the essential nor the final purpose of interpreting the text, but rather a particular means to elicit a prescribed response intended by the parable.

---

75. For a fuller discussion see Cadbury, "A Proper Name for Dives"; and for a summary see Fitzmyer, *Luke*, 1130.

76. E.g., in the manner of Cadbury.

77. The majority of commentators are happy to note a very similar allusion to Archelaus in the parable of the pounds (Luke 19:11–27).

78. On the geographical significance of Jesus' ministry in relation to Antipas, see Chilton, "Friends and Enemies," 72–77. Chilton maintains that Jesus deliberately avoided cities throughout his ministry in order to elude the grasp of Antipas, whose influence largely determined Jesus' choice of itinerary.

79. Darr, *Herod the Fox*, 212.

In no other parable do the Father, the Son, and the Kingdom of God have such a conspicuous absence, and it is obviously for this reason that the majority of commentators have struggled to see anything other than an uncomfortably timeless condemnation of wealthy self-centeredness.[80] But if Antipas is indeed veiled behind the nameless rich man, the parable acquires potent historical connotations that cannot be ignored, even though they cannot be verified. Here one can identify four major features of the parable itself that draw us in this direction, each of which will be highlighted through a Messianic reading of the parable through this historical lens.

The Clothing

First is the question of purple clothing worn by the rich man. While of itself this is not sufficient to demand that we picture a king (purple was more widely available in this era), it is certainly consistent with the assumption of royal overtones.[81] Indeed, Fitzmyer states that the rich man's garments, "described in Old Testament terms (Prov 31:22), insinuate that he lived like a king."[82] Here it is worth glancing forwards to Jesus' trial, where Antipas has him dressed in the fine clothing of royalty, a deliberate mockery of the sort of pitiful king such a figure as Jesus had proved to be. It was in essence God's kingship that was on trial. Hoehner summarizes the clear statement thus made to Pilate: "The king in all his glory is handed back to you."[83] The contrast between all that God's anointed king was thought to be and the pathetic state of the voiceless

---

80. The issue of wealth and poverty is clearly a theme that runs throughout Luke 16, and obviously is present in the parable itself. However, its presence does not necessarily make it the sole or even the main point of the parable. The Julicher-Jeremias tradition of single-point interpretation of these parables may have prevented them from being heard both as social *and* political rhetoric without it fragmenting into a multivalent allegory. To read the parable as a cryptic political statement does not thereby displace the social statement, but animates it by making it specific to a particular situation.

81. See Danker, "Purple," 558.

82. Fitzmyer, *Luke*, 1130.

83. Hoehner, *Herod Antipas*, 243. Though this is by no means the only way of understanding the significance of the clothing at Jesus' trial. Darr, for instance, regards the clothing as a symbolic expression of Jesus' innocence even from his supposed enemy. The weakness in Darr's argument however is that despite the apparent innocence of Jesus as a Messianic trouble-maker, Jesus was still dubbed king of the Jews by Pilate, even if he was not the sort of king that was considered a threat. Jesus was not found innocent of being a king.

Galilean peasant spoke for itself. It is the precise contrast the parable is designed to draw out.

Antipas never attained the status of "king" (although he was conferred the title "Herod"), but, being the closest thing the Israelites had to a king, was probably often regarded as such.[84] If Antipas was indeed the rich man, then ignorance of the crippled beggar outside his gate amounted to the ignorance (be it deliberate or otherwise) of Moses and the Prophets which, as previously noted among the Herodian dynasty, and which the parable implies of the five brothers. Such ignorance is twofold: both of the responsibilities required of a King of Israel, and ignorance that God's anointed King was destined to suffer (see above). One need not look outside Luke's own Gospel for these applications of Moses and the Prophets because they are both accentuated at crucial moments of his narrative. In the Lukan Manifesto, Jesus outlines the nature of his calling with a citation from Isaiah (Luke 4:18–19): Jesus it seems treated this text (Isa 61:1–2) as Messianic, and the recipients of the Messianic message could not better be personified than in the character of Lazarus as Luke describes him. In the parable, ignorance of such a person on one's own doorstep may be understood as a departure from the Messianic manifesto, most applicable to one such as Antipas who embodied Israel's most successful pretence to such a role. That the privileges conferred upon the king and the people of Israel were not for their own sake (thus resulting in the ignorance of Lazarus) but for the sake of rest of the world, is highlighted in the conclusion to the Gospel where Luke's Jesus speaks as though he has already parted company with his disciples.

> Then he said to them, "These are my words which I spoke to you, while I was still with you, that everything written about me in the law of Moses and the prophets must be fulfilled." Then he opened their minds to understand the Scriptures, and said to them, "Thus it is written, that the Christ should suffer and on the third day rise from the dead, and that repentance and forgiveness of sins should be preached in his name to all nations, beginning from Jerusalem.[85]

---

84. For instance, Matt 14:9, where Matthew describes Herod as King, even though he has demonstrated his knowledge of Herod's true status by referring to his technically correct title, "tetrarch" (Matt 14:1). This suggests that despite it being technically incorrect, there was sufficient latitude to regard Antipas as King.

85. Luke 24:44–47.

A Christ destined so to suffer constitutes a very different picture of the heaven-sent Monarch from that witnessed in the fine apparel, lavish banqueting and becoming royal serenity of the Herodian dynasty. And yet Jesus' re-conception of Messiahship, though radically opposed to prevailing contemporaneous designs, was nothing new. It was drawn naturally from scripture, thus fulfilling Jesus' introductory statement to the parable about the law and the prophets fully retaining their validity (Luke 16:17). Lazarus represents one who suffers and as such is identified both with the intended recipients of good news and with the suffering herald of good news (Luke 16:16).

Lazarus

If the rich man represents Antipas, it seems natural to suggest that Lazarus be identified with Jesus. It would be a mistake however to establish such an identification prematurely.[86] The present discomfort of Lazarus is set against the comfort that lies beyond his death, a clear contrast with the present comfort and future discomfort of the rich man. But this is not simply a story of otherworldly consolation/retribution. The story is firmly embedded in the plight of Israel. This recalls the ministry of the Baptist and the introductory verses 16–18. The call for Israelites to be baptized was in itself a negation of Israel's natural birthright to be the people of God. As John himself had declared, he could make descendants for Abraham out of stones (Luke 3:8). Abrahamic descent, as the rich man discovered, was of little avail. Prophetic denunciations of ethnic Israel's presumed legitimacy to be the people of God, issued either by the Messiah or his forerunner, were by no means inconsistent with, but actually a faithful expression of "Moses and the Prophets." These witnesses were until John, after which time those who remain faithful to scripture will rejoice in the arrival of the Messiah, hence the tragic reality that "*everyone*" responds violently. This recalls Bonhoeffer's *who* question, namely who constitutes Israel. As subsequent chapters will explore, the categories that determine who is "in" and who is "out" of the kingdom are comprehensively redrawn by this parable. At this stage one need merely mention that the person of Lazarus is clearly "out." Furthermore, if Lazarus is to be identified with Abram's servant, Eleazar, in Gen 15—

---

86. See for instance Glombitza ("Der reiche Mann und der arme Lazarus: Luk.xvi 19–31, Zur Frage nach der Botschaft der Textes") who identifies Lazarus with Jesus on the basis of the name signifying the location of God's help.

an issue addressed at length in chapter 6—then strictly speaking Lazarus is a Gentile.[87] And yet it is this outsider figure who is "helped by God." The *who* question thus resurfaces, as the question of exactly *who* now carries the Abrahamic gene has become thoroughly ambiguous.

Jesus is to be identified with Lazarus as he is to be identified with all outsiders who long to be insiders,[88] an identification encapsulated in the derogatory dismissal of his Messiahship with which chapter 15 began, "This man receives sinners and eats with them" (v. 2). As Lazarus is welcomed to the eschatological feast in the bosom of the patriarch, the same might equally be said of Abraham. Israelite assumptions about who is in and who is out of the Kingdom are brought under the spotlight when one widely regarded as the Messiah aligns himself with the supposedly wrong crowd. Israelite "logology" can then either allow itself to be effectively put to death by this Anti-Logos, or it can finally reject him violently. The type of *who* question accentuated by Bonhoeffer is thus powerfully visited upon those who understand this parable. Had Antipas been willing to hear Moses and the Prophets, the pathetic figure he robed in mockery might not have appeared so different from the sort of Messiah destined to restore the "outsiders" and to suffer violence. Behind the security of his gate, the rich man assumes himself to be safe from the wrath of the *who* question.

The Gate

The level of sheer affluence portrayed could certainly only refer to a tiny minority,[89] so that those who did not move in royal circles are hardly likely to be imagined by those who heard the parable. The type of gate depicted is suggestive of such tremendous wealth, since *pulon* refers especially to "the large gate at the entrance of temples and palaces."[90] Throughout the middle and "prosperous" era of his reign (25–12 BC)[91] Herod the Great conducted an extensive building program that includ-

---

87. Cf. Cave, "Lazarus and the Lukan Deuteronomy," 323–25.

88. Barth, "Miserable Lazarus (Text: Luke 16:19–31)," 261.

89. For instance, the verb for his "feasting" (εὐφραινόμενος) which elsewhere in Luke refers to major social events and merry-making (12:19; 15:23, 32), is employed to describe what the rich man enjoys on a daily basis (16:19).

90. Bauer, Arndt, and Gingrich, "*pulon*" in *A Greek-English Lexicon of the New Testament and Other Early Christian Literature*, 729.

91. Hoehner, "The Herodian Dynasty," 325.

ed the construction of his royal palace in Jerusalem and above all the thoroughgoing restoration of the temple. Such activity was designed to legitimate the Herodian dynasty, of which Antipas was a representative. If from the parable it is inferred that the divine favor is resting upon those who dwell outside the gates of the palace / temple, then it may be heard as the "illegitimization" of the Herodian dynasty. The rich man is bastardized even as he is addressed as "son" (16:25).

This is in full accord with the Magnificat (1:46-55), a text that many commentators connect with this parable.[92] Of particular importance are the statements that,

> he has brought down rulers from their thrones but has lifted up the humble. He has filled the hungry with good things but has sent the rich away empty. He has helped his servant Israel, remembering to be merciful to Abraham and his descendants for ever..."[93] (52-55).

If Antipas is the historical referent for the rich man, then the application of the Magnificat is focused much more sharply. The thrones become a specific throne and, in line with the parable, the descendants of Abraham are radically distinguished from those who sit on it. One may also hear the implied redundancy of the dynasty in Luke's description of Jesus' entry to Jerusalem, in which the glory of the Herodian building program is prophesied as having little future.

The Brothers

Why *five* brothers? Is it simply to be regarded as a random number? If this parable were simply meant to compare rebel Israel with the rich man, more significant numbers than five might well have been chosen. It is more likely that the number of brothers mentioned is deliberately intended to bring to mind a historical character. Antipas is a prime candidate, since in his "father's house," there might well have been five surviving brothers at the time the story was told.[94] But what of their capacity to be convinced by one risen from the dead? Antipas" views concerning resurrection are difficult to establish. In a point omitted by Luke, Mark

---

92. E.g., Craddock, *Luke*, 189.

93. Luke 1:52-55.

94. Hoehner suggests this as a possibility (*Herod Antipas*, 109), as does Leaney (*The Gospel According to Saint Luke*, 226).

and Matthew have Herod believing that Jesus is John the Baptist raised from the dead (Matt 14:1–2; Mark 6:14–16; Luke 9:7–9). However one is to take Herod's statement, it constitutes at the very least the confusion of having put a stop to an awkward but popular political activist openly denouncing his right to be in authority on the basis that Israel's true king is now approaching, only for identical action to be rekindled with equal ferocity by a similar protagonist. If at some stage Herod did actually believe that Jesus was John raised from the dead, he was not convinced by the time of Jesus' trial, as has already been seen.

The trial itself is a telling incident when considered alongside the parable, especially when Jesus' silence is considered. Bearing in mind that Antipas represents the generation that "seeks a sign" (Luke 11:29), he is frustrated in that he neither sees (a sign) nor hears (a word). The reader's mind is drawn back to Herod's initial who question in response to Jesus' ministry, when after the execution of John he asks, "'Who then is this about whom I *hear* such things?' And he sought to *see* him" (Luke 9:9). Naturally, this echoes Jesus' reason for teaching about the kingdom of God in parables, in that for some, "though seeing they may not see, though hearing they may not understand" (Luke 8:10; Isa 6:9). Similarly, the brothers in the parable, according to Abraham, will be convinced neither by seeing a resurrected Lazarus (a sign) nor by hearing Moses and the Prophets (a word).[95] In fact the two are linked, since Abraham declares that if they are unable to hear the latter they will not be convinced by the former (Luke 16:31). This supports our argument in chapter 4 above that one's attentiveness to the text is inextricable from one's stance towards the world. Since Herodians had little need to hear scripture,[96] it is most likely that in the presence of those who would desire to see and yet not see, to hear and yet not hear (Matt 11:15),[97] any words uttered by Jesus would fall upon deaf ears. If they will not hear Moses and the prophets, they would certainly not be convinced by one who was resurrection personified. Hence Jesus remains as silent as the Lazarus of his parable.

---

95. According to Lorenzen, this is a point made by the parable itself (Lorenzen , "A Biblical Meditation on Luke 16:19–31: From the Text toward a Sermon," 42).

96. See pp. 125–32.

97. It is noteworthy that this reference in Matthew concludes the parallel tradition to Luke 16:16.

For those who do seek to be attentive to Moses and the prophets, the resurrected Jesus will be revealed as demonstrated in the Emmaus road encounter. In Luke 24:13–35, Moses and the prophets [like John the Baptist] pave the way for resurrection to be encountered, since the law and the prophets were until John. The disciples who *hear* Moses and the Prophets will also see—in the fullest sense—the resurrected one (as will be argued in chapter 6 below). However, the parable offers a negative paradigm of seeing and hearing, with Herod as the archetypal enemy representing not the outsiders or Gentiles (like Pilate) but the Jews who ought to respond joyfully to the arrival of God's kingdom (16:16). His desire to see does not arise from his capacity to be transformed by encounter—be it with text or person—but rather is motivated by something more closely akin to the Heideggerian category of curiosity.[98] As Darr's insightful study of Luke's Antipas concludes, "Herod is among those who, because of their abuse of power and lack of repentance, are never able truly to see and hear the revelation of God in Jesus."[99]

Lazarus Christology

To identify the rich man with Antipas is not the end of the interpretive task. To be confronted with the particular historical challenge of the parable, it is necessary to allow interpretive assumptions of the bible in general and this parable in particular to be transformable in the light of historical reading, and to allow historical reading itself to be confronted by Christology. This "Herodian" reading of the parable is best appropriated through the Christological categories noted above, as they highlight how such a reading informs the notion of Christ as Anti-Logos, as presence and as the mediator of history.

For Bonhoeffer the designation "logos" referred to the human means of ordering and classifying that which is encountered as novel, and some convergence with Derrida's assault upon logocentrism readily suggests itself. Crossan rightly understands the parable of the rich

---

98. Heidegger, *Being and Time*, 159–62. Curiosity for Heidegger refers to a detached observation of the world, which regards events with interest but indifference.

99. Darr, *Herod the Fox*, 212. Darr footnotes: "In this sense, Herod is like the Pharisees who also hear and observe Jesus and yet utterly fail to identify him." If we take the parable of the rich man and Lazarus as an example of Darr's insight, the presence of the Pharisees—who would not usually want to be identified with the Herodians—in the wider context of chapters 15 and 16 need not detract from regarding Herod as the primary historical referent of the rich man.

man and Lazarus as a parable of reversal,[100] which in accord with the deconstructive method, disrupts reader expectation and thereby assaults the human *logos*. However, the recent history of interpretation of this parable shows that familiarity with the tradition has defused this dangerous story, relieving it of its subversive potential. This is illustrated by the numerous commentators who have sought justification for the all-too-familiar reversal to which the parable leads. It is difficult to find a commentator who does not rely on the shocking reversal to read sense back into to the build-up to that punch line, committing what Derrida calls "teleological retrospection." Placing the cart before the horse in this manner relieves the parable of its explosive impact. Recipients of this anachronistic tradition then respond to the parable, "Oh I see, the rich man was bad and the poor man good—otherwise they would not end up in their respective destinies," and thereby allow this parable of cata-strophe to atrophy into one of urbane predictability. Understood in this way, the undisturbed human logology may simply respond to this parable, "Thank you God that I am not like this Pharisee / *rich man*" (Luke 18:11) and thereby shield itself from the Anti-Logos. As Bonhoeffer perceived, the human logos is all too ready to accommodate the Anti-Logos within the confines of its own structures.

With its sharply defined set of historical referents the Herodian reading of the parable leaves no room for timeless truths about poverty and wealth, but stands as a permanent deconstructive force that reasserts the *who* question upon readers of the parable. Herod epitomizes those who not only refuse, but are destined in their refusal to hear, see and respond to the good news of the kingdom of God (16:16). To hear this parable is to have one's conceptions of messiahship confronted. Here one moves inexorably to Bonhoeffer's second Christological focus.

Barth's reading of the parable focuses on the character of "miserable Lazarus" as the presence of God himself in the world. Barth's interpretation is remarkably consistent with our Herodian reading as he relates Lazarus to Moses and the state of the nation of Israel as a whole:

> It is about this condescension of God toward a nation that Moses . . . witnessed. Who is the Servant of the Lord about whom they preached: "He hath no form or comeliness; we looked upon him, but there was no beauty that we should desire him"? and when the time and the prophecies were fulfilled,

100. Crossan, *In Parables*, 75.

> there was the fullness of all God's word and presence: the Child in the stable at Bethlehem, the Son of Man who had no place where he could lay his head, who was ostracized in the name of God and crucified in the name of Caesar. "In our needy flesh and blood the eternal God was mantled." Immanuel—"God is with us"—in the Holy Scriptures from beginning to end means: Lazarus, the miserable, who lay before the door of the rich man, full of sores. Who seeks him, called God, in the Holy Scriptures, must seek him in Lazarus.[101]

For such a radically Christocentric theologian as Barth, biblical interpretation cannot afford to ignore this Lazarus Christology. Having stated the importance of attending to Lazarus, Barth moves to ask who Lazarus really is. Far from restricting him to those who are materially poor, Barth opens up the identity to those, in accordance with the name Lazarus, "who need God's help." This is not to identify every person in any sort of need as Christ himself, even though we nevertheless encounter Christ *in* that person.[102] The outcome is a Christology of mutual dependence, where "as brothers of Lazarus we would see that we need one another, one Lazarus needing the other and each and all alike needing Christ. Oh that we may be made to see!"[103] This is no pious application of the parable, but gets to the heart of the inseparability of world and text. After all Barth's emphasis echoes that of the parable as it rests upon *seeing* rather than *doing*.[104] By implication, the way that one encounters Christ in other people has enormous bearing upon the way that one will read of Christ in scripture. If Christ is not engaged outside the text, one can hardly expect to engage with him when a text is opened. In short, Christ will not be confined to the textuality of the text.

A parallel Christology is found in Matthew's parable of the sheep and the goats(Matt 25:31–46) where the King judges that the way in which outcasts are treated is inseparable from the way the king himself is treated: "Truly I tell you, just as you did it to one of the least of these my brothers, you did it to me"(Matt 25:40). Divinity and destitute humanity are as inseparable as text and world. When Lazarus is identified in all who are in need, when the Messiah of Israel takes up residence in real

---

101. Barth, "Miserable Lazarus (Text: Luke 16:19–31)," 261.
102. E.g., Matt 25:31–46.
103. Barth, "Miserable Lazarus (Text: Luke 16:19–31)," 268.
104. Barth, "Miserable Lazarus (Text: Luke 16:19–31)," 262.

people, the proper response is not the curiosity of the "how" question, but the disruption of the "who" question. However, the presence conferred in a Lazarus Christology is, of course, not subject to the Derridian critique of presence that underwrites the structures by which communication is thought to occur. It is rather the presence whose ultimate security does not short-circuit the necessity to suffer transformation. The Lazarus present in others perpetually confronts us with the "who" question, inviting ever-renewed response to the annunciation of the good news of the kingdom of God (16:16).

The parable is prefaced with a statement about the dawn of a new historical epoch, in which the good news of the Kingdom of God is announced. However, it would be ridiculous to suppose that the character of Lazarus is intended to serve as the mediator of history. Nevertheless, to conceive of Lazarus as suggested above certainly informs one's notions of history. If the law and the prophets were until John, then contemporary readers postdate both John and Pentecost and dwell in what is described above as the age of the Spirit. It is the Holy Spirit who mediates the presence of Christ, and, as Barth contends, the face of Christ looks like that of Lazarus. In the age of the Spirit Christ-centered readers of scripture are awakened by the Spirit to *see* Christ in Lazarus.

This brings us all the way back to Derrida's conception of messianic time. Derridian eschatology, as argued previously, in true historicist fashion assigns to history itself the awesome potency of conferring unexpected newness upon the present. But Derrida draws antecedent conclusions about the otherness the future brings, and is, therefore, destined to respond violently to the arrival of an actual historical messiah. The two-dimensional history of all such historicism itself reflects the Adamic sin in its lust for power and its need of redemption. If, as Bonhoeffer perceived, Christ is the "the mediator of history,"[105] the character of Lazarus offers a glimpse of Christ's role. Anticipating our final chapter on eschatological reading, one may note that, over against technologist attempts to enter and conquer the future, Lazarus embodies the ongoing darker side of history. And yet it is here, in the history that knows it has no future, the history that is helped by God that the *who* question is posed even of history. As Moltmann argues, "the Messianic hope was never the hope of the victors and the rulers. It was always the hope of the defeated and the ground down. The hope of the poor is nothing other

---

105. Bonhoeffer, *Christology*, 65 as cited above.

than the messianic hope."[106] The Magnificat is replete with references to the God who "remembers" those caught on the wrong side of history, "from generation to generation" as his mercy extends "to Abraham and his descendants forever" (1:50, 55). God's action in history is to be found in helping Abraham's offspring; and just *who* those descendants are is the question taken up in our next chapter.

CONCLUSIONS: CHRISTOLOGY FROM WAY BELOW

If technologism en-frames humanity to the extent that it reduces the world in general and the text in particular into something manageable, the resurrected Anti-Logos poses the reverse question of the interpreter's own identity.[107] As interpreters of the text address this question in the light of the Anti-Logos, scripture is truly encountered. That is, the reader not only exposits scripture, but is exposed to scripture in such a way that it is no longer conceived as "standing-reserve,"[108] but presents a content-full otherness with the capacity to dethrone one's interpretive assumptions.

As the figurehead of a generation that seeks a sign (Luke 11:29), Antipas thereby epitomises the stubborn refusal to hear scripture. Biblical interpretation, if its categories are derived from scripture, will seek first and foremost to foster a Christ-centred (that is, a wilful readiness to be transformed by Christly speech and action) disposition of the affections and will. Given that all gospel Christology is unavoidably and deliberately "Christology from below," Lazarus is a disturbing picture of just how low is this "below," or as Luke's Jesus declares—probably with an autobiographical tone—" . . . the least among all of you is the greatest" (Luke 9:48). Such is the social location of Israel's Messiah. If he cannot be heard there, he cannot be heard in scripture, in person, or indeed anywhere else. Christ will not remain confined within the textuality of the text but as Anti-Logos reaches beyond the world of the text and whatever lies in front of the text. To hear scripture, then, is not to devise a tight hermeneutic strategy that would enable a clear and easy route out of the technologist *Gestell*. Rather, to hear scripture is to cultivate

---

106. Moltmann, *The Way of Jesus Christ*, 13.
107. See pp. 141–44 above.
108. Heidegger, "The Question Concerning Technology," 322.

an attentive disposition. This necessitates the pursuit of humility as the capacity to be transformed by the content-full otherness of Christ. The formation of this disposition is neither a simple nor straightforward theory, but the development of an attitude that is forged in the furnace of life in the body of Christ.

6

Somatological Reading as Charis[1]

INTRODUCTION: THE AMBIGUITY OF "COMMUNITY"

CERTAIN TECHNOLOGIST READING STRATEGIES have introduced regime change to Holy Scripture. No longer must the reader be confronted by an undemocratic voice issued from on high, bringing the disruptive force of otherness to the reading community. Instead, a more domesticated hermeneutical subsistence compels readers to conform to the dictates of their own community's conventions. This, it was argued in chapter 2, is the theological substance of Fishian notions of scripture, which graciously permit the Almighty a backstage role in shaping—or more precisely, endorsing—the reading conventions of the community.

In the first part of this chapter, it will be argued that while belonging to a reading community is essential, indeed (as Fish would concede), unavoidable, it is also important to note that membership of a community is not a divinely ordained scriptural hearing aid. Again in accordance with Fish, it is impossible to short-circuit the conventions of the context in which readers find themselves, so to read anything at all in any way at all, is to read "in community."[2] Furthermore, the wide consensus that the so-called meaning of a text is saturated by the prior concerns of the reading community is accompanied by a conspicuous reticence for

---

1. Why *"charis"* rather than the more straightforward and comprehensible term, grace? "so long as we endeavour to speak about grace," notes Barth, "our speech must labour under a necessary obscurity" (*Church Dogmatics*, I.1, 224).

2. At least, in Fish's sense of the term "community."

substantial dialogue about the nature of such a community. Community is a rather blunt tool when used without care or precision, which is why it is vital that the internal and external dynamics of such a community be carefully considered. The second part then offers a reading of Luke 16:19–31 which takes careful account of the nature of the community as suggested by the parable, informing and being informed by the *charis*-derived way of reading outlined in the first part of the chapter.

PART I: READING IN THE COMMUNITY OF CHRIST

Since Kierkegaard, the pervasive influence of the human environment upon textual interpretation has been widely acknowledged by Nietzsche, Heidegger, Wittgenstein and Barth, and remains high on the agenda of contemporary figures including Fish and Watson. However, despite this widespread acknowledgement these figures follow widely divergent paths as they develop interpretive schemes that take full account of social contingency. Francis Watson's outstanding survey of theological hermeneutics,[3] offers a way of reading that both encourages readerly exposure to the otherness of scripture, and also affirms the primacy of belonging to Christ-centered community.

Watson's hermeneutic principle is based on the biblical notion of *koinonia*, that God wills through Jesus Christ to establish true community, a *koinonia* characterized by mutual transformation. It is this practical communal transformation that Watson finds curiously absent in Barth's vision of the church. For sure, Barth heralds the theoretical claim that the Christian believer is called not to a private unmediated relationship with God, but to participate as an active limb in the body of Christ.[4] However, Barth's failure to embody this claim with any substance may be perceived as bordering upon a textual form of Gnosticism. His Christology focuses so exclusively upon Christ, that he is seen as a representative of humanity to such an extent that humanity is almost bracketed out of the covenant.

> [Barth's] interpretation of the theme of the body of Christ emphasises the singleness of the church at the expense of the inner-ecclesial love which binds together its very diverse members in

---

3. Watson, *Text, Church and World*.
4. See Barth, *Church Dogmatics*, VI.1, 687–89.

the one Spirit, losing the Pauline sense of community in order to maintain the narrow Christological focus.[5]

Arguing that Barth is preoccupied with a Christ who is uncomfortable in the Christian community, Watson regards Barth's Christ as somehow detached from concrete human existence. The requirement to acknowledge and recognize the fulfillment of God's covenant purposes in the death and resurrection of Jesus, as propounded by Barth, eclipses the prerequisite context of full ecclesial participation in that resurrection life. Watson, however, is at pains to point out that God is not encountered in such unmediated recognition, but rather within the dynamic of God's *philanthropy* as embodied in Jesus Christ.[6] This philanthropic love is not an independent power source, just waiting to find expression in action—rather, it is that very active dynamic that constitutes divine love. In short, Watson values Barth's emphasis on the vertical aspect of God's self revelation in Jesus Christ, but feels compelled to look elsewhere (namely, to Yoder's *Politics of Jesus*[7]) for the co-essential horizontal dynamic of God's philanthropic revelation.

Watson's exegesis is firmly based upon this notion that to hear scripture is to engage in the koinonia of the body of Christ in which mutual transformation constitutes the manifest presence of resurrection life. However, such a strategy fails to relieve theological hermeneutics of the ambiguities that Watson himself has perceptively identified. The actual dynamic of the Christian community, though essential to all would-be recipients of revelation, remains curiously beyond the perceived scope of interpretive endeavor. While Watson may be justified in the claim that Barth's conception of the church's identity can appear a static rather than a dynamic relationship, to take full account of this insight necessitates trespassing further into the ethical territory than Watson seems willing

---

5. Watson, *Text, Church and World*, 244.

6. Far from picturing God as a benevolent Victorian do-gooder, such *philanthropy* is the grammar of revelation—it is within the fluidity of interpersonal grace that revelation occurs. See Sanders, *The Historical Figure of Jesus*, 38.

7. Yoder's own work however is not without problems. His *Politics of Jesus* implies that Jesus' central message was to encourage ethnic Israel to become better at being ethnic Israel, failing to address the manner in which Israel is not simply restored but reconstituted, as argued in the second part of this chapter.

to encroach,[8] in order to question how this horizontal relationship is perceived as a manifestation of divine philanthropy.

If scripture is to be encountered by the reader as a source of genuine otherness, it must be read as *Holy* Scripture, embodying a voice that does not originate with the democratic exertions of the community itself. As was argued in chapter 2, the Holy Spirit's active role in interpretation cannot simply be reduced to a "behind-the-scenes" shaping of the community into a receptive frame of mind. Nevertheless, without the Holy Spirit's capacity to activate a communal dynamic of grace, the spirit of the community will remain far from holy.[9] The community of God's people, although instituted by Christ (in that there is a fundamental givenness about what it actually is) is constituted by the Holy Spirit (in that its life blood and essential togetherness arises from his presence).[10] In the absence of the Spirit, a community is no more than a pragmatic association. If the Holy Spirit were truly present in a community, then a radical otherness would impinge upon the everydayness of the community's life that would prevent it from being conceived as a monolithic, static institution.

Herein lies the danger of offering mere academic assent to the belief that belonging to a church is essential to hearing the voice of scripture: there is no such thing as "the church." The body of Christ should not, indeed cannot, be too readily construed as a *Ding an sich*. The "church," Bonhoeffer perceived, "is nothing but a section of humanity in which Christ has really taken form."[11] Echoing Watson's comments on philanthropic love, one may claim that the church is not a thing in itself that occasionally springs into action, but rather is constituted in active grace. The body of Christ is not a couch potato. If, as Emil Brunner thought, "the church exists by mission as fire exists by burning,"[12] it might with equal justification be suggested that the church exists by *agape* as a river exists by running, or equally that it exists by *charis* as the wind exists by blowing. Opting into an ecclesial crowd comprised of sheep and goats (Matt 25:31–46) in itself brings no guarantee of hearing Holy Scripture,

---

8. Stephen Fowl makes a similar assessment of Watson in *Engaging Scripture*, 22–23.

9. This is the burden of Barth's lectures on the Spirit (Barth, *The Holy Spirit and the Christian Life*.)

10. Smail, *The Giving Gift*, chapter 8

11. Bonhoeffer, *Ethics*, 64.

12. Brunner, quoted by Taylor, *Go Between God*, 133.

as the rich man of the parable finally discovered to his cost. Community remains a problematic concept. One of the criticisms of Stephen Fowl's excellent research on communal hermeneutics, is the vagueness that surrounds the make-up of the community,[13] a major criticism of Fish's exploits as described in chapter 2. Fowl's defense is to draw attention to the danger of seeking to become so prescriptive about describing the community, that other places where Christian community is genuinely at work can be excluded and ignored. While this may appear as a reasonable insight, it only remains a danger as long as the church is viewed in static, monolithic terms. The path taken by this chapter seeks instead to unpack the relational dynamics of a community, which reframes the understanding of how a Christian community is actually constituted. As will be argued below, the parable makes its own statement to this effect. Though the renewed emphasis by Fowl and others on the import of membership in the body of Christ is to be welcomed, that recognition is of itself no more use than the mere recognition and acknowledgment which Watson criticizes in Barth's Christology.

Simply entering into or claiming membership of a Christian community is not necessarily to engage in the fundamental dynamics of grace-based community. As previously stated, the rich man and his brothers belonged fully and firmly to their appropriate interpretive community, and yet remained unable to hear Moses and the Prophets. Membership of a religious community is no backstage pass granting unrestricted access to the voice of scripture from which non-community members are excluded. In fact, as argued in chapter 4, this very communal brand of Gnosticism is the main target of Jesus' prophetic challenge to Israel;[14] and, as Part 2 of this chapter will show, it is a primary concern of this parable in particular. As will be suggested below, community membership might well buttress the reader's pride, rebellion and idolatry, as she finds others who confirm her in her prejudice, encourage her in her quest for self-enlightenment and affirm her in her desire for control. Such a community might be merely an amplified form of individualism, a delusional counterfeit of the community in which

13. Fowl, *Engaging Scripture*, 2.

14. Proponents of the Third Quest frequently note that renewal movements in Jesus' day, including Jesus' own, critiqued presumptions that certain elements of Israel constituted a community which was the unconditional beneficiary of God's exclusive grace, over against the gentile nations and the outcast Israelites (e.g., See Sanders, *The Historical Figure of Jesus*, 189–237; Theissen and Merz, *The Historical Jesus*, 130–47).

individualist conceptual frameworks are sacrificed as an act of spiritual worship (Rom 12:1–2).

The authority of the Christian interpretive community is an authority derived from the antecedent presence of grace. However, grace does not hitherto lie dormant in the Christian community, awaiting an opportune time to erupt. Nor is it finally the property of the believers' collective spirit. Grace is the God-given dynamic that radically distinguishes the body of Christ from the schematics of the worldly environment. Hence the charismatic community is not a self-legitimating body, but a *governed* community with acute eschatological awareness. Writing as a theological ethicist, Bernd Wannenwetsch describes a community in which mutual authority of members relates to an authority that is external to the community. His reading of Rom 12 locates authority in a distinctive but convincing notion of grace. He takes seriously both the disruptive presence of Christ in the community's relationships, a presence that challenges the influence of the world that schematizes the believing community, and the political distinctiveness of the community's way of being, in his essay, "'Members of one another': *Charis*, Ministry and Representation, A Political Reading of Romans 12."[15]

> In order to be able to witness to the worldly city with *transforming* power, the church must acknowledge the *formative* power of the dominant patterns of reaction within the worldly city. Though Christ has deprived this power of rule, the schemata are nevertheless still powerful, and the new understanding and practice of political authority within the Church must be formulated over against these conceptualisations . . . "[16]

Wannenwetsch observes that Paul's account of the body of Christ as depicted in Rom 12 is addressed not to a collective of individuals but a body of members. Thus Paul employs a speech-act that on the one hand directs his readers toward obedience, but on the other carries the authority not of the speaker but of the shared reality embracing both speaker and listeners. The basis of Paul's exhortation is παρακαλεῖν, a speech-act that sets the stage for the more detailed account that subsequently unfolds.

---

15. Bartholomew, *A Royal Priesthood*, 196–219.
16. Wannenwetsch, "Members of One Another," 197.

> The kind of exhortation that *"parakalein"* denotes, mirrors the particular address ("brothers"), which is in itself an appeal to a reality (the brotherhood of the children of God) that embodies an inherent moral imperative. And it seems that the detailed exhortation that follows is merely specifying the imperative inherent in the invoked reality. Thus, the appeal is not directed to "moral subjects" as a summons to realize what is not yet real or not yet fully there; rather the appeal is to a given reality.[17]

Paul's appeal, therefore, is for the body to be aware of and responsive to the given authority embodied in the community life of which they are already participants. But, if this is the case, on what basis can Paul expect his exhortation to be *obeyed*? On the basis that it is in accord with the very "mercies of God" that constitute the church. "The nature of this political language is intelligible only in a community for which 'authority' is never a monolithic concept—a community, which is less concerned with divine legitimation of temporal authority but with human *mediation* of divine authority."[18] Hence the church's appeal for authority cannot be made directly to the heavens, because to do so would be to give way to a private inner prompting, and thereby to short-circuit the public life, death and resurrection of Jesus' historical facticity.[19]

The horizontal axis of the church's political life is then cast in terms of transformation. The world's capacity to schematize, that is, to shape the being of the Christian community, is to be resisted by believers, as they bring their worldly conceptions of authority to the altar of sacrifice.[20] The presenting (standing together) of the believers' bodies (plural) as a living sacrifice (single) is a spiritual act of worship grounded not upon mystic notions of individual union, but rather is a living sacrifice because in the fullest sense it embraces the whole, physical, political, living community. In this event of worship natural notions of community arising from the schematics of the worldly environment are baptized. (It should hardly need stating that this baptism is not the waving of an ecclesiastical wand simply to pronounce "community is good," but the radical exposure of those human ideas to the public reality of the death and resurrection of Israel's Messiah). The result is a transforma-

---

17. Wannenwetsch, "Members of One Another," 200.
18. Wannenwetsch, "Members of One Another," 204.
19. A point Wannenwetsch finds in O'Donovan, *Resurrection*, 141.
20. Wannenwetsch, "Members of One Another," 206.

tion (implying continuity and contrast) of previous identity, i.e., "the renewal of your mind."[21] This renewal however, is concurrent both with the unmasking of the world's incessant schematizing capacity and the concrete reception of a new political schematics. Renewal of the mind is not achieved as a one-off human accomplishment, but appearing in the passive voice, it issues in the transformation that is effected by the gracious action of God.

> The renewal of mind is necessary, given the schematising power of the *aion*. *Me syschematizesthe*: "do not be conformed to this world." Here, the passive voice is no less in place than it is in the subsequent call to be transformed. The latter case is certainly a matter of *passivum Divinum*—the transformation cannot be a simple "rethinking" of things as an increased effort of the human mind itself; transformation requires nothing less than a renewal of the mind. And a new mind can only be a gift, part and parcel of the *kaine ktisis*, God's creation of a new humanity, so that the imperative can only mean to watch out for God's activity of renewing the mind.[22]

Although the resistance to worldly schematization carries a general validity for all aspects of Christian life, in this context its primary referent is the world's potential ecclesio-politico effects.

> The schema of rule in the secular world ("the rulers of the nations lord over them, and those in authority are called benefactors") in which "natural authority," the authority of means dictates status, is confronted ("but not so with you") with a new way of understanding and exercising authority: "The greatest among you must become like the youngest and the leader like one who serves."[23]

The divine transformation effected in the Christian community inverts authority schemes based upon greatness, re-framing the very meaning of greatness itself in terms of one's readiness to allow the greatness of others to flourish rather than be eclipsed by one's own pretensions to that greatness.

Paul's discussion of this renewed ecclesiological mind appears through the prism of his enigmatic phrase "members of one another,"

---

21. Wannenwetsch, "Members of One Another," 206.
22. Wannenwetsch, "Members of One Another," 207.
23. Wannenwetsch, "Members of One Another," 208.

which far from being "a slightly odd variation of the body metaphor"[24] implies a radical re-envisioning of political practice. In stark contrast to a model of community based upon expertise, Paul argues for politics in which the otherness of other members is a source of joy. In an expertise model of community, members are free to rejoice in the expertise of others, so long as it does not encroach upon their own. A church may run like a well-oiled machine, with each expert fulfilling her allotted task, but such a community's schematics are drawn from the secular world characterized by fragmentation and over-specialization. Within such a scheme Paul's instruction is interpreted as the charge to use *my* individual gift to the very best of *my* ability, and with everyone fulfilling their role in similar fashion, the church runs smoothly. However *charis*, as the basis and authorization of each individual's charisma, is a spanner in the works of this ecclesial machine.

> Of course, it is more difficult to accept the charisma of the other than it is to accept his or her weakness. Their weakness is an opportunity to express my strength, but their charisma is a possible threat to my charisma, letting comparison and competition become the regular order of relationships . . . Accepting the other as "a member of my own (body)" goes beyond accepting his or her charisma as such. It is precisely accepting the ministry of the other *towards* myself.[25]

In employing the subversive term, "members of one another" Paul replaces the economy of fragmentation and specialization with the economy of grace. Wholeness is found not in the security of my *charismata* over against the claims of others, but rather in accepting the ministry of others towards me in my humble readiness to be the recipient of their gifts. In fact my reception of the other's gift is a source of joy since I am made whole as my weakness is highlighted and complemented by their gift. Naturally, human pride is the final obstacle to engagement in this economy of grace, but, in seeking the gifts of members to be used in a way that embodies *charis*, it is recognized that their gift is not their private property but the property of the community.

> It is exactly this acceptance of mutual representation that allows the Church to become a community of discernment that probes

---

24. Dunn, *Romans*, 724, quoted by Wannenwetsch, "Members of One Another," 210.

25. Wannenwetsch, "Members of One Another," 210.

and explores God's will (Rom 12.2). For to know God's will is to do it, and it is only in doing God's will that it will be known. The political existence of the Church is itself the practice of exploring God's will.[26]

So representation is not the realization of a gift that a congregation had lacked prior to the member's presence. Rather re-presentation is the redeployment of that grace which is already present in the body. The congregation does not become that which it was not before, but rather is transformed into that which it already is. To exercise a particular gift is by no means to be the possessor of it, because this would remove the prefix from re-presentation. All that would then remain are gifted individuals who *grace* the church with their presence, as though they were contributing to rather than also drawing from the life of the community. For instance, congregational listening is part of the gift of teaching, just as congregational discernment is part of the gift of prophecy. Those who fulfill the ministry of teaching or prophecy then do not graciously bestow their ministry upon the congregation, but as catalysts serve as channels through whom the reflexive impact of grace makes its presence felt to and through the members of the body. This is the political form of the body of Christ.

If the political form of this community lies in the members of the one body offering themselves in bodily sacrifice to "the consumption of God's rule" then Paul's exhortation "invokes the political *morphe*, which the authority of Christ takes on through the authorisation of the Spirit's gifts."[27] However, there is a hiddenness about this activity, embedded in the relationships of members who belong to one another, which the disengaged observer is unable to distinguish from, say, a religious expression of secular institutional form. Nevertheless, the different levels of representation highlight the intrinsically distinctive and fundamental principle of *charis*. "The recognition of office [e.g., teacher] is a way of recognising ministry [e.g., teaching], which is a way of recognising charismata [e.g., teaching, prophecy, pasturing, etc.], which is a way of recognising *charis*."[28] In sum, the community of discernment is grounded on a *charis* that allows the use of gifts in the Church to be measured against its very own nature:

26. Wannenwetsch, "Members of One Another," 211.
27. Wannenwetsch, "Members of One Another," 214.
28. Wannenwetsch, "Members of One Another," 215.

> Does the concrete way in which the office/service is exercised account for the gift character of grace? Or does it instead subvert grace in making its exercise look like an achievement, expecting praise, gratitude, and so on? Does it live up to the communal character (panti), or does it reclaim the charisma for the office-holder, denying the participation of others in it?[29]

Having sharply identified the intrinsic character of the body of Christ as expressed in Rom 12, Wannenwetsch (gesturing towards Rom 13) outlines an extrinsic dynamic between the church and secular authorities. The dialectical representation offered in this exposition draws its authority from the common good of the body, and in so doing suggests that "Political office as such is only authorised by its ordination to represent the common good, yet must be tested against it by exactly calling into question the representative quality in every action."[30] In other words, office-holders on the one hand are not beholden solely to lobbyists, but on the other are not authorized to claim unmediated access to the common good. Secular authority structures cannot be directly identified with those of the church, lacking from a theological perspective, the *charis* granted by the Holy Spirit. However, the notion of representation based upon dialectical recognition of the common good justifies the claim that " . . . rulers do not simply represent the people, nor do they represent God (a pagan idea), but rather they represent quite simply "rule."[31] This rule is the property of the whole, which means that the political leader's authority is not elevated above but grounded in the body.

Thus, Wannenwetsch offers a way of understanding the body of Christ as a (governed) community, which has (derived) authority over its members. The hermeneutic spelt out by Wannenwetsch stands in stark contrast to that envisaged by Fish, as outlined in chapter 2. While Fish uses the term *community*, this term in itself is little more than a rhetorical device, and in his writings remains frustratingly abstract and elusive. If it exists at all, it was argued in chapter 2, Fish's so-called community is at the mercy of the rhetorician who is able to exert authority through manipulation and sophisticated mob rule. As Wannenwetsch stresses, Paul's hermeneutic employs the *body* metaphor (with all the

---

29. Wannenwetsch, "Members of One Another," 216.
30. Wannenwetsch, "Members of One Another," 217.
31. Wannenwetsch, "Members of One Another," 217.

political and communal overtones it carried), but, rather than allowing it to shape his view of the church, Paul transforms the concept of body, allowing the reality of the Christian community to reshape it radically. Fish's "authority of the interpretive community"[32] stands contraposed to the authority embodied in the interpretive dialectic of the body of Christ, which transforms the entire concept of community. A communal authority at the mercy of the rhetorician is precisely the negative image of an authority exercised by appeal to "the mercies of God."

Communal Hubris

To insist upon the unavoidable and extensive influence that the reader's communal environment has upon interpretation, and to affirm the validity of that influence is unlikely to scandalise the post-modern mindset. After all, it has now become apparent that "[t]o speak and act out of one's communal experience is the American way."[33] However, it is the purpose of this chapter to expose this communal hermeneutic to the light of the resurrection, and to see how its perceptions might thereby be reshaped. If, in harmony with the insights of Wannenwetsch, the experience of *charis* is allowed to shape our understanding of community rather than vice versa, the conception of community will be radically different from that of other patterns for communal life.[34]

Having witnessed his mighty acts, the villagers from Jesus' hometown were not merely expressing amazement, but voicing contempt when they asked, "Is not this the carpenter, the son of Mary and brother of James and Joses and Judas and Simon, and are not his sisters here with us?" (Mark 6:3). The point is made with more clarity in Luke, where it is precisely the *charis* of Jesus' proclamation that is the very source of their offence (Luke 4:22). When the interpretive community is scandalized by the presence of *charis* (and from this it may be inferred the *otherness* that accompanies it), their hurried defense is to point out that this pseudo-prophet is in reality a mere product of their own community.

---

32. The subtitle of *Is There a Text in This Class?*
33. Freedman, "Don't Blame the Jews for this War."
34. A parallel argument is made by O'Donovan, who argues that rather than starting with what we know about politics and moving to the unknown about the kingdom of God, the direction must be reversed—starting with the Kingdom of God as the revealed core of political practice. See O'Donovan, *Resurrection*, 113.

This claim to familiarity at the expense of recognizing *otherness* leads to their rejection of him.

Contentment with the way things are is characteristic of Fish's entire project,[35] and enables him to allow for a Christian belief in God as the hidden shaper of the community. Those on the other hand, who don"t happen to belong to arguably the most privileged community experienced by humanity (i.e., those with no share in the twenty-first century North American affluence of which Fish is a beneficiary) might be less content to see a divine cause behind their current plight. However, such people are of little concern to a Fishian community that cannot by definition, comprehend anything that happens beyond its own borders, or in parody of the gospels—"a prophet cannot be recognised unless he remains in his own country" (cf. Matt 13: 57; Mark 6:4; Luke 4:24; John 4:44). Like the rich man of the parable, as far as Fish is concerned, Lazarus does not exist: he is beyond the gates of the community and his existence is incommensurable with the community's interests.

Communities can be wrong. In its modern guise, nevertheless, individualism appears to stand in opposition to community, which is why post-modernist theorists have perceived in community the potential for a liberating counter-hermeneutic. The New Testament, however, hardly conceived of either individualism or community in this way. Whatever traces of individualism might be found in the New Testament are secondary to the aboriginal experience of community.[36] This renders the appeal to scripture, in order simply to claim that we must read in community, nonsensical. Fish would endorse this critique—since there is in reality no alternative but to read in community. The question addressed by the New Testament rather concerns the "nature" of the community to which readers belong. It is, after all, possible to belong to a religious

---

35. It is for this reason that the position of Fish the lawyer/literary critic is comparable to that of the scribes who, being portrayed by the gospels as lawyers/literary critics, frequently supplied the antithetical backdrop to the proclamation of the Kingdom of God. This claim is buttressed by Watson's discussion of the widespread antipathy toward the new *koinonia*. If there is a foundational prescriptive non-realism in Fish's hermeneutics, then as Watson points out: "Lack of realism is . . . characteristic of those who, like the scribes of Jerusalem . . . are broadly contented with the way things are, and therefore manifest in their different ways the world's hatred towards the new *koinonia* (Watson, *Text, Church and World*, 255).

36. For a more detailed discussion on the differences between modern western individualism and its ancient Israelite counterpart, see O'Donovan, *Resurrection*, chapter 2, who argues as above. The opposite case is put by Sanders, *Jesus and Judaism*, 233–34.

community that opposes the Messiah: "The Kings of the earth take their stand, and the rulers gather together against the Lord, and against his anointed One" (Ps 2).[37] Indeed, as was argued in chapter 5, the rich man and his brother unwittingly constitute such a community. The significance of this brand of communal authority is identified by O'Donovan, who notes,

> In his darkest remark . . . [Luke] tells us that collaboration over the case of Jesus sealed a political friendship between [Pilate and Herod] . . . (23.12). What bound them together was their mutual consciousness of impotence. They were professional flatterers, who sang to the tune that their masters, the mob, piped for them. This, then, was the meaning of the authority of the kings of the Gentiles; this was the secret of the title "benefactor." Their authority was from below, and they held on to it by dutiful obedience to what was required of them.[38]

The authority of the interpretive community culminates in relentless implacability with the resounding demand, "Crucify him, crucify him" (Luke 23:21). With a single voice, the gospels present this as the climactic human interpretation of God's Messiah. The Roman legal system and the Jewish religious system combine to present crucifixion as the ultimate hermeneutic strategy. But after the Sabbath at the centre of history, the resurrection is revealed as God's interpretation of the world. With this the authority of the interpretive community is divested of its pretentious absolutism. Or in Paul's words, ". . . having disarmed the powers and authorities, *he* made a public spectacle of *them* by the cross" (Col 2:15). Resurrection is the divine response to the ultimate human initiative. If theological hermeneutics is to embrace the recognition of community, then the interpretive community is to recognize the resurrection.

The communal pride endemic in the human condition cannot with legitimacy be bracketed out from theological hermeneutics, since it constitutes a fundamental aspect of the all-encompassing influence of the interpretive environment. Absent from many admirable notions of community is the down-to-earth engagement in a community of *charis* which is by no means always welcome in anthropocentric—even

---

37. See also Acts 4:25–26.
38. O'Donovan, *Resurrection*, 140.

philanthropocentric—community but rather by definition depends upon readiness to embrace the divine initiative that is resurrection.

Human community is no antidote to the human rebellion against God that colors the interpretive enterprise. Nor can refuge be found in trading the term *community* for a more scriptural counterpart (e.g., *soma*, *ecclesia*, Israel), since even these pictures fall prey to the interpretive pride that finds expression in the technologist strategies as outlined in Part I of this study. There, it was noted that the most important distance between readers and biblical texts is not historical but ethical. Whilst hermeneutics attends to the notion of historical distance, when biblical interpretation remains exclusively preoccupied with such a problem it is destined to remain technologist in the sense that the actual, personal transformation of the reader can be legitimately bracketed out of the core activity of reading. For instance, it is far from inconceivable for a group of Christians to read scripture together, to rejoice in one another's perspectives, to marvel at the richer yield that multiple readings can produce, and to be grateful at the personal enlightenment that ensues. They might even be able to articulate how that experience has challenged and transformed their personal experiences. And yet such an activity in no way requires the cultivation of an attentive disposition that is necessary for the hearing of scripture. This supposed activity of communal reading can all too readily result in a pseudo-transformation of character that occurs in strict adherence to the dictates of technologism, maintaining a public/private dualism and confining moral transformation to the latter, thereby endorsing the individualism from which it supposes itself to be liberated. The attentive disposition without which scripture cannot be heard is cultivated through active participation in the body of Christ. In accordance with the insights offered by Wannenwetsch, this participation does not simply mean attending a church and bringing to it one's gifts of which other members may be the grateful beneficiaries. Participation in the body of Christ is an experience of ongoing transformation, of dying and rising with Christ as one receives oneself back from the body in which Christ is pleased to dwell. If there is a hermeneutical circle/spiral, this daily death and resurrection is what causes it to turn. It is the readerly appropriation of Luther's call to be baptized every day.[39]

---

39. Luther, "Small Catechism," in Kolb and Wengert (eds.), *The Book of Concord*, 360.

This brings us back to Wannenwetsch's exegesis, in which *re-presentation* offers a means of countering the hubristic schematization inherent in the hermeneutics of Fish. Interpretation, according to Fish's brand of technologism as presented in chapter 2, is prone to manipulation by expertise (in the form of the manipulative rhetorician), and in turn exercises a manipulation of the text. Within the body of Christ, however, authority functions not merely to govern the members (or, for that matter, the text); instead, it animates among its members the mutual *presentation* of bodies as "a living sacrifice." This "living sacrifice" substantiates the insistence upon checking humanity's congenital propensity to master the text. For the readers of scripture to partake of the "living sacrifice" is to undergo a death and resurrection, a baptism. The living sacrifice of individualist schematics is essential for somatological reading as an act of true worship. Individualistic attempts to gain direct access to the Almighty, thus yielding divine legitimation for private readings of scripture, transparently bypass the economy of grace in which vertical and horizontal dimensions of revelation must be distinguished without being isolated from one another. Watson argues this point with some force, concluding that,

> . . . it is not the case merely that a vertical divine-human relation is complemented by a human interrelatedness on the horizontal plane. Rather, the divine-human relation overflows from the vertical into the horizontal planes, comprehending within itself a new human interrelatedness, and abolishing the alienating dichotomy between vertical and horizontal dimensions which leads to a construal of love of God and of neighbour as separate claims upon us which may even be played off against each other.[40]

The nature, therefore, of a community of such renewed human relatedness is founded upon nothing other than the *charis* that in origin and practice comes as a gift from beyond the community. This is a central issue for biblical interpretation because for the speech-act of God to be welcomed fully, it must also be recognised and accepted as a "gift act."[41] That is, as something that impacts upon the reader and the reading community as a constant presence of otherness that demands a constantly renewed humility. In chapter 5 this humility was presented as the capacity to be transformed by the presence of Christ, and this pres-

---

40. Watson, *Text, Church and World*, 280.
41. A phrase used by Isolde Andrews (*Deconstructing Barth*, 148).

ence is encountered through participation in relationship with others in the body of Christ, as being "members of one another." Or in a more Johannine tone, and bearing in mind that to listen is fundamentally the capacity to be transformed by one's encounter with another, it might simply be noted "if you cannot listen to your brother whom you have seen, how can you listen to God whom you have not?" (cf. 1 John 4:20). This requires not only a readiness to be remade by one's encounter with other members of the community, but equally, as Watson highlights, the essential transformability of the community itself, as it reaches beyond its own boundaries, and remains open to the reflexive challenge issued from beyond itself.[42] In short, moral transformation is the communal appropriation of the resurrection.

PART II: A SOMATOLOGICAL READING OF LUKE 16:19–31

Abraham's Community

Rudolf Bultmann saw the parable of the rich man and Lazarus as evidence that "universal (cosmological) eschatology is displaced by an individualistic one, i.e., one which does not expect a new aeon, but simply the continuation of individual life after death."[43] As argued above, however, individualism in its twenty-first century manifestation is of an entirely different order from any experienced in the Judaisms of the first century where membership of a covenant community was fundamental to any subsidiary individual concerns. On the surface, the parable may appear to involve individuals; but, as will be demonstrated below, the story erupts with a seismic shock that displaces every grain of Abrahamic sand. To call Abraham "Father" is to state one's commitment to a faith community.

This parable is not the first scriptural story of which Abraham and Lazarus have been joint tenants. The name Lazarus is an abbreviated transcript of Eleazar, a character who lingers at the brink of the Old Covenant's foundation as recounted in Genesis 15. This text is a tradition deeply embedded in the psyche of first-century Jews, although it has often been overlooked by interpreters of the parable.[44] Abraham

---

42. Watson, *Text, Church and World*, chapter 15.

43. Bultmann, *Existence and Faith*, 297.

44. The presumption that the parable is primarily about wealth may have obscured

had received a promise of children (Gen 12:2, 7; 13:16), but seemed to take the doubtful precaution of adopting one of his servants, Eleazar, as his heir.[45] This rather pitiful picture of faithlessness is reversed by v. 6, where Abraham's apparent belief in God's renewed promises of offspring sees him credited with righteousness. Wenham sees here a paradigmatic display of faith that is to be imitated by Abraham's descendants: "it is the response of believing obedience to the word of God, not righteous deeds, that counted for righteousness. To be sure, such faith, when genuine, issues in righteous deeds, but that is not what the text says: faith counts for (instead of) righteousness."[46]

Taken as a whole, Genesis 15 recounts the covenant with Abraham's offspring that is foundational to a community of first-century Jewish stars, as illustrated by allusions and references by the apostle Paul (Rom 4:3; Gal 3:6) and other NT authors (Jas 2:23, 26).[47] This is hardly surprising if, in accordance with Sanders and Wright, one accepts that "the idea of covenant was central to Judaism in this period."[48] Indeed, Galatians 3 is an extended exposition of Genesis 15 explicating the validity of Torah and offers some insight into the Christian significance of this initial Abrahamic covenant. Our brief reflection on this passage offers only a way of reading that is consistent with our exposition of the kingdom of God as presented in chapter 4 and follows again the insights of Wright. Other literature parallel with the parable will be drawn out further below, but for now Wright's assessment of the passage is most illuminating:

> This passage simply asserts that the Torah as it stands is not the means of faith, since it speaks of "doing" which is best taken in the sense of "doing the things that mark Israel out" . . . and hence

even those commentators who allude to Genesis 15 from drawing out its fundamental significance, thus leaving them to go no further than noting a common name. (E.g., Kreitzer, "Luke 16:19–31 and 1 Enoch141"; Evans, "Uncomfortable Words—V," 228; Schweitzer, *The Good News According to Luke*, 261.)

45. Tanghe ("Abraham, son fils et son,") has suggested that Eleazar's role as envoy should determine the manner in which the parable is read. However, Tanghe fails to offer a convincing defence of this theory, not least because of his lack of attention to the wider context in which the parable is placed by Luke.

46. Wenham, *Genesis 1–15*, 1:334–35.

47. See Dodd, *According to the Scriptures*, 107, where Dodd notes the frequency with which Genesis 15 appears throughout the NT, but also notes that the references cited above refer primarily to the nature of faith.

48. Wright, *The New Testament and the People of God*, 260. See also Sanders, *Paul and Palestinian Judaism*, 420–22.

> cannot be as it stands the boundary-marker of the covenant family promised to Abraham and spoken of by Habakkuk, i.e., the family that is a single worldwide family, the family that is created the other side of judgment, the family characterised by *pistis* . . . He is expounding covenantal theology, from Abraham, through . . . to Jesus the Messiah, and is showing, albeit paradoxically, that the Torah *per se* rules itself out from positive participation in this sequence . . . The climax of exile has been reached . . . in a great event of recent memory, and now the true restoration was beginning, a restoration in which Gentiles were, quite properly being invited to share.[49]

The Torah in Paul's eyes was incapable of effecting the faith which, according to Genesis 15, constituted the covenant community that is Abraham's family.[50] Abraham's true offspring are those who actively believe,[51] and would constitute a community that reaches beyond the boundary of ethnic Israel (Gal 3:6–8). Paul is re-envisioning the identity of the people of God, i.e., the family of Abraham, such that many who presumed themselves to be "in" were in fact "out" and vice versa. Our next chapter will make full use of the in/out categories, but at this stage it is worth noting that Paul's conception of a reconstituted Israel is deeply reminiscent of that pronounced by Luke's Jesus:

> There will be weeping and gnashing of teeth when you see Abraham and Isaac and Jacob and all the prophets in the kingdom of God, and you yourselves thrown out. Then people will come from east and west, from north and south, and will eat in the kingdom of God. Indeed, some who are last will be first, and some who are first who will be last.[52]

This obvious statement that the Abrahamic covenant is being redrawn to include many Gentiles and exclude many Jews prefigures more detailed arguments presented in Paul's writings. However, it is inconceivable that such an influential passage as Genesis 15 did not enjoy a privileged place in the mental library of any first-century rabbi,[53] and it

---

49. Wright, *The Climax of the Covenant*, 150–51.

50. Wright, *The Climax of the Covenant*, 151.

51. Note again the verbal dynamism rather than the static monolith of Christian community.

52. Luke 13:28–30.

53. E.g., Sanders, *Jesus and Judaism*, 141; Theissen and Merz, *The Historical Jesus*, 126; Wright, *The New Testament and the People of God*, 260.

is impossible therefore to regard the parable's allusion to it as accidental. In fact the very opposite may be supposed—that this bedrock text forms the parable's foundation. It is quite reasonable to suppose that Genesis 15 is clearly in mind as Luke's Jesus deliberately reshapes covenant thought amongst his contemporaries in the telling of the parable.

Lazarus

It is often asserted that Lazarus is the only figure in any of Jesus' parables who is mentioned by name, a mistake as astonishing as it is widespread.[54] Abraham also appears in this and no other parable—which suggests that their joint appearance is more than coincidence. The *relationship between* Abraham and Lazarus is clearly of the highest significance, even if interest in it has been unanimously displaced by the relationship between Lazarus and the rich man. In the parable Lazarus is a repulsive figure, just as in the Genesis text, Eleazar represents Abram's inability to believe the promise of God. He is the very antithesis of covenant faith(fullness). But with the renewal of God's promise to Abram, what is to become of the patriarch's hapless servant? Yahweh's covenant with Abraham (and, therefore, with the people of Israel) begins with the very pronouncement, "This man shall not be your heir" (Gen 15:4). It comes as little surprise, therefore, when in the parable Lazarus is depicted lying outside the gates of the great wealth bestowed upon Abraham's "true" descendant.

It is highly likely that antipathy toward the disgusting figure of the dog-licked Lazarus, far from displaying an unjust immoral disposition, might rather be regarded as evidence of covenant faithfulness. If Genesis 15 were a foundational text for Jesus" hearers, then when the Lazarus who represents the mere servant/slave of Abraham, finds himself on Abraham's lap, and the rich man finds himself excluded from Abraham's presence, the provocative injustice of the story would not go unmissed. Commentators have sometimes noted the rich man's persistent refusal to see Lazarus as anything other than a slave, but far from concluding

54. Most major commentators inherit and endorse this odd opinion. A notable exception is Cadbury ("A Proper Name for Dives,") who notes the unusual absence of a name for the rich man when placed alongside the named Lazarus, but instead of taking this to highlight the importance of the relationship between Lazarus and the other named character, Abraham, he seeks to ascribe a proper name for the rich man that enables the dynamic (between the rich and the poor man) which is a secondary dynamic to become primary.

that this is because the rich man was a self-centered, hell-worthy sinner[55]—it might on the contrary demonstrate that he was in fact someone who took the covenant seriously, and knew well enough that Lazarus was, in truth, a servant.[56] Not his own servant, one might add—since the rich man makes no request directly to Lazarus—but Abraham's, as Gen 15:2 and Luke 16:24, 27 clearly show. The rich man requests that Abraham himself send his own servant, Lazarus.

By placing Lazarus in the bosom of Abraham, and excluding Abraham's expected beneficiary, Jesus is clearly making radical statements about the Abrahamic covenant. Whether in the parable Lazarus can be cast as a Gentile is doubtful (although the reference in 16:21 to dogs licking his sores may be designed to provoke this thought),[57] but it is certain that Lazarus is an outcast, just as Eleazar is "cast out" in the Genesis text. So by turning the covenant inside out, is Jesus thereby negating it? By no means—as Paul argued at length (Rom 9-11). Instead, he is redefining just who the offspring of Abraham really are. Bearing in mind that prior to the parable Jesus has claimed that the law and the prophets were until John, it is worth remembering John's call to baptism (implying as insufficient any status the so called people of Israel might claim to enjoy)[58] and his call to repent (warning that Abrahamic ancestry is no guarantee of favored status). Faith is replacing ancestry as the primary boundary marker of the covenant community.

Moses and the Prophets

Quite literally, the parable of the rich man and Lazarus is a parable about a renewed covenant. What then is to become of the old writings, namely Moses and the prophets? Are they null and void? Again it is noted that the parable is prefaced with Jesus' claim that "it is easier for heaven and

---

55. This is implied at least in Caird, *Saint Luke*, 192; Marshall, *The Gospel According to Luke*, 637–38; Morris, *Luke*, 277, and stated explicitly by Bock, *Luke*, 275; Fitzmyer, *Luke*, 1133 and Thompson 1972, 215. This insight, however, only finds its true significance if the connection is made with a Jewish covenantal arrogance that looked down upon those who are "outside."

56. See further on Luke's perception of this below.

57. St Bede (673–735) follows Gregory the Great (590–604) in making connections both between Lazarus and the Gentiles, and between the rich man and the Jews. Quoted in S. I. Wright, *The Voice of Jesus*, 92.

58. One may think for instance of John the Baptists warnings to that the multitudes should not count on their Abrahamic descent (Luke 3:8).

earth to disappear than for the least stroke of a pen to drop out of the Law" (v. 17). This statement is followed immediately by an allusion to covenant faithfulness, or the implied lack thereof: "anyone who divorces his wife and marries another woman commits adultery, and the man who marries a divorced wife commits adultery" (v. 18). There is a striking similarity here with Paul's commentary on the Genesis 15 covenant, especially Gal 3:10, which reads, "All who rely on observing the law are under a curse, for it is written: 'Cursed is everyone who does not continue to do everything written in the Book of the Law.'"[59]

By very different routes, Paul and Jesus seem to have arrived at the same point. Israel was called to be a light to the nations. "Understand then," writes Paul, "that those who believe are the children of Abraham. The scripture foresaw that God would justify the Gentiles by faith, and announced the gospel in advance to Abraham: 'All nations will be blessed through you'" (Gal 5:7-9). Far from being an agent of *charis* to the world, Israel had by and large come to see herself as an agent of judgment.[60] As such, she had been unfaithful to the covenant, in such a way that she and all of her proselytes are subject to the curse of the law that is inevitably visited upon unfaithful/adulterous Israel. From this very fitting reference to covenant adultery (against Fitzmyer who sees this verse as awkwardly placed),[61] Luke's Jesus launches immediately into the parable that highlights both the efficacy and insufficiency of Torah.

Is there any way that the rich man's brothers (the "in" community of self-convinced Abrahamic seed) might avoid the curse foretold by Moses and the prophets? The rich man's request for a revived Lazarus to announce coming judgement is denied, on the basis that Moses and the prophets are quite sufficient to issue this warning. But to hear this warning necessitates belonging to the right interpretive community, namely Abraham's true offspring—the *believing* community, and in particular, those who are able to believe one who has been raised from the dead. Such a community is re-presented by two disciples travelling towards Emmaus.

---

59. An exposition consistent with this approach is found in Wright, *The Climax of the Covenant*, 137-56.

60. See chapter 4.

61. Fitzmyer, *Luke*, 1125.

The Road to Emmaus

In the parable, the rich man's brothers are denied a resurrected interpreter to assist them in their application of Moses and the prophets. This hardly seems fair when considered against Cleopas and his companion on the road to Emmaus, where it was only with the assistance of the resurrected Jesus that Moses and the prophets set their hearts aflame (a different order of flame, one might add, from that experienced by the rich man). In the parable, Abraham claims that Moses and the prophets are sufficient for the rich man's brothers; on the road to Emmaus, they are not—and a resurrected interpreter retells the story that the ex-disciples had until that point, failed to hear. Why the inconsistency?

Before answering this question, a prior question must be addressed, namely the question of just what it was that Moses and the Prophets were supposed to be saying. Without exception, traditional interpretation has presumed that it is exclusively to look after one's neighbor, and the injustice of a beggar at the very gates of affluence has invited widespread condemnation for the rich man, simply leaving the parabler the inevitable and satisfying task of passing sentence.[62] This would be a most convenient reading if one wanted to identify the implications of this parable for reading in community.[63] Unfortunately, despite the fact that the injunction to love one's neighbor is central to Moses and the prophets, this is not their primary function in the parable. It is not splitting hairs to point out that all that the rich man's brothers might hear from Moses and the prophets is how to avoid the fate of their unfortunate brother. Nothing more than this is to be gleaned from the parable itself.

This is by no means to suggest that the traditional interpretation is entirely mistaken, but must one seriously believe that the parable is told simply to announce that the practice of philanthropy is a sure-fire way of avoiding Hades? One of the early church's greatest interpreters of the law and the prophets would certainly not agree, as a brief reading of 1 Cor 13:1–3 reveals. Whilst one may affirm that a true hearing of scripture inevitably results in the sort of neighborly love that the rich man failed

---

62. Such is the approach exemplified for instance by Blomberg (*Interpreting the Parables*), Johnson (*Luke*), and Morris (*Luke*).

63. The sharpest reading of the parable from this perspective is offered by Kreitzer ("Luke 16:19–31 and 1 Enoch 22,") discussed below, who sees here both an injunction to be one's brother's keeper, and to widen the concept of brotherhood.

to display, to reach this conclusion prematurely is to short-circuit an essential component of the parable.

The contrast between the two groups represented by the rich man and Lazarus are outlined in Jurgen Moltmann's study of Christian eschatology, where his description of comfort is also reminiscent of Fish, as was seen in chapter 2.

> The person who possesses power is concerned that history should continue to run its course towards the goal he has designed for it. He understands future as the prolongation of his own present, so he swears by economic growth and scientific progress, and seeks the increase of the power he already has . . . But the people who are dominated and powerless have no interest in the long-term prolongation of this history. On the contrary, they are concerned that it should find a speedy end. Better an end with terror than a terror without end, says a German proverb. Those who are dominated, hope for an alternative future, for liberation from present misery and deliverance from their helplessness . . . The person who possesses power fears the end of that power; the person who suffers under it hopes for its end. The people who enjoy the modern world because they live "on the sunny side of the street" fear the downfall of their world; the people who suffer on the underside of this world hope for that very downfall. For the one group, apocalypse is a word for the catastrophe that brings their world to an end; for the others it is an expression for the disclosure of reality, and the fact that the truth will at last emerge and liberate them.[64]

The rich man wishes to warn his brothers of the catastrophe that awaits them. This is not merely the catastrophe that they are bound for hell when they die, although chapter 7 will argue that this implication may be present. But in the light of resurrection as described in chapter 4, the catastrophe is that "the way things are" (the Israelite "in" crowd presuming the privilege of God's favor) is for a limited period only. How does the rich man expect his brothers to avoid his own fate? By repentance, and this repentance is best understood in the light of Moltmann's description of the direction in which the lives of the comforted and wealthy are heading. It is the abandonment of "the goal he has designed" for history.[65] Unfortunately, such repentance would do violence to all

---

64. Moltmann, *The Coming of God*, 135.
65. Moltmann, *The Coming of God*, 135.

that is precious to the rich man's brothers (see Luke 16:16) and would certainly require what Paul has deemed a living sacrifice (Rom 12:1). And it is from Moses and the prophets that this call for repentance is to be found. It is a repentance then, not solely from being wealthy and selfish, although it may incorporate this, but a repentance from the security of a future planned for one's own community. Writing more than a century ago, F. H. Capron, whose analysis of the use of the term "son" in this parable offers weighty backing to the interpretation offered in this chapter, rightly perceives in it a heavy attack on the vanity which accompanied this armchair comfort:

> This comfortable doctrine . . . is absolutely discountenanced by Christ . . . Do not place a vain reliance on your physical descent from Abraham, for it will not avail you. And in the Parable of the Rich Man, the vanity of this expectation is being exposed. Thus the Rich Man instantly and persistently claims the benefits which he expected would result from his relationship, by addressing Abraham . . . as "Father."[66]

If only the brothers could see that this covenant community, as they perceive it, has no future, they would repent; but, as Abraham points out, the futurelessness of such a community is already pronounced by Moses and the prophets.[67] Tragically, it is a future that is not easily abandoned in the present.

Only with this recognition can the difference between the parable and the Emmaus tradition be understood. The Emmaus-bound disillusioned ex-disciples were hardly a picture of covenant comfort and content. Their hope for regime change had come to an abrupt end when the would-be realization of covenant promise was nailed to an execution stake. The reversals promised and realized throughout Luke's Gospel are as dashed by the cross as the one who promised them. Their interpretive stance was on the opposite side of that of the brothers in the parable. But this means that, as Watson has seen, their farrowed hope was ripe for receiving the word of a stranger.

> The only possible consolation in the face of the tears of the oppressed is the gospel's promise that the conditions that produce those tears will be fundamentally changed: "blessed are you that

---

66. Capron, "'Son' in the Parable of the Rich Man and Lazarus," 523.

67. The germinal form of this exact message may be found in Luke 16:18, which hints at the curse facing those who have practised unfaithfulness.

weep now, for you shall laugh . . . Woe to you that laugh now for you shall weep" (Luke 6.21, 25). In announcing that the law and the prophets bear witness to the death and resurrection of the Christ, the stranger asserts that this promise and this threat were not made in vain. Jesus' mission of preaching good news to the poor and setting at liberty those who are oppressed (4.18) has not come to an end, but, on the contrary, assumes in his death and resurrection its intended, definitive form. There are therefore grounds for hope that the future will not eternally repeat the past but will ultimately issue in an event in which all things are made new and in which human community . . . is perfected.[68]

In sharp contrast to Fish's stance in which novelty is excluded and in direct contravention of the returned-from-exile contentment illustrated by Moltmann's assessment of the powerful,[69] the disciples were ready to hear a new covenant story. In fact, Jesus did *not* reveal himself directly to these disciples as the rich man had requested Lazarus visit his brothers. Instead, he comes as a stranger and constructs an alternative narrative framework, which not only sets hearts ablaze, but also leads to their recognition of his identity in the highly symbolic breaking of bread.[70] Without entering this new story, the appearance of Jesus would have been a curious piece of unintelligibility. The brothers of the rich man would have been unwilling to hear this new story because their old covenant was (albeit for a limited period only) serving them well. It may be for this reason that "it is easier for a camel to pass through the eye of a needle than for a rich man to enter the kingdom of God" (Matt 19:24; Mark 10:25; Luke 18:25), or for that matter, to hear the word of God.

Lukan Context

It is not only to the end of the gospel that one might look in order to make sense of this parable. A return to its immediate context in the Lukan narrative sheds light on both the parable and the narrative. Since the parable has usually been seen to offer moral commentary on wealth and poverty, it appears to be very much at home in Luke 16, but very few have attempted to see how the parable fits with the subsequent narrative

---

68. Watson, *Text, Church and World*, 286–87.

69. See p. 201 above. See also Moltmann, *The Coming of God*, 135.

70. The breaking of bread draws its significance from the Exodus tradition which Luke himself has taken up to describe Jesus' mission (Luke 9:31). Framing Jesus' activity in Jerusalem within such a picture suggests the notion of covenant renewal.

of chapter 17. Larry Kreitzer, one of the parable's few commentators to tip his hat to Genesis 15, has drawn out at length the parable's similarity with the pseudepigraphical text, 1 Enoch 22, and in turn has highlighted its allusions to the Cain and Abel story of Genesis 4.[71] Kreitzer suggests then that the point of the parable might be to answer the question, "Am I my brother's keeper?" and whilst answering in the affirmative, the question of who belongs to my brotherly community reaches beyond the "brothers" with whom I am familiar, thus extending the bounds of that community. This redrawing of the community's boundaries is certainly in accord with the general direction of the parable as interpreted in this chapter, but one may follow further some of the signposts Kreitzer has planted. Importantly, having presented the parable as calling for philanthropic love, he allows it to run smoothly into the subsequent text: "In 17:1–4 Jesus offers instruction to the disciples about how they are to treat one another, how they are to demonstrate care for one another. Thus the parable moves directly into a short discourse on the nature of responsibility for others."[72] Kreitzer's thesis would be more convincing if it were understood within the context of the covenant. For one thing, the tradition following on immediately after 17:4 can be read as a deliberate reference to the Abrahamic covenant, as the disciples exhort Jesus, "increase our faith"—after all, Abraham's descendants are now identified by faith rather than race. Furthermore, their unusual description here as "apostles," may echo the status of Lazarus who in the parable is twice petitioned to be "sent." This is more than coincidental when it is considered that Eleazar was a servant, and that Jesus moves straight into a parable about the servant-hood of his "sent ones" (17:7–10).

If Abraham's heirs are now those who were servants, the possibility of them wallowing in their ethnic privilege is minimized.[73] A state of perpetual humility is to be sought by those privileged enough to be graciously counted heirs of the covenant, which reveals an essential thrust of this servant-hood parable. It does not propound a general truth about the timeless quality of humility, but rather it makes a particular demand about the covenant quality of humility. There are echoes here of the central point made by Wannenwetsch cited above, where grace can be subverted by the demand for praise and gratitude. The servant is

---

71. Kreitzer, "Luke 16:19–31 and 1 Enoch 22."
72. Kreitzer, "Luke 16:19–31 and 1 Enoch 22," 141.
73. Cf. Luke 3:8.

not the deserving recipient of divine favor, but rather the undeserving recipient of grace, and as such has no legitimate claim to the national pride for instance that many historians have perceived in some pre-70 AD Palestinian Jewish movements.[74] The status of the beneficiaries of the new covenant mirrors the status of Lazarus in relation to Abraham. The very name Lazarus carries strong overtones of passivity (meaning literally helped by God) and suggestively precludes the possibility of such servant/recipient status from yielding legitimate grounds for pride.

The parable about servant-hood is itself immediately followed by a tradition, also peculiar to Luke, that buttresses the message heard in the rich man and Lazarus tradition. On his way to Jerusalem, Jesus encounters ten lepers, who were cleansed on request. The only one that returned to thank him was a "foreigner," possibly because unlike the Jewish ex-lepers he could presume no ethnic privilege that would justify his healing. Again, one hears echoes of the Abrahamic covenant being opened up beyond its traditional bounds, especially as Jesus implicitly affirms the foreigner as a descendent of Abraham when he declares, "your *faith* has saved you" (17:19).[75] Again this serves as evidence that "People will come from east and west, from north and south, and will eat in the kingdom of God. Indeed, some who are last who will be first, and some who are first who will be last" (Luke 13:29–30).

CONCLUSION: A HEARING COMMUNITY

Taken as a whole, the material surrounding this parable confirms our interpretation, and is illuminated by it. In telling it, Jesus has entirely reconceived the exclusivity and inclusivity of the Abrahamic covenant. If Abraham had been blessed with a great nation, a nation through whom God would bless the world, then that nation had been unfaithful, as hinted at by the reference to covenant infidelity in v. 18. It had become a community impenetrable from beyond its own boundaries (as illustrated by the brother's incapacity to hear Moses and the scriptures) and largely unconcerned for the world beyond its own boundaries (illustrated by the Lazarus outside their gates whose only support it seems,

---

74. E.g., Bockmuehl, *This Jesus*, 74; Kümmel, *The Theology of the New Testament*, 40; Sanders, *Jesus and Judaism*, 36–38.

75. The word used for salvation here is σέσωκέν.

came from dogs). This rendered the rich man's familial community ultimately untransformable, and constitutes the final tragedy portrayed by the parable. In effect YHWH, instigating dramatic reversal, says of the rich man to Abraham, "this man will not be your heir" (thereby inverting Gen 15:4).

Nevertheless, this chapter has sought to draw out the implications of resurrection (as spelt out in chapter 4) for a model of communal biblical interpretation. Part I began by recognizing the extensive reach of the interpretive environment and its dominant capacity to shape the reading of texts. Part II, presented this environment in the form of the Abrahamic covenant as conceived by those whose membership of it was solely by birthright. In Part I it was argued that if scripture is acknowledged as holy, but loses its ability to confront readers and reading conventions, the reading environment has become self delusional. In Part II this was perceived in the rich man's readiness to care for his brothers (i.e., his own fellow beneficiaries of the Abraham community), but unable to see Lazarus as worthy of his attention since he hailed from beyond his covenant community, thus illustrating Israel's failure to be a light to the nations. Part I continued by outlining the importance of grace as a community's down-to-earth internal dynamic that witnesses to the world beyond the community. Part II referred to Luke 24:13–35, where two disciples demonstrated their capacity to be transformed by the stranger who, as resurrected interpreter, reshaped their interpretive schematics. In Part I, however, the continuing power of communal hubris was acknowledged as a disruptive force in hermeneutics. In Part II this was recognized in the covenantal pride of the brother's community, although attention was drawn to Luke 17 in which the need for the maintenance of a servant attitude is clearly emphasized. Part I concluded by this recognition that if the doctrine of the resurrection is to have its impact upon hermeneutical strategies, then this will be evidenced in the transformation of the communities and their members. In Part II the parable of the rich man and Lazarus has been read as the radical transformation from the Old Covenant to the new, from a static ethnic community, to an active believing community. Luke 16:19–31, it was argued, is a parable about the transformation of God's chosen community.

The new covenant creates a transformed and a transforming community, an expectation found both in Genesis 15 and in the parable. But, as Wannenwetsch emphasized, worldly schematics remain powerful.[76] Moses and the prophets were not in themselves able to break through them to reach the brothers, who were caught up in the schematics of a generation that sought a sign. This chapter has attempted to distinguish between a hermeneutical "ecclesiolatry" akin to the nationalist idolatry that duped the rich man's brothers and their community, and the active, dynamic, hearing community that is the body of Christ. However, a community of listening, though constituted by its vivified interaction, is not therefore a community of ceaseless hermeneutic activity. It is a community that also knows how to celebrate Sabbath.

---

76. See pp. 183–88 above.

7

Eschatological Reading as Sabbath Celebration

INTRODUCTION: THE AUTHORIZED CONSTRUCTION OF TEXTUAL MEANING

ALL READING IS ESCHATOLOGICAL. Everyone reads for an end, although the question of how the end functions in reading is complex and elusive.[1] Chapter 1 argued that the prominent force in contemporary hermeneutics is technology, an empirical means of establishing security, order, peace and sense out of the neutral expanse of potential that constitutes the future. Technology, it was argued, has incarcerated a pseudo-liberated humanity in the *Gestell*, an enframed, prescriptive structure determining what can be made out of the future. In order to be liberated from this technological *Gestell*, interpretation must attend to Sabbath. However, to oppose the technologism is not to oppose legitimate human work as such, since technologism is a particular brand of human activity. That is, one that treats the world (and one may infer, the text) as raw material devoid of the capability of offering serious resistance to the machinations of human progress. Given such a blueprint for interpreta-

---

1. This question is addressed at length in Paul Fiddes' illuminating study, *The Promised End*. While thanking Derrida for stressing the deferral of meaning, Fiddes integrates the Derridian approach with that of Frank Kermode, (for whom the end of the text animates the sense of its whole), Northrop Frye, (for whom the end expresses human desire), and Paul Ricoeur (for whom the end opens up new possibilities).

tion, the text is incapable of wielding influence over those who would hear it. But there remains a proper place for human making, for working co-operatively with the world, its "resources" and its texts. Biblical interpretation is human work, and it is the burden of this chapter to emphasize the importance of the foundation of such work: Sabbath. The first part of the chapter retraces some of Bultmann's steps, and presents Sabbath as a hermeneutical imperative, while the second part offers an eschatological reading of the parable of the rich man and Lazarus.

PART I: SABBATH AS AN ESCHATOLOGICAL LENS

Bultmann's Eschatology

Bultmann shifted the focus of eschatology from the consummation of the space-time order and to an event which now can only come by means of natural calamity (e.g., a meteor strike) or technological mishap (e.g., nuclear war).[2] The locus of eschatological encounter is made exclusively present: "Always in your present lies the meaning of history . . . In every moment slumbers the possibility of being the eschatological moment. You must awaken it."[3] Bultmann's overriding concern is that readers be exposed to the dynamism of the kerygma which demands existential response.

In Bultmann's reading of apocalyptic predictions, the embarrassingly delayed *parousia* caused NT authors to reframe their hope in order to create a tension between the events which they had already witnessed and experienced (the so-called "now") and the second coming of Jesus (the "not yet"). This new tension relieved the previously overstrained tension that arose from taking supposedly mythological statements literally.[4] More radically, for John the death and resurrection of Jesus, along with his supposedly future *parousia* are presented in a single homogenous sphere of a-temporal activity. Thus Bultmann removes the sting from history's tail.

---

2. See chapter 1 above, and Bultmann, *Jesus and the Word*, 296.
3. Bultmann, *History and Eschatology*, 155.
4. In Paul for instance, Bultmann sees a tendency towards demythologizing the *parousia* with a radical emphasis on existential call, since "death has been swallowed up in victory" (1 Cor 15:54).

> It is the paradox of the Christian message that the eschatological event, according to Paul and John, is not to be understood as a dramatic cosmic catastrophe but as happening within history, beginning with the appearance of Jesus Christ and in continuity with this occurring again and again in history, but not as the kind of historical development which can be confirmed by any historian. It becomes an event repeatedly in preaching and faith. Jesus Christ is the eschatological event not as an established fact of past time but as repeatedly present, as addressing you and me here and now in preaching.[5]

This provocative reconstruction of New Testament eschatology has invited widespread critique, but Bultmann's intention to allow scripture to confront a scientific world that is going existentially deaf is highly commendable, though it was argued in chapter 1, unaccomplished by his own strategy. This chapter posits a twofold critique of Bultmann that paves the way towards a reconfigured emphasis on the existential decision for which Bultmann called. Firstly, Bultmann's emphasis on the believer's present faith comes at the expense of faith in a future *parousia*. His existential rolling pin flattens out the cosmological contours of past event, interim period and future return, into a neatly packaged a-temporal order of decisive personal events. According to Bultmann's reading of the New Testament, the essential truth that finds expression in the crude myths of rabbinical and early Christian mythology, linking the cosmic order with human history, is that the old aeon is characterised by sin, the new by freedom. "For the past that is ended is not only a cosmic situation—although it is also this for mythological thinking—but rather *my* particular past in which *I* was a sinner. And the future for which *I* am freed is likewise *my* future."[6]

This highlights the second important shortcoming in Bultmann's eschatology; namely, its thoroughly individualistic basis. Bultmann cites the parable of the rich man and Lazarus as evidence of an emerging concern amongst New Testament authors "in which universal (cosmological) eschatology is displaced by an individualistic one, i.e., one which does not expect a new aeon, but simply the continuation of individual life

---

5. Bultmann, *Eschatology and History*, 151–52. See also Bultmann, *Jesus and the Word*, 32–34.

6. Bultmann, *Existence and Faith*, 301 (emphasis added).

after death."⁷ Despite the variety of influences on Bultmann's theology,⁸ it is undoubtedly his appropriation of Heidegger's earlier thought that surfaces in this aspect of demythologization. The angst that arises with facing one's own death compels the individual to resolute decision for authentic existence. Such individual appropriation is necessary but not sufficient to understand this parable, as will be suggested below. The importance of such individual decision is not to be doubted, but, as Moltmann points out, this imperative takes its place within Bultmann's eschatology at the cost of one's involvement in world history, in creation, in personal relationship with other human beings and as part of the body of Christ.⁹

However, the Last Day for Bultmann, is not necessarily concerned with an individual's death. Bultmann's eschatology no longer perceives Jesus Christ as the Alpha and Omega, but rather places the end of time into human hands, in full accord with historicist practice. Technology has now endowed humanity with the capacity to invoke "the consummation of the age"(Matt 28:20). If the sky is to be lit up from the east to the west, it will be at the flick of a switch rather than the blast of a trumpet. Both images are equally mythological,¹⁰ even if the power centre has descended from the heavens to the Pentagon. The call to decision is so prominent in Bultmann that the end of time, like all else, is quite literally in the hands of human decision-makers. Humans have to take responsibility for their own appropriation of time,¹¹ because past, present and future constitute the human environment.

Bauckham and Hart perceive that the dominant eschatology of contemporary Western society is the lingering belief in the "myth of progress." Within this worldview, they claim, technology attempts to master the future by controlling it—and in so doing it defuses it. No longer does eschatology carry the explosive charge of a wholly other; it is now a projection of the humanly controlled present. And this control

---

7. Bultmann, *Existence and Faith*, 297.

8. See pp. 26–28 above where it is also argued that Bultmann's individualism is to be understood in relation to the "mass" or "herd" mentality.

9. Moltmann, *The Coming of God*, 21.

10. Most would agree that technology is sustained by its own myths. See for instance Bauckham and Hart's identification of technology with the "myth of progress" (*Hope Against Hope*, chapter 2).

11. Bultmann, *History and Eschatology*, chapter 7.

of the future empties the future by subjecting it to the perceptions of the present.[12] Thus the future becomes an open space, waiting to be conquered by the crusading forces of human responsibility. As a beneficiary of the technologist enterprise, Bultmann's own belief system would be seriously threatened if, instead of subjecting the dangers of the future to the objectives of the present, it were subjected to the unexpected intrusions of a future eschatological event that instantaneously deconstructs historical human objectives.

Bultmann's eschatology and hermeneutics are considered here in the light of resurrection, as discussed in chapter 4. Bultmann is to be applauded for his dogged call for existential decision, and critiqued for portraying an anthropocentric eschatology that deprives the future of the capacity to answer back. This chapter posits an eschatological way of reading in the present that earths the future without eclipsing it. Bultmann thought it possible for this dual emphasis to be retained, given that a certain paradox be upheld; namely, that the time-stopping eschatological event both begins in and continues through human time. "To me the paradox seems to be that for our vision, for which time is the setting of the eschatological event, this event seems to be temporal although it puts an end to time. Might one say, perhaps, that the paradox is that God's "time" comes into our (secular) time."[13] Thus Bultmann expressed himself in a letter to Barth whose own earlier work had portrayed an eschatology similar to that of Bultmann, shifting the focus of a final event to a present decision.[14] Future event is eclipsed by the decisive eschatological present, which transforms human time. Unlike Bultmann, however, Barth developed his eschatological categories to embrace the present without empirically annexing the past and future.[15] It is in Barth's writings that the notion of Sabbath provides a framework for a hermeneutics in which God enters our fallen time, without vacating eternity.

12. See Bauckham and Hart, *Hope Against Hope*, chapter 2.

13. Barth and Bultmann, *Letters*, 94. This particular letter was written in response to a controversial public lecture delivered by Barth, entitled "Rudolf Bultmann: Ein Versuch ihn zu verstehen."

14. E.g., Barth, *Church Dogmatics*, I.1, 497. "this is the secret of time which is made known in the moment of revelation, in that eternal moment which always is . . . "

15. See for instance Barth, *Church Dogmatics*, III.1, 445–58, where he explicitly and incisively critiques Bultmann for reading the resurrection as a mythical aspect of the disciples" Easter faith.

A Palace in Time[16]

A. J. Heschel's study of the Sabbath sets the celebration in deliberate contrast with technological civilization and its goal to achieve security through the ceaseless toil of productive activity.[17] For Heschel, this incessant technological drive to conquer space is afforded only as a result of the sacrifice of time, even though time itself was meant to be "the heart of existence".[18] The technologist worldview enframes humanity within a specific understanding of time. The future is pregnant with new possibilities, an undiscovered territory which, given the right strategies, will yield fruit for an enterprising humanity that hungers after security. However, as with Derrida's and Fish's hermeneutics, so also with Bultmann's, the concept of novelty is sterilized. The future is at the mercy of the present, and arises so thoroughly out of the present that the possibility of genuine novelty is eclipsed. On the other hand, as Moltmann has shown, a consideration of the German word *Zukunft*, brings us closer to the biblical notion of *parousia*.[19]

The Greek *parousia* refers literally to the presence of a person. On initial reflection, this coheres with Bultmann's exclusive focus on the *eschatos* rather than the *eschaton*.[20] Indeed, the phrase *parousia* is reserved in the NT for the future coming of Christ into the world, thus animating temporal existence with future hope. Interestingly, Bultmann himself has succumbed to the supposed myth of a delayed *parousia*, and others are now demythologising Bultmann.[21] Some have argued convincingly that many of the supposed future predictions of the Gospel accounts refer primarily to the destruction of the Temple, and that there is no evidence after AD 70 of any disappointment or frustration with the failure of Jesus to return.[22] This raises the question about why the myth of

---

16. A phrase used by A. Heschel as he contrasts technologism with Sabbath (Heschel, *Sabbath*, 12).

17. E.g., Heschel, *Sabbath*, 3, 13.

18. Heschel, *Sabbath*, 3.

19. Moltmann, *The Coming of God*, 22–29.

20. By *eschaton* is meant the events that might be described as the "consumation of the age"(Matt 28:20). By *eschatos* is meant Christ who, as cosmocrator is the one who is the alpha and the omega (Rev 1:8).

21. See Bauckham "The Delay of the Parousia"; Hengel *Between Jesus and Paul*; Wright *The New Testament and the People of God*, 459–64.

22. Until recent decades it was commonplace for biblical scholars to regard many of Jesus' statements of judgment as reference to the second coming. Thus an appar-

a delayed *parousia* has held such privileged status in scholarly circles. For sure, the expulsion of *parousia* from biblical interpretation coheres perfectly with the technologist enterprise. Indeed, the belief in a future coming of Christ contrasts two different models of time: the technologist—in which the future is to be tamed, controlled and conquered; and the eschatological, in which the future confers life upon the present. In short, these two concepts of time are characterized by two different directional currents. Technologism sees humanity marching forwards into the future. Eschatology sees the future as coming towards humanity.

The verbal root of Sabbath is the Hebrew noun, *shabat* to stop. In the light of a frenzied hyperactive desire to carve meaning out of the future, the Sabbath command is to stop, and to be re-oriented in creation.[23] To "sabbath" is to embrace an eschatological openness, by ceasing work and entering the time God has for us. The use of Sabbath as an eschatological image, implicit within the New Testament,[24] is made explicit in the thinking of Augustine. The Manichees had argued that the Old Testament was riddled with untrustworthy anthropomorphism, exemplified in part by the revelation (Gen 2:3) that after a week's busy creating, God decided to take a well-earned rest. This belief was intolerable to the Manichees, who believed that God had no such need. It was in response to this line of thought that Augustine emphasized the eschatological nature of Sabbath, as a means of describing the rest encountered after the consummation of history, which nevertheless can be anticipated and appropriated in the present.[25] For Augustine, Sabbath came to signify the humility of receiving grace-driven activity. He understood the Sabbath command as human labor being characterized by an openness to God's influence.[26] Bauckham and Hart observe the counter-intuitive reception of Augustine's exhortation.

---

ently "delayed parousia" was construed as a major problem. A focus on the first century Jewish context of many of Jesus' sayings, seems instead to accentuate the historical referents to many of Jesus' sayings. See for instance Wright *Jesus and the Victory of God*, 362. Sanders similarly takes seriously the importance of the Temple and its foretold destruction (*Jesus and Judaism*, 77–90) as a feature of Jesus' ministry.

23. E.g., Psalm 46.
24. Most notably Hebrews 4.
25. Augustine, *City of God*, 22.30.
26. Augustine (*Against the Manichees*, 1.22.33–34; *City of God*, 11.9, 22.30). See also Aquinas (*Summa Theologica*, II.II q.144), Luther (*Treatise on Good Works*, vol.44) and Calvin (*Institutes*, 2.8).

Modern people do not wish, like Augustinian humanity, to find in God the rest for their restless hearts; they want ever new worlds for their restless spirits to conquer. If there is "heaven," it should not be the end of the road, wary humanity's homecoming, but rather like struggling over the brow of the hill to find a vast new vista of unexplored country ahead of us. The appropriate adage is "to travel hopefully is better than to arrive."[27]

Bultmann's de-eschatologised future thus continues to enjoy privileged status, and is thoroughly critiqued by Barth, whose understanding of Sabbath, informed by Augustine, along with Luther and Calvin, offers an alternative eschatology. Furthermore, since Sabbath lays claim to *all* human activity, it is an injunction to which biblical interpretation must pay close attention.

Barth on Sabbath

Part I (chapters 1–3) of this study outlined the technologist nature of three hermeneutical models, arguing that the meaning they derive from texts is *exclusively* the product of human labour. As such, they are bereft of the radical otherness that confronts the readers of Holy Scripture. Recognition of this otherness arises from the celebration of Sabbath, in which humanity encounters something other than its own projected self. Barth's discussion of Sabbath is a theological account of human rest and right human action. Following in the footsteps of Calvin, Barth regards the Sabbath command as the prime commandment, from which the meaning of all the others is derived.[28] It sets the framework for right human action, which is both commissioned and enabled by the Creator. As such, it diverts man's attention from pride in his human [hermeneutical] achievements, towards a conscious dependence upon the gracious action of God.

Barth is by no means suggesting that God's foundational commandment is merely, "Have a break". After all it is possible to remain "plugged in" to the technologist culture throughout a period of so-called "rest and relaxation", but this would be a sub-conscious, unreflective and passive

---

27. Bauckham and Hart, *Hope Against Hope*, 157. An alternative model is offered by Fiddes, who argues both for a sense of openness or "journeying", alongside a definite sense of closure, i.e., a human "passion for the possible" alongside an openness to the future as a gift. This is closer to the proper context of Sabbath as argued below.

28. Barth, *Church Dogmatics* III.4, 53.

form of continuing action, since it remains fundamentally attuned to the mesmerizing broadcast of fallen notions of time. This is to be sharply distinguished from the active celebration of Sabbath that humbles and "pacifies" human activity, subjecting it to divine leading; the sacrifice of personal ambition that necessarily precedes personal transformation. In so decisively de-centering the self, Sabbath celebration establishes a logic of external constitution, that is, it affirms the human self as being grounded in that which is not itself.

Here, Barth is resting on his exposition of the creation accounts,[29] in which he noted that Adam was created on the sixth day, so that his first full day of human responsibility was the Sabbath. Consequently, this Sabbath rest in God is not merely the regrettable necessity for recuperation after an exhausting week of toil so much as it is the basis of human action in the first place. To observe the Sabbath is to take one's bearings in the creation, in deference to the creative purposes of God. As the Sabbath is the "meaning and intention" of the covenant as recounted in Genesis,[30] so it also serves as the foundation of the new covenant as depicted in the NT. For the first Adam, Sabbath is the day of formation; for the last Adam it is the day of transformation.

Sabbath for Barth, then, is foundational to God's covenanted walk with His people. Every Sabbath is a liturgical checkpoint in Israel's walk with God. Throughout Israel's history, God constantly summons His people into fellowship with himself, calling worshippers into the time that God has for them, in which there is "genuine intercourse" between God and his people. Barth follows Calvin in reading Hebrews 4 as the climactic fulfillment of this summons in Christ. His exposition of the first creation account reaches its Christological conclusion by regarding the resurrection as the ultimate fulfillment of Sabbath. Was the church's move to celebrate on the eighth instead of the seventh day of the week justified?

> If it is correct that the truth and faithfulness of God in the blessing and sanctification of the seventh day are revealed in the resurrection of Jesus Christ; if the history of the covenant and salvation between God and man inaugurated in the former is concluded in the latter; if in the latter life began in the new time of a new world, we have to admit that they were right; that this first day of

---

29. E.g., Barth, *Church Dogmatics* III.1, 228.
30. Barth, *Church Dogmatics* III.1, 218.

this new time had to become literally as well as materially the day of rest which dominates life in this new time.[31]

The ethical context of Barth's discussion of Sabbath (III.4) presupposes the foundations laid in his exposition of the creation accounts (III.1). Sabbath forms the ethical basis of the Christ-centred life because it demands that receptivity to the gracious action of God underlie human knowledge, work and activity. "What it really forbids him is not work, but trust in his work."[32] The eschatological implications of the Sabbath are made explicit in that it is celebrated on the day of the resurrection. (The first reason for this has already been noted: it was the salvific fulfillment of the covenant). The second reason is that the early Christians saw in the resurrection the first hint of his final return, the consummation of the age, the promise of the general resurrection, redemption and eternal life. His future as the last day is both awaited and remembered in focusing on this event, and, as Barth claims, this focus leads us to reassess radically the structure of human thinking, willing and acting.

> If we link the significance of the holy day in salvation history and its eschatological significance, and if we remember that in most instances we are concerned with its relationship to the particularity of God's omnipotent grace, we shall understand at once, and not without a certain awe, the radical importance, the almost monstrous range of the Sabbath commandment. By the distinction of this day, by the summons to celebrate it according to its meaning, this command sets man and the human race in terribly concrete confrontation with their Creator and Lord, with his particular will and Word and work, and with the goal, determined and set by Him, of the being of all creatures, which means also the inexorable end of the form of their present existence.[33]

It claims the whole man, his good and his bad works. It is the reception of grace at the expense of self-justification, rendering necessary a certain self-denial. It is the cessation of his presumptuously unrestricted access to textual meaning and the acceptance that this comes legitimately only as gift.

The celebration of the Sabbath most decisively de-centers the self. This self-renouncing faith is the essence of the commandment. Sabbath

---

31. Barth, *Church Dogmatics* III.1, 228.
32. Barth, *Church Dogmatics* III.4, 54.
33. Barth, *Church Dogmatics* III.4, 57–58.

is a time of commissioning in which man is freed both *from* himself and his work, and therefore freed *for* God and divine service. Sabbath is the basis of human existence because only by celebrating Sabbath can one truly *ek-sist*.[34] At this point Fish resurfaces, most specifically his critique of Toulmin's injunction that we should with great frequency, "enter the courts of rationality,"[35] stepping out of our context and engaging in unadulterated rational reflection. However valid Fish's critique that escape from one's communal context is impossible, it does not apply to the Sabbath command. This is partly because observing the quiet of Sabbath is by no means equivalent to humanly achieved rational reflection, as Heschel had noted: "The Sabbath is not holy by the grace of man. It was God who sanctified the seventh day."[36] Secondly, Barth makes clear that Sabbath is not an individualistic affair—it must be celebrated in the assembly of God's people. It is participation in a worshipping congregation that distinguishes this day of rest from a day of sublime inactivity. This communal aspect of celebration does not merely signify attendance at church. The action of going to church will not be meaningful if it is not based on the self-renouncing basis of the command, which means that both the divine service of the congregation and resting from work are to be regarded as secondary issues.[37] This emphasis on communal reflection distinguishes Barth's hermeneutics from the thoroughgoing individualism of Bultmann's. However, quite how this communal celebration is fleshed out remains unclear in Barth, as Brian Brock points out.

> In his salutary emphasis on Sabbath as command, he fails to emphasise that it is at the same time the basic experience of right human action, or rather right human resting in God. Barth can make it sound as if Sabbath is behind us at creation, or before us as an eschatological ideal to be celebrated and remembered, when we must also emphasise that Sabbath is a corporate experience of place before God which is the raw data of all human transformation as well as theologising. That place is the experience of not needing to fashion idols to be at peace and in right relation with all things.[38]

34. Heidegger, "On The Essence of Truth," 26; see also *Being and Time*, 302.

35. Toulmin *The Construal of Reality*, 500; quoted by Fish, *Doing What Comes Naturally*, 438.

36. Heschel, *Sabbath*, 76.

37. Barth, *Church Dogmatics* III.4, 69.

38. Brock, *Discovering Our Dwelling*, 214.

Sabbath and Interpretation

Like all human works, interpretation can be an idolatrous pursuit, in that it may be seized upon by a humanity eager to create *ex nihilo* its own world of intelligibility. God has not dropped revelation like emergency aid by parachute, leaving hungry humanity to work out how to get at it and what to do with it. Neither can hermeneutics be regarded as the ingenious human response to a mythically encrypted divine message (à la Bultmann), because interpretive appropriation of the text (à la Barth) is itself part of that revelatory gift. To treat hermeneutics as an end in itself, a separate sphere from the gracious action of God's self-revelation, is to play into the hands of technologism. Sabbath is essential to the act of interpreting because it fundamentally calls our interpretive pride into question. The observance of Sabbath appropriated into hermeneutics is the interpreter's joyful acknowledgement that humanity simply does not have the (God-given) tools (e.g., scriptural texts, language, dictionaries, rational minds) or the "know how" (techniques, methodologies, reading strategies) to forge meaning out of the raw scriptural material. Instead, as John Webster repeatedly affirms,[39] reading scripture is an activity that takes its place within the wider economy of God's gracious communication with His people. Sabbath brings into hermeneutics the conscious recognition that hearing Moses and the Prophets is an activity granted solely to *One Whom God Helps*, i.e., Lazarus.[40]

Human receptivity to the gracious action of God is the only means of escaping the *Gestell* in which Bultmann's technologist hermeneutics remain ensnared.[41] As outlined in chapter 1, Bultmann has sought a technologist solution to the technologist problem and thereby accentuated the technologist problem identified by Heidegger. Heidegger's own route out of the *Gestell* rested on a distinction between earth and world. This important aspect of Heidegger's later thought, surfacing most explicitly in his 1935 lecture "The Origin of a Work of Art,"[42] was outlined in chapter 1 is now worth briefly revisiting.

Heidegger attempts to counter the potentially exclusive dominance of the technologist category by introducing a bipolar opposition

---

39. Webster, "Hermeneutics in Modern Theology."

40. As noted above, the name Lazarus is an abbreviated transcription of Eleazar, "Helped by God".

41. See chap 1 above.

42. Heidegger, "The Origin of a Work of Art," 143–203.

between the historical activity of people (world) and the ontological stuff of nature (earth).[43] "World" is human conquest and discovery; "earth" is nature's resistance and revealing. However, the distinction between the two does not render them separate, but mutually engaged. Heidegger's description of the relationship between earth and world as 'strife" depicts the waters of chaos threatening to rob the universe of order,[44] while the forces of human order seek to tame the chaotic wild. Nevertheless, earth and world are not simply contraposed but interdependent, since earth needs world in order for its being to be made manifest; and, conversely, world needs earth since it provides its decisive basis.[45] Human work itself constitutes this perpetual strife between earth and world. The work of art is an aspect of work that impacts upon both earth and world, as it reveals elements of earth in such a way as to disrupt and create history in the world. Art brings forth the being of earth as a revelation to and reshaping of world.

As noted above, the weakness of Heidegger's secular Sabbath is that it leads inexorably towards a worshipful reverence for earth in order to counter the technologist world category. Conversely, Sabbath, while embracing the categories of human bodily action and relationship inextricably related to participation in the created order, does not stand exposed to the wild forces of being, but to the infinitely more dangerous forces of grace. Sabbath is not the open field of comportment,[46] nor is it a court of rationality.[47] Rather, Sabbath is the time that God has for us, the *locus* of transformation, the basis of all true human work. It is, therefore, an imperative in the divinely enabled human endeavor of hermeneutics.

---

43. Heidegger, "The Origin of a Work of Art," 174–76.

44. Heidegger's veiled allusion to ancient creation mythologies is deliberate, but his own claims interpret those myths by suggesting that the struggle itself is not only an primeval divine event, but ongoing one in which humanity participates.

45. Heidegger, "The Origin of a Work of Art," 174.

46. Heidegger, "On the Essence of Truth," 122–23.

47. Fish, *Doing What Comes Naturally*, 438.

PART II: AN ESCHATOLOGICAL READING OF LUKE 16:19–31

Heaven and Hell

Given the context and referents of the parable, it is unlikely that its purpose was to offer a literal description of the afterlife that would provide useful information for those who want to discuss the nature of heaven and hell.[48] Neither can the parable be held up as an accidental glimpse into Jesus' view of the afterlife, because—as we have argued—the parable serves to bring the reality of resurrection from some future eschatological event, into the political and social reality of his present community.

> Resurrection, for Luke, is not only the truth of what happened to Jesus, and the truth of what will happen to the righteous at the end. It is also a truth which comes to birth, anticipating those literal and concrete events, in other events which, though equally concrete, use the language of resurrection metaphorically. Luke has clearly not flattened out the ultimate future promise . . . But the most striking thing about Luke's special material is the way in which "resurrection" becomes a metaphor for what is going on in the ministry of Jesus itself.[49]

For Wright, Luke offers a "realized eschatology" without abandoning the traditional final resurrection. And since the parable functions metaphorically, all that may be gleaned about post-mortem existence from the parable itself, is Jesus' possible belief that death is not the final human experience. However, the eschatological storyline of the parable is a well used one in first century Palestine. The fact that Jesus adds a new twist to this familiar storyline, questions even his own commitment to that narrative structure of a journey to death and back again.

Jesus can hardly be conceived as an heir to the story-telling tradition of Plato[50] and Plutarch,[51] who have clearly constructed myths to convey their own understanding of the afterlife. Since H. Gressmann's 1918 publication on the potential parallels and sources,[52] the reliance of the parable on extra-biblical stories has been an area of protracted

---

48. Tertullian, for instance, does not regard Luke 16:19–31 as a parable, but a historical account of the soul surviving the grave (*De Anima*, 7).
49. Wright *The Resurrection of the Son of God*, 420.
50. See Plato's story of Er the Pamphylian (*Republic*, 10.614a–621d).
51. *De Sera Numinis Vindicta* 22–33.
52. Gressmann, H. *Vom reichen Mann und armen Lazarus*.

debate. Gressmann had focussed on an Egyptian folktale in which death leads to a reversal of conditions for a rich and a poor man. Si-Osiris is the reincarnated tour guide who shows his father around the realm of the dead, Amente.[53] The story's intention is clearly to illustrate that the unrighteous may have their punishment postponed beyond death, whereas the righteous receive them in life so as to avoid penalty after death. These and similar sources have been postulated similarly by Jeremias, Bultmann, and Crossan.[54] However, the most comprehensive survey of possible parallels to this parable and the eschatological significance they carry, has been conducted by Richard Bauckham.[55]

For Bauckham, a first-century Palestinian Jew would hear stories about post-mortem reversal of plight for the rich and the poor with the full expectation of hearing how that reversal is made known to the living, possibly leading to the repentance of the rich man's five brothers. So when this proposed return is denied, despite the persistence of the rich

---

53. Griffith, *Stories of the High Priest of Memphis*, 42–43. The rich man's burial was an impressive spectacle of wealth, compared with the unceremonious transportation of the poor man, carried along to Amente on a straw mat. Si-Osiris reveals to his father, however, that the rich man is now subjected to agonizing punishment (the socket of his eye being used as the hinge of a door), whereas the poor man is elevated to a position of honor. Gressmann argued that this Egyptian tale had entered Jewish folklore as the tale of Bar Ma'yan, a wealthy tax collector in Ashkelon, who dies on the same day as a poor biblical scholar. The disparity of their economic status is again fully expressed in their respective funerals, and one of the scholar's friends becomes deeply troubled by this marked contrast. It is revealed to this friend in a dream, however, that the scholar is in paradise, whereas the tax collector is punished with tantalization, perpetually but unsuccessfully attempting to drink from a river. The scholar's one bad deed is rewarded by a low-class funeral, the tax collector's one good deed is rewarded by a high-class funeral. [This tradition is translated by Manson (*The Sayings of Jesus*, 297)]. Gressman believed that the story had been imported to Palestine by Alexandrian Jews, and subsequently metamorphosized to become the tale of Bar Ma'yan.

54. Hock has listed the tradition of theories. For Crossan's view, see chapter 5.

55. Bauckham, "The Rich Man and Lazarus." Bauckham identifies a variety of parallel stories, which together imply that the general folkloric theme of post-mortem reversal of fortune for rich and poor was a popular one in ancient Palestinian culture, a theme that provided the framework for a variety of differently colored stories. However, he also contrasts the parallels with the parable. He notes firstly that both Jewish and Egyptian versions converge against the parable on three major points. Firstly, the focus falls mainly on the burials rather than on the preceding lives of the rich and poor characters. Secondly, those who attend the funeral learn of the post-death destinies of the deceased by means of some special revelation. Thirdly, the ultimate fate of the deceased is the just desert of their moral behavior in life.

man (evidence itself of the deeply rooted expectations aroused by this entire narrative framework), this is worthy of close attention.[56]

Before turning to this question however, it must be noted that neither heaven nor hell are mentioned in this parable. Less still, can traditional assumptions about places of never-ending torment for the wicked and eternal bliss for the righteous, be read back into this parable. The rich man—we are not told why—ends up in Hades, whereas Lazarus is in "Abraham's bosom." The latter image suggests a feast, in which Lazarus is reclining alongside the patriarch. The scene is clearly a banquet, the manner of banquet previously enjoyed by the rich man. And unlike heaven, the banquet is a frequent image in the parables of Jesus. In this instance, the post-mortem feast is hosted by Abraham himself. If Lazarus is indeed to be identified with the Eleazar of Gen 15 (as argued above), then not only has Abraham invited the wrong person to his feast,[57] but that wrong person has become Abraham's honored guest, i.e., sat on his lap at the feast.

Here, the great theme of reversal is fully grasped. This is not simply a story like countless others, in which death reverses the fate of wealthy and the poor. If this were the case, then Abraham's services as an eschatological usher are being employed on the wrong side of the unbridgeable chasm. This is rather, a story bringing the final realities of death and resurrection forward, into the ministry of Jesus. In this sense, for readers of Luke, the parable reads like a direct fulfillment (and specific reading) of the so-called *Magnificat* (Luke 1:46–55). If the rich man of the parable is to be identified with Herod Antipas (as argued above), then even the meaning of dethroning the mighty finds its clearest exposition in this parable. Jesus was not inciting a political revolution, as was widely expected, but revealing the temporal and flimsy basis of the authority structure that presently governed Israel. The wealthy and the royal members of Israel's society are not enjoying their current lifestyle of authority and luxury because it has been divinely bestowed upon them. Confronted with the God of Abraham, their status—far from being upheld—is, in fact, reversed.

---

56. For an outline of the Jewish myth, see Jeremias, *The Parables of Jesus*, 178–79, 183.

57. Though in strong continuity with the parable of the Great Banquet, Luke 14:15–24.

The parable functions then, to reconfigure the notion of who is *in* and who is *out* of the kingdom of God. But what can be done here and now to warn those with wealth and power, like the rich man's five brothers? It is at this point the parable departs from conventional stories of this nature. As Bauckham's review of parallel stories has shown, the distinctive point about this parable is that no return from the dead to the living is granted. No resurrected herald of woe is to be granted because no herald is necessary. "Moses and the Prophets" are perfectly sufficient to instruct the five brothers on how to avoid their brother's fate.

A Resurrected Interpreter?

Of course, there are no warnings in Moses and the Prophets that refer to an afterlife. And even if there were, Herod and his family were notoriously ignorant of Moses and the Prophets. What is more, Antipas himself was fascinated by Jesus, and wanted to see him perform a miracle (Luke 23:38). The parable explains the refusal to grant this wish. For such a person to hear Moses and the Prophets would be no less a miracle than someone rising from the dead.

However, this is not simply to state that it takes a miracle (like a resurrection or a camel squeezing through the eye of a needle) to open a wealthy man's ears to the Scriptures. The ability to hear Scripture is rather implicitly bound up with resurrection.[58] After all, the parable is introduced with the explicit claim that, since the coming of John the Baptist, the Law and the Prophets have not been negated but fulfilled (Luke 16:16–18). However, to engage with those prophets, that is to *hear* them, and such hearing (as discussed in Wannenwetsch's work, above)

---

58. The "resurrection" nature of Jesus' ministry is never far below the surface of Luke's narrative. It is not to be sought primarily in traditions where Jesus actually resuscitates people from death, although the example of Jairus' daughter (Luke 8:40–56) is perhaps the most illustrative. Jesus is on his way to heal a twelve-year old girl and en route confronts a twelve-year old hemorrhage. The woman concerned would have been excluded from the community on account of her illness, but after her encounter with Jesus is restored. This little incident is textually hemmed in on either side, by the narrative of the dead girl being raised to life. The audacious bleeding outcast's interruption to the resuscitation story illuminates the wider context of Jesus" resurrection ministry, demonstrating that when outsiders are welcomed in, resurrection is happening. And in full accord with Luke's thematic of status reversal, it was the excluded woman who tasted resurrection before the synagogue ruler. Crossan (*In Parables*, 75) identifies six parables of reversal, five of which are Lukan (Matt 22:11–14; Luke 10:25–37; 14:7–11; 15:11–32; 16:19–31; 18:9–14) and display Luke's own capacity for effecting reversal.

Eschatological Reading as Sabbath Celebration 225

is an act of death and resurrection, as the capacity to be broken and remade. Read in the light of Heidegger and Barth, Bultmann, Fish, and Derrida, the parable makes its own point to this effect.

The rich man does not hear Scripture. To do so would require a two-way movement in which beliefs about who is *in* and who is *out* of the kingdom are radically challenged. To begin with, the rich man and his festal guests (his rich brothers[59]), i.e., his interpretive community, must engage with that which is beyond the gate of the community. Only then, can they encounter Lazarus.

For sure, any who came to and from the house would have encountered Lazarus in some sense. But the Lazarus they encountered was a faceless individual with no capacity to evoke existential response from them. Society being what it was, Lazarus was an accepted and familiar expression of how some within that accepted societal structure are destined to live. To encounter in Lazarus, the King of Israel,[60] requires that which, for Fish, is impossible. To do so would require stepping out of one's interpretative context. Here, the existential injunction to "ek-sist,"[61] literally, to stand out of one's context leads Heidegger to a similar conclusion: "Only a god can save us." And yet, in the parable, Lazarus is "he whom God helps." To step into the presence of Lazarus, is a concrete manifestation of Sabbath Celebration. To Sabbath, as outlined above, is not simply to step into a value-free zone, or a "court of rationality." To Sabbath is to be radically exposed to the content-full presence of the God of Israel. Only in such an encounter is Lazarus' true identity revealed.

To encounter Lazarus, not only must the rich man venture out of his interpretive community, but welcome in the stranger like Lazarus.[62]

---

59. The brothers are not stated as present, but since this rich man was feasting every day and his first thought was of his brothers, it is fair to assume they would be among his regular guests.

60. I.e., Christ in Lazarus as argued above by Barth.

61. Heidegger, "On the Essence of Truth," 26; see also Being and Time, 302.

62. The theme of outsiders being welcomed in is a thread that weaves its way through the whole of the Gospel. It surfaces not only in the actions of Jesus, but also in his teaching and his parables. Chapter 15 for example, has the parable of the prodigal son climax with the paradigmatic phrase, "this brother of yours was dead and is alive again" (Luke 15:31). For an example of resurrection in his teaching one turns to the Lukan beatitudes (Luke 6:17–26). Jesus is joined by those who have sought him out because they want to be healed. It is in this setting, remote from the national power centre and its heirs, to a people unlikely to be regarded as beneficiaries of the kingdom, that Jesus declares his provocative inversions. "Blessed are you who are poor, for yours

The rich man, feasting as he does, has kept the outsiders outside, where they belong. Again, in accordance with Fish, to do so would require a total reconfiguration of the interpretive community to cope with the shifting boundaries of intelligibility. However, such disruption is likely to be a disturbing and unwelcome enterprise, and Fish's community are under no obligation to welcome the stranger.

As the archetypal outsider,[63] Lazarus was also meant to be a beneficiary of the covenant blessings God had bestowed upon Israel. The nation is meant to be a light to other nations, rather than hoard its god-given blessings.[64] It is hardly surprising then, that those who fail to engage with Lazarus as Lazarus, should be unable to hear Scripture or believe in a resurrected guide to the afterlife.

Contrary to the parallel stories in Jewish and Middle Eastern culture—a visit from beyond the grave is presented by the parable as a pointless exercise. Those who cannot *hear* a person or a text under their nose, will be incapable of welcoming the impact of resurrection when it happens. Here, the parable makes explicit the mutually inseparable nature of the readiness to interpret a text and the ability to engage with another person. The capacity to hear Moses and the Prophets (texts which already were centuries old in Jesus' day), has little to do with applying a correct model of interpretation, or even with the help of a messenger from the dead.

Given that Hermes is the messenger from the gods to the mortals, and from the dead to the living, hermeneutics itself is made redundant by the worldview to which this parable invites the reader. That is, hermeneutics as the correct understanding of a text as though such a practice could be pursued in isolation from other dimensions of the reader's life. Moses and the Prophets (according to the Abraham portrayed by Luke's Jesus,) have a voice of their own which requires no supernatural or hermeneutical assistance. Bauckham's summary of the parable is right in this respect: "The point is no more than the law and the prophets say—and that no more than the law and the prophets say is required."[65]

---

is the kingdom of God . . . Woe to you who are rich, [here one may imagine Jesus nodding towards Jerusalem] for you have already received your comfort" (Luke 6:20, 24).

63. "This man will not be your heir" (Gen 15), as discussed in Chapter 6 above.

64. E.g., the parable of the talents, Luke 19:12–28.

65. Bauckham, "Rich Man and Lazarus," 245. Bauckham's view is shared by the majority of commentators, but Tanghe offers a fascinating alternative. In a plausible

The interpretation of the parable offered here, suggests that it is other dimensions of the reader's *ethos* that determine how that reader encounters the text. The ability to hear Moses and the Prophets is inseparable from the ability to hear Lazarus. As such, reading is an ethical activity that engages the full-blown moral comportment of the reader and hence, for figures like Barth, will make Sabbath celebration a crucial aspect of the reading process. To read well, in a manner that goes beyond technically correct translation of words and concepts, necessitates Sabbath.

Conclusion: Sabbath as Gracious Reversal

Far from negating the legitimacy of interpretive endeavor, Sabbath is the centre of interpretive gravity. It is a rhythm that goes to the heart of all genuine pursuit of hearing God's voice. Hermeneutics is human work, and as such is grounded in the recognition that it is both dependant wholly upon and directed finally towards the glory of God. But it remains a necessary labor to be engaged upon with rigor and effort, a labor that is not negated but validated by Sabbath observance.

Sabbath has thus served as a useful theological category for hermeneutics, gathering unto itself a breadth of essential components absolutely vital for interpretation. It lays claims to the whole person, not simply the human intellect or interest, and demands participation in the created order. It seeks to affirm rather than escape this creation. It looks back to an eighth day of creation, in which world history entered a new era, and looks forward to the future as a gift to be received rather than a chaos to be conquered. The Sabbath is the quiet space, where the mystery

---

(but not entirely persuasive) article ("Abraham, son fils et son envoye,") he suggests that Abraham is being sarcastic. That when he declares to the rich man that his brothers "have Moses and the prophets," he is actually understood to imply, "and I told you they were not sufficient." Tanghe suggests that the context was a Judaism that rejected Jesus because it already had in its possession the Law and the Prophets. Tanghe's arguments are not easily dismissed, just as they are not easily verified. A similar view is adopted by Esler (*Community and Gospel in Luke-Acts*, 119). Finally, this line of interpretation does not cohere with the readings of the parable offered in this thesis. For instance, the parable may be summarized with the incident in Luke 11:27-28 "As Jesus was saying these things, a woman in the crowd called out, "blessed is the mother who gave you birth and nursed you [reaffirming his bloodline]." He replied, Blessed rather are those who hear the word of God and obey it [demanding instead obedience to Moses and the Prophets]." Such a beatitude is finally at odds with Tanghe's defense of the insufficiency of scripture.

of God's resurrection is worked. This resurrection is both metaphor and historical event. Historical events had, according to Wright, led some Jews to take resurrection as a metaphor: The return from exile was a historical hope for which resurrection served as the climactic metaphor. However, the death of the Messiah, the Sabbath day, and Easter morning, reversed this scheme. For the early Christians, resurrection lay at the centre of their historical beliefs, and became the truth for which the return from exile became a metaphor.[66] At the centre of these reversals lay God's Sabbath.

Sabbath celebration enables the reading community to ek-sist[67] without becoming de-historicized, and without being morally immobilized by the textuality of the text. The lack of serious historical engagement has been a thorn in the side of Bultmann's hermeneutics, which demand a pseudo-historical resurrection, a pseudo-historical parousia, all for the sake of what can then only amount to a pseudo-historical faith. Sabbath is rooted in history because resurrection is historical. Thomas Torrance has highlighted this historical ground of the resurrection, noting that

> . . . an astonishing thing about the resurrection is that instead of cutting Jesus off from his historical and earthly existence before the cross it takes it all up and confirms its concrete factuality by allowing it to be integrated on its own controlling ground, and therefore enables it to be understood in its own objective meaning. Far from being "violated" the historical Jesus comes to his own within the dimension of the risen Jesus, and the risen Jesus is discerned to have no other fabric than that in the life and mission of the historical Jesus. It is the resurrection that really discovers and gives access to the historical Jesus, for it enables one to understand him in terms of his own intrinsic *logos*, and appreciate him in the light of his own true nature as he really was—and is and ever will be.[68]

In order to be liberated from the technologist *Gestell* and its diminished capacity to encounter otherness, Christian hermeneutics must embrace readiness for the gracious transformations wrought by the *Eschatos*, transformations which have real consequences in the

---

66. Wright, *The New Testament and the People of God*, 459.
67. Heidegger, "On the Essence of Truth," 26; see also Being and Time, 302.
68. Torrance, *Space, Time and Resurrection*, 165–66.

real world. Sabbath ek-sistence necessitates participation in the creation without demoting it below the importance of *my* decisive faith (Bultmann) and equally without promoting it to become an object of worship (Heidegger). On the contrary, "every sabbath celebration is a messianic intermezzo in time"[69] and, as such, it constitutes the beating heart of biblical interpretation. We come to God as presumed *outsiders* and enter *into* his rest, his kingdom and his scriptures by no other means than gracious unmerited invitation and extraordinary divine enabling.

---

69. Moltmann, *The Coming of God*, 138.

CONCLUSION
Resurrection as the Pulse of Scripture

THE FIRST PART OF this book explored the extensive reach of technologist influence, especially as it determines the manner in which texts are read. Heidegger's notion of technologism referred to a propensity to make use of the earth, its resources and, as inferred above, its texts. The text, like any other entity, is regarded by the technologist interpreter as a resource to be utilised, or as a chaos to be tamed. Regardless of the lip service paid to its holiness, this thesis has argued that despite the sound convictions and worthy intentions one might consciously bring to the biblical text, the decisions about how the text might exert its own force back upon the reader have been decided in advance, thus imposing severe restrictions upon the transformative scope of reading. This, it was argued, was the case not only for those who seek to "master the text," but remains so even for those who seek to be mastered *by* the text, in that such readers may still be reading into the text the sort of authority they want to extract out of it, regardless of whether that authority structure is alien to the text itself. To read technologically is to deny *poiesis*, to silence the otherness embodied by the text, to safeguard oneself from the disruptive encounter that constitutes serious engagement with the text. This technologist structure was presented as having several ramifications for the Christian reading of scripture, bringing it into conflict with some central Christian convictions.

Firstly, as discussed especially in chapters 2 and 4, the notion of "historicism" is inextricably related to that of technologism. Historicism is the belief, more likely to be held unwittingly than consciously,[1] that history is devoid of external causality, which in turn means that both creation and eschatology lose their status as events. As Strauss traced the movement, history lost its standing as an overarching reality and became the study of localized movements, the fates of nations and societies. This meant that no single moment of history could be privileged over any other, because every historical event and reality was relative to every other. As thoroughly historically and culturally situated beings, the human subjects of history had no access to trans-historical events that might be perceived to embrace all cultures, societies, nations and times.

Against their own intentions, the three hermeneuticists discussed in the first part of this thesis accorded well with the central tenets of historicist thought. Bultmann exemplified historicist faith by placing the future into the hands of human decision makers, denying the sort of eschatology that would draw history to a close from outside. Fish demonstrated it similarly by severing history from eternity and advocating a thoroughgoing relativism in which no trans-historical principles can be recognized as such. Derrida revealed his historicist faith by effectively turning the future into a vast expanse of unexplored potentiality, again without the inconvenience of actual eschatological interruption from a God who is wholly other.

For those who adhere to the convictions of historicist belief, there can be no resurrection that occurs as an event within (yet from beyond) history, in such a way as to transform history. The historicist is rather compelled to promote the two-dimensional unfolding of time as it stretches along the plane of history, and in so doing distances contemporary readers from ancient figures, rendering historical characters thoroughly inaccessible. This means that historicists require the construction of hermeneutical bridges that will provide some means of tentative access to those ancient figures. Thus it was argued that when biblical interpretation is perceived merely as the practice of bridging the gaps perceived by historicism, its breadth and scope are severely limited. This has not been to deny the legitimacy of hermeneutics as the necessary attempt to listen to texts and authors that are historically distant, but the distance is prone to exaggeration when it arises from a movement that embodies

---

1. Bultmann, Fish, and Derrida each would want to distance themselves from historicism, but as argued above, each of their respective interpretive strategies display the very symptoms by which historicism is to be identified.

the fundamental rejection of trans-historicality. Biblical interpretation embraces much more than historicist hermeneutics is able to conceive.

Secondly, this thesis advances the claim that technologist reading cannot get beyond the world of the text. If textual meaning is ever secured, it is thereby destined to remain textual. That is, it need not reach beyond the world of the text to transform the life of the reader.[2] Again, this is thoroughly consistent with the technologist security measures designed to defend oneself from the otherness embodied by the text. Not that technologist reading strategists are deprived of the *language* of personal transformation (as demonstrated by the chapter on Bultmann), of community (as demonstrated by the chapter on Fish) or of otherness (as demonstrated by the chapter on Derrida). In each case, however, these extra-textual entities have been domesticated in advance. Technologism informs but never transforms. This is because, despite the validity of historical distance as perceived by historicist hermeneutics, this distance is not the only distance between reader and text. Of much greater import is the moral distance that separates the world of the text from the life of the reader. Because it is set up to cope with a historical gap, historicist hermeneutics is powerless to attend to this most important gap faced by theological interpretation. When the historicist's work is done, the results will only ever be textual. Of course, one can then adopt a hermeneutic strategy and then subsequently talk of one's own transformation as a result of it, but this will always be a subsidiary concern that may take place in accordance with both the perceived expectations of orthodoxy and yet also with the privatized morality that safeguards itself against radical otherness. Technologist hermeneutics cannot cope with the difficulty described in chapter 4 as the problem of "the textuality of the text," the distance that remains even when the apparently "true" meaning has been wrested out of the text, between that text and the moral life of the reader.

Thirdly, the ethical life or "ethos" of the reader—being crucial both to the manner in which a text is first read and the subsequent appropriation of that text—is not addressed fully by an interpretive framework that remains exclusively preoccupied with "horizons." Hermeneutics

---

2. Although technologism as applied in many theological hermeneutics retains the language of "transformation." However, such transformation is conceived in terms of Kantian moral applicationism that captures the so-called "meaning" of a text, prior to a separate and subsequent act of applying it.

remains effectively focused solely upon the horizontal plane, with little if any attention paid to the vertical aspect of interpretation. For those writing on biblical interpretation from a Christian perspective, the Holy Spirit is either left out of the discussion almost entirely,[3] or else strained attempts at orthodoxy are offered;[4] but in such instances the role of the Spirit is often regarded as a private or mystical matter and as such bracketed out from the real business of biblical interpretation. Conversely, the "division of labor" model can be applied to the Trinity resulting in an overspecialized Holy Spirit whose interpretive role is extremely limited.[5] The Spirit does not simply ensure that the meaning of the text is correctly understood, less still can the third person of the Trinity be conceived as invisibly enabling readers to understand dictionaries and lexicons. Nor does the Spirit arrive late in the day, enabling the reader to apply personally the meaning of a text they have already understood. The proposals for interpretation offered in this study do not struggle to make room for the Spirit's presence in and through the entire process of reading scripture, a process that embraces the full blown ethical comportment of the reader. The Spirit is active in shaping and reshaping the life of the reader, transforming the reader from one degree of glory to another (2 Cor 3:12-18), and in so doing the practice of reading scripture becomes what it is. Only by the Holy Spirit is the life of the reader to be transformed, and it is this lived context, a disposition of the affections, the desire and will that predetermines the strategies and methods that are already in place when a text is encountered. If reading scripture is an element of the worshipping life of the Church, this setting cannot with legitimacy be re-

---

3. E.g., the Holy Spirit gets the most fleeting mentions in Jeanrond, *Theological Hermeneutics*, and Morgan and Barton, *Biblical Interpretation*.

4. Even Thiselton is vulnerable to this critique. His masterly study of contemporary hermeneutics makes little mention of the Holy Spirit until the final pages, and even there it can seem as though the role of the Spirit is simply to ensure the reader extracts the correct meaning from the text.

5. See for instance Vanhoozer, *After Pentecost*. Vanhoozer's insights are generally to be welcomed, especially since he is acutely aware of the importance of the Spirit's transformation of the reader. However, in equating Father-Son-Spirit with sender-message-receiver, and virtually restricting the Spirit's activity to enabling perlocutionary effects, the wider thesis becomes questionable. This pattern causes Thiselton reservations concerning "its neat polarities, over-exclusive alternatives, and uniformly triadic patterns to be correlated with Trinitarian modes of action." (Thiselton, *After Pentecost*, 106) Vanhoozer has a convincing alibi for each member of the Trinity, but they were each seen elsewhere when the speech-act occurred.

garded as an extrinsic or secondary aspect of biblical interpretation. The acknowledgement of the Holy Spirit's presence in the reading process defies the smooth running of the technologist interpretive mechanisms, but remains a core consideration in the interpretive process.

In sum, it has been argued in the first part of this thesis that for biblical interpreters the primary textual problem is that deemed the "textuality of the text," the distance between world of the text and the daily life of the reader. A textual problem of this magnitude simply does not have a textual solution. So long as its solution is sought in textual methodology, technologism will continue to dominate theological interpretation. However, the practice of reading scripture is not only an exercise in reconstructing the history of the text, but in reconstructing the life of the reader—which locates reading in the sphere of moral activity, and highlights the centrality of the Holy Spirit and the reading community. This reconstruction of the reader, it has been argued, is a core aspect of biblical interpretation, and since it is best described through the biblical category of resurrection, is fundamentally an act of the Holy Spirit. Far from being a methodological alternative to technologist ways of reading (which renders it vulnerable to becoming just another technologist strategy), resurrection is an event recounted in scripture. But it is not simply an objective fact that sits there in history. Taken together with the crucifixion it transforms history, and provides the shape for the Christian moral life. Since it embraces the entire life of the reader, it is not a thesis that can be deconstructed, but a theopraxis in which the life of the reader is deconstructed. In the end, technology seeks to shelter the reader from this deconstruction, whereas resurrection demands it. The alternatives posed by these contrary means of approaching scripture were thus summarized in a single sentence: *Resurrection displaces technologist reading categories that seek to make use of scripture, with the cultivation of an attentive disposition which enables the reader to be transformed by the God encountered in scripture.*

It is the cultivation of this attentive disposition that constitutes legitimate human productivity.[6] In terms of interpretation, it is a means of making sense of scripture whilst consciously and decisively seeking to be Christ-centered, communally active and eschatologically aware. It is

---

6. The word cultivate, whose Latin root refers to the notion of reverence and respect for that which is being used, is deliberately used to retain the recognition that otherness be allowed to flourish.

Conclusion: Resurrection as the Pulse of Scripture

within this economy of grace as outlined in the second part of the thesis, an environment in which the reader learns how to listen, that scripture is then to be heard as Holy Scripture. Listening here is to be understood not as the capacity to behave politely in conversation, but refers rather to the readiness to be transformed by encounter with otherness. In this sense, in relation to the on going moral transformation of the reader, the so-called "hermeneutical circle" makes the greatest sense. This circle is not to be understood as gradually divesting oneself of theoretical hindrances to pure correctness of understanding, so much as the on-going exposure to the radical otherness of the incarnate God as experienced simultaneously in transforming relationships within the body of Christ, through the saving action of the Holy Spirit, and through the continuing struggle to appropriate the meaning of scripture. John Webster has appropriated brilliantly the importance of resurrection for biblical interpretation, describing it in terms of the Spirit-led moral transformation that is required by those who would hear scripture:

> . . . [A] Christian theological anthropology will envisage the act of reading Scripture as an instance of the fundamental pattern of all Christian existence, which is dying and rising with Jesus Christ through the purging and quickening power of the Holy Spirit. Reading Scripture is thus best understood as an aspect of mortification and vivification: to read Scripture is to be slain and made alive. And because of this, the rectitude of the will, its conformity to the matter of the gospel, is crucial, so that reading can only occur as a kind of brokenness, a relinquishment of willed mastery of the text of the encounter with God in which the text is an instrument.[7]

This brings us all the way back to Schweitzer, whose interpretation of the parable of the rich man and Lazarus was not exclusively textual, but spilt over into the world beyond the text with transformative effect. To be sure, interpretation must include rigorous historical critical work and cannot but make use of hermeneutic strategies. But this thesis has argued that if scripture is to inform the reader it must also at the same time be encountered so as to transform the reader. In this crucial sense scripture is Penuel, the location where Jacob wrestled with God and in so doing earned the name "Israel" (Gen 32:22–32). Holy Scripture is the given site where readers engage with otherness, the place in which death

---

7. Webster, *Word and Church*, 11.

and resurrection are experienced, the activity in which the Holy Spirit graciously effects the transformation of the believer's character from one degree of glory to another (2 Cor 3:18). Ultimately and primordially, the life of the reader is an enacted interpretation of the text she deems authoritative.

Bibliography

Alexandre, M. "L'interpretation de Luc 16:19-31 chez Gregoire de Nysse." In *Epektasis: Melanges patristiques*, edited by J. Fontaine and C. Kannengiesser, 259-68. Paris: Beauchesne, 1972.

Andrews, Isolde. *Deconstructing Barth: A Study of the Complementary Methods in Karl Barth and Jacques Derrida*. Studien zur interkulturellen Geschichte des Christentums 99. Frankfurt: Lang, 1996.

Aquinas, Thomas. *Summa Theologica*. Translated by the Fathers of the English Dominican Province. 3 volumes. New York: Benziger, 1947.

Augustine. *The City of God against the Pagans*. Edited by R. W. Dyson. Cambridge: Cambridge University Press, 1998.

Bailey, Kenneth E. *Poet and Peasant and Through Peasant Eyes: A Literary-Cultural Approach to the Parables of Luke*. Combined Edition. Grand Rapids: Eerdmans, 1983.

Baker, J. "Luke, the Critical Evangelist." *Expository Times* 68 (1957) 123-25.

Ball, Michael. *The Radical Stories of Jesus: Interpreting Parables Today*. Macon, GA: Smyth and Helwys, 2000.

Balmforth, Henry. *The Gospel According to Saint Luke*. Oxford: Clarendon, 1930.

Baltzer, Klaus. "The Meaning of the Temple in the Lukan Writings." *Harvard Theological Review* 58 (1965) 263-277.

Bammel, Ernst. "Is Luke 16, 16-18 of Baptist's Provenience?" *Harvard Theological Review* 51 (1958) 101-6.

Barclay, William. *The Gospel of Luke*. 2nd ed. Daily Study Bible Series. Philadelphia: Westminster, 1956.

Barraclough, R. "A Reassessment of Luke's Political Perspective." *Reformed Theological Review* 38 (1979) 10-18.

Barth, Karl. *Anselm, Fides Quaerens Intellectum: Anselm's proof of the Existence of God in the Context of his Theological Scheme*. Translated by I. W. Robertson. London: SCM, 1960 [1931].

———. *Church Dogmatics*. Vol. I.1: *The Doctrine of the Word of God*. Translated by G. W. Bromiley. Edinburgh: T. & T. Clark, 1975 [1936].

———. *Church Dogmatics*, Vol. I.2: *The Doctrine of the Word of God*. Translated by G. T. Thompson and H. Knight. Edinburgh: T. & T. Clark, 1956 [1938].

———. *Church Dogmatics*, Vol. III.1: *The Doctrine of Creation*. Translated by G. W. Bromiley and T. F. Torrance. Edinburgh: T. & T. Clark, 1958 [1945].

———. *Church Dogmatics,* Vol. III.4: *The Doctrine of Creation.* Translated by G. W. Bromiley and T. F.Torrance. Edinburgh: T. & T. Clark, 1961 [1951].

———. *Church Dogmatics,* Vol. IV.1: *The Doctrine of Reconciliation.* Translated by G. W. Bromiley. Edinburgh: T. & T. Clark, 1961 [1953].

———. *The Epistle to the Romans.* 6th Ed. Oxford: Oxford University Press, 1968 [1933].

———. *The Holy Spirit and the Christian Life.* Translated by R. Birch Holyle. Louisville, KY: Westminster John Knox, 1993 [1929].

———. "Miserable Lazarus (Text: Luke 16:19–31)." *Union Seminary Review* 46 (1934–35) 259–68.

———. "Rudolf Bultmann—An Attempt to Understand Him." In *Kerygma and Myth,* vol. II, edited by Hans-Werner Bartsch, 83–132. Translated by Reginald H. Fuller. London: SPCK, 1962.

———. *The Word of God and the Word of Man.* Translated by S. A.Weston. Boston: Pilgrim, 1928.

Barth, Karl, and Rudolf Bultmann. *Karl Barth-Rudolf Bultmann: Letters 1922–1966.* Grand Rapids: Eerdmanns, 1971.

Bartholomew, Craig G., Colin J. D. Greene, and Karl Möller, editors. *After Pentecost: Language and Biblical Interpretation.* Scripture and Hermeneutics Series 2. Carlisle: Paternoster, 2001.

———. *Renewing Biblical Interpretation.* Scripture and Hermeneutics Series 1. Carlisle: Paternoster, 2000.

Bartholomew, Craig G., et al., editors. *Out of Egypt: Biblical Theology and Biblical Interpretation.* Scripture and Hermeneutics Series 5. Milton Keynes: Paternoster, 2004.

———. *A Royal Priesthood?: The Use of the Bible Ethically and Politically: A Dialogue with Oliver O'Donovan.* Scripture and Hermeneutics Series 3. Carlisle: Paternoster, 2002.

Bartsch, Hans Werner, editor. *Kerygma and Myth: A Theological Debate.* Vol. 2. London: SPCK, 1964.

Batiffol, P. "Trois Notes exegetiques: Sur Luc 16, 19" *Révue Biblisque* 9 (1912) 541.

Bauckham, Richard. "The Delay of the Parousia." *Tyndale Bulletin* 31 (1980) 3–36.

———. *God Will Be All In All: The Eschatology of Jurgen Moltmann.* Edinburgh: T. & T. Clark, 1999.

———. "The Rich Man and Lazarus: The Parable and Parallels." *New Testament Studies* 37 (1991) 225–46.

Bauckham, Richard, and Trevor Hart. *Hope Against Hope: Christian Eschatology in Contemporary Context.* London: Dartman Longman & Todd, 1999.

Bauer, Walter, W. F. Arndt, F. W. Gingrich, and Fredrick Danker. *A Greek-English Lexicon of the New Testament and Other Early Christian Literature.* 2nd ed. Chicago: Chicago University Press, 1979.

Berchmans, J. "Some Aspects of Lukan Christology." *Bible-bhashyam* 2 (1976) 5–22.

Bergquist, James A. "'Good News to the Poor'—Why Does This Lukan Motif Appear to Run Dry in the Book of Acts?" *Bangalore Theological Forum* 18 (1986) 1–16.

Berger, K. "Zum traditionsgeschichtlichen Hintergrund christologischer Hoheitstitel." *New Testament Studies* 17 (1970–71) 391–425.

Bethge, Eberhard. *Dietrich Bonhoeffer: Theologian, Christian, Contemporary.* Translated by E. Mosbacher, P. Ross, B. Ross, F. Clarke, W. Glen-Doepel. Edited by E. Robertson. London: Collins, 1970.

Beutel A. "Luther's Life." In *The Cambridge Companion to Martin Luther*, edited by Donald K. McKim, 3–19. Cambridge: University Press, 2003.
Biggar, Nigel. *The Hastening That Waits: Karl Barth's Ethics* Oxford: Oxford University Press, 1995.
Bishop, E. F. "A Yawning Chasm." *Evangelical Quarterly* 45 (1973) 3–5.
Blomberg, Craig. *Interpreting the Parables*. Downers Grove, IL: InterVarsity, 1990.
Bock, Darrell L. *Luke*. The IVP New Testament Commentary Series 3. Downers Grove, IL: InterVarsity, 1994.
Bockmuehl, Markus. *The Cambridge Companion to Jesus*. Cambridge: Cambridge University Press, 2001.
———. "A Compleat History of Resurrection: A Diaologue with N.T.Wright," *Journal for the Study of the New Testament* 26.4, (2004) 489–504.
———. *This Jesus: Martyr, Lord, Messiah*. Edinburgh: T. & T. Clark, 1994.
———. "Matthew 5:32; 19:9 in the Light of Pre-rabbinic Halakhah." *New Testament Studies* 35 (1989) 291–95.
Bonhoeffer, Dietrich. *Act and Being*. London: SCM, 1962.
———. *Christology*. London, Collins, 1960.
———. *Ethics*. London: SCM, 1972.
Bornhauser, K. *Studien zum Sondergut des Lukas* Gutersloh: Bertelsmann, 1934.
———. "Zum Verstandnis der Geschichte vom reichen Mann und armen Lazarus: Luke 16, 19–31." *Neue Kirchliche Zeitschrift* 39 (1928) 833–43.
Bornkamm, Günther. *Jesus of Nazareth*. Translated by Irene and Fraser McLuskey with James M. Robinson. New York: Harper & Brothers, 1960.
———. *Paul*. Translated by D. M. C. Stalker. New York: Harper & Row, 1971.
Bono. "Grace." *All That You Can't Leave Behind*. London: Universal Island Records, 2000.
Bouttier, M. "L'humanite de Jesus selon Saint Luc." *Recherches de science religieuse* 69 (1981) 33–44.
Boyle, Nicholas. *Sacred and Secular Scriptures: A Catholic Approach to Literature*. London: Darton, Longman, and Todd, 2004.
Brock, Brian Reid. "Discovering Our Dwelling: A Theological Examination of Contemporary Deliberation about the Development of New Technologies, with Reference to M. Heidegger, M. Foucault and G. Grant." PhD dissertation. King's College, London, 2003.
Brown F. B., and E. S. Malbon. "Parables as a Via Negativa: A Critical Review of the Work of John Dominic Crossan." *Journal of Religion* 64 (1984) 530–38.
Brown, Raymond Edward. *The Death of the Messiah: From Gethsemane to the Grave: A Commentary on the Passion Narratives in the Four Gospels*. 2 volumes. Anchor Bible Reference Library. New York: Doubleday, 1994.
Browning, W. R. F. *The Gospel according to Saint Luke*. Torch Bible Commentaries. London: SCM, 1960.
Bruyne, D. "Chasma, Lc 16, 26." *Revue Biblique* 300 (1921) 400–405.
Bultmann, Rudolf. *Existence and Faith*. London: Fontana Library, 1964.
———. *History and Eschatology*. Edinburgh: University Press, 1975 [1955].
———. *The History of the Synoptic Tradition*. Oxford: Basil Blackwell, 1963 [1931].
———. *Jesus and the Word*. London: Collins, 1958 [1926].
———. *Jesus Christ and Mythology*. New York: Scribners, 1958.
———. *Jesus Christ and Mythology*. London: SCM, 1960.
———. *Kerygma and Myth*. Vol. 1. Edited by H. Werner Bartsch. London: SPCK, 1962.

———. *Theology of the New Testament*. 2 vols. Translated by Kendrick Grobel. London: SCM, 1952.
Burnside, W. F. *The Gospel according to St Luke: The Greek Text*. Cambridge: University Press, 1913.
Cadbury, Henry J. "A Proper Name for Dives." *Journal of Biblical Literature* (1962) 44–46.
———. *The Style and Literary Method of Luke*. 2 vols. Harvard Theological Studies 6. Cambridge, MA: Harvard University, 1919–20.
Caird, George B. *The Gospel of Saint Luke*. The Pelican New Testament Commentaries. Baltimore: Penguin, 1963.
———. "Jesus and Israel: The Starting Point for New Testament Christology." In *Christological Perspectives: Essays in Honor of Harvey K. McArthur*, edited by R. F. Berkley and R. F. Edwards, 58–68. New York: Pilgrim, 1982.
Cantinat, J. "Le mauvais riche et Lazare." *Bible et Vie Chretienne* 48 (1962) 19–26.
Capron, F. H. "'Son' in the Parable of the Rich Man and Lazarus." *Expository Times* (1901–2) 31.
Caputo, John D. *The Prayers and Tears of Jacques Derrida: Religion Without Religion*. Indiana Series in the Philosophy of Religion. Bloomington: Indiana University Press, 1997.
———. *Radical Hermeneutics: Repetition, Deconstruction, and the Hermeneutic Project*. Studies in Phenomenology and Existential Philosophy. Bloomington: Indiana University Press, 1987.
Carleton Paget, J. "Quests for the Historical Jesus." In *The Cambridge Companion to Jesus*, edited by Markus Bockmuehl, 138–55. Cambridge: Cambridge University Press, 2001.
Carson, D. A. *The Gagging of God: Christianity Confronts Pluralism*. Leicester: Apollos, 1996.
Castelli, Elizabeth A., et al., editors. *The Postmodern Bible*. New Haven, CT: Yale University Press, 1995.
Catchpole, D. R. "On Doing Violence to the Kingdom." *Journal of Theology for Southern Africa* 25 (1978) 50–61.
Cave, C. H. "Lazarus and the Lukan Deuteronomy." *New Testament Studies* 15 (1968–69) 32–39.
Chesterton, G. K. *Saint Thomas Aquinas: The Dumb Ox*. New York: Doubleday, 1933.
Chilton, Bruce. "Friends and Enemies." In *The Cambridge Companion to Jesus*, edited by Markus Bockmuehl, 72–86. Cambridge: Cambridge University Press, 2001.
Clarke, Neville. *Interpreting the Resurrection*. London: SCM, 1967.
Colle, R. "Zur Exegese und zur homiletischen Verwertung des Gleichnisses vom reichen Mann und armen Lazarus: Luk. 16, 19–31." *Theologische Studien und Kritiken* 75, (1968–69) 652–65.
Conzelmann, Hans. *The Theology of Saint Luke*. Translated by Geoffrey Buswell. London: Faber & Faber, 1953.
Copplestone, Frederick C. *History of Philosophy*. Vol. 1: *Greece and Rome*. London: Burns & Oates, 1961.
Craddock, Fred B. *Luke*. Interpretation, a Bible Commentary for Teaching and Preaching. Louisville, KY: John Knox, 1990.
Cranfield, C. E. B. *The Gospel According to Mark: An Introduction and Commentary*. Cambridge Greek Testament Commentary. Cambridge: University Press, 1959.
Creed, John Martin. *The Gospel According to St. Luke*. London: Macmillan, 1942.

Crossan, John Dominic. *Cliffs of Fall: Paradox and Polyvalence in the Parables of Jesus.* New York: Seabury, 1976.

———. *The Historical Jesus: The Life of a Mediterranean Jewish Peasant.* Edinburgh: T. & T. Clark, 1991.

———. *In Parables: The Challenge of the Historical Jesus.* New York: Harper & Row, 1973.

———. *Raid on the Articulate: Comic Eschatology in Jesus and Borges* New York: Harper and Row, 1976.

Cullmann, Oscar. *Christ and Time: The Primitive Christian Conception of Time and History.* Translated by F. V. Filson. London: SCM, 1951.

Dalberg, John E. E. (Lord Acton). *Essays of Freedom and Power.* New York: Free Press, 1949.

Danker, F. W. *Jesus and the New Age According to St. Luke.* St. Louis: Clayton, 1972.

———. *Luke.* 2nd ed. Proclamation Commentaries. Philadelphia: Fortress, 1987.

———. "Purple." In *The Anchor Bible Dictionary,* 557–60. Vol. 5. London: Doubleday, 1992.

Darr, John A. *Herod the Fox: Audience Criticism and Lukan Characterization.* Journal for the Study of the New Testament Supplement Series 163. Sheffield: Sheffield Academic, 1998.

Dawsey, J. M. *The Lukan Voice: Confusion and Irony in the Gospel of Luke.* Macon, GA: Mercer University, 1986.

———. "The Temple-Theme in Luke." *Melita Theologica* 38 (1987) 26–32.

———. "The Unexpected Christ: The Lucan Image." *Expository Times* 98 (1987) 296–300.

———. "What's in a Name? Characterization in Luke." *Biblical Theological Bulletin* 16 (1986) 143–47.

Derrett, J. D. M. "Fresh Light on St Luke xvi: II. Dives and Lazarus and the Preceding Sayings." *New Testament Studies* 7 (1960–61) 364–80.

Derrida, Jacques. "Plato's Pharmacy." In *Dissemination.* Translated by Barbara Johnson. London: Athlone, 1981 [1972].

———. "The Double Session." In *Dissemination.* Translated by Barbara Johnson. London: Athlone, 1981 [1972].

———. *Of Grammatology.* Translated by Gayatri Chakravorty Spivak. Baltimore and London: John Hopkins University Press, 1976.

———. *Specters of Marx: The State of the Debt, the Work of Mourning, and the New International.* Translated by Peggy Kamuf. New York: Routledge, 1994.

———. *The Gift of Death.* Translated by David Willis. Chicago: University of Chicago Press, 1995.

———. *Given Time, I: Counterfeit Money.* Translated by Peggy Kamuf. Chicago: University of Chicago Press, 1991.

———. "Khora." In *On The Name.* Translated by David Wood, John P. Leavey Jr., and Ian Macleod. Stanford: Stanford University Press, 1995 [1993].

———. "Sauf le nom (Post Scriptum).'" In *On The Name.* Translated by David Wood, John P. Leavey Jr., and Ian Macleod. Stanford: Stanford University Press, 1995 [1993].

———. "Faith and Knowledge." In *Religion,* edited by J. Derrida and G. Vattimo, 1–78. Stanford: Stanford University Press, 1998.

Dewey, A. J. "Quibbling Over Serifs: Observations on Matt 5:18, Luke 16:17." *Forum* 5.2 (1989) 109–20.
Dodd, C. H. *According to the Scriptures: The Sub-Structure of New Testament Theology*. London: Fontana, 1952.
———. *The Founder of Christianity*. London: Collins, 1970.
———. *The Parables of the Kingdom*. London: SCM, 1961 [1935].
Domeris, W. R. "The Holy One of God as a Title of Jesus." *Neotestamentica* 19 (1985) 9–17.
Donnelly, P. J. *Rhetorical Faith: The Literary Hermeneutics of Stanley Fish*. Albany: State University of New York Press, 2002.
Downing, F. G. "Freedom from the Law in Luke-Acts." *Journal for the Study of the New Testament* 26 (1986) 49–52.
Drury, John. *Tradition and Design in Luke's Gospel: A Study in Early Christian Historiography*. London: Darton, Longmann, and Todd, 1976.
Dunkerley, R. "Lazarus." *New Testament Studies* 5 (1958–9) 321–27.
Dunn, James D. G. *Christology in the Making: An Inquiry into the Origins of the Doctrine of the Incarnation*. London: SCM, 1989.
———. *Romans 1–8*. Word Biblical Commentary 38A. Dallas, TX: Word, 1988.
———. *Unity and Diversity in the New Testament: An Inquiry into the Character of Earliest Christianity*. London: SCM, 1990.
Dupont, J. "L'apres mort dans l'oevre de Luc" *Review of Theological Literature* 3 (1972) 3–21.
———. "Le salut des Gentiles et la signification theologique du Livre des Actes." *New Testament Studies* 6 (1959–60) 132–55.
Eagleton, Terry. "The Estate Agent: *The Trouble with Principle* by Stanley Fish." *London Review of Books* 22.5. (2000) 10–11.
———. *Ideology: An Introduction*. London: Verso, 1991.
Easton, Burton Scott. *The Gospel According to St. Luke: A Critical and Exegetical Commentary*. New York: Scribner, 1926.
Elliott, M. A. "Israel." In *Dictionary of Jesus and the Gospels*, 356–63. Leicester: InterVarsity, 1992.
Ellis, E. E. *The Gospel of Luke: New Century Bible* London: Oliphants, 1996.
———. "Present and Future Eschatology in Luke." *New Testament Studies* 12 (1965–66) 27–41.
Ellul, Jacques. *Propaganda: The Formation of Men's Attitudes*. New York: Random House, 1965.
Ernst, J. *Das Evangelium nach Lukas, übersetzt und erkalrt*. Regensburg: Pustet, 1977.
Esler, P. E. *Community and Gospel in Luke-Acts: The Social and Political Motivations of Lucan Theology*. Cambridge: Cambridge University Press, 1987.
Evans, Christopher F. "Uncomfortable Words—V." *Expository Times* 81 (1969–70) 228–31.
Feuillet, A. "La parabole du mauvais riche et du pauvre Lazare (Lc 16, 19–31) antithèse de la parabole de l'intendant astucieux (Lc 16:1–9)." *La nouvelle revue théologique* 101 (1979) 212–23.
Fiddes, Paul S. *The Promised End: Eschatology in Theology and Literature*. Challenges in Contemporary Theology. Oxford: Blackwell, 2000.
Fish, Stanley. *Doing What Comes Naturally: Change, Rhetoric, and the Practice of Theory in Literary and Legal Studies*. Oxford: Clarendon, 1989.

———. *Is There a Text in This Class?: The Authority of Interpretive Communities*. Cambridge, MA; Harvard University Press, 1980.

———. *There's No Such Thing as Free Speech: And It's a Good Thing Too*. Oxford: Oxford University Press, 1994.

———. *The Trouble with Principle*. London: Harvard University Press, 1999.

Fitzmyer, Joseph A. "Divorce among First-Century Palestinian Jews." *Eretz-Israel* 14 (1978) 106–10.

———. *The Gospel According to Luke (X–XXIV)*. New York: Doubleday, 1985.

Flender, Helmut. *St. Luke: Theologian of Redemptive History*. Translated by R. H. and I. Fuller. London: SPCK, 1967.

Fowl, Stephen E. *Engaging Scripture: A Model for Theological Interpretation*. Blackwell Readings in Modern Theology. Oxford: Blackwell, 1998.

Fowl, Stephen E., and L. Gregory Jones. *Reading in Communion: Scripture and Ethics in Christian Life*. Grand Rapids: Eerdmans, 1991.

Francis, F. O. "Eschatology and History in Luke-Acts." *Journal of the American Academy of Religion* 37 (1969) 49–63.

Freedman, Samuel G. "Don't Blame the Jews for this War." *USA Today* (Apr 4–6 2003) 11A.

Gadamer, Hans-Georg. *Truth and Method*. Translated by J. Weinsheimer and D. G. Marshall. London: Sheed & Ward, 1960.

Gaventa, Beverly R. "The Eschatology of Luke-Acts Revisited." *Encounter* 43 (1982) 27–42.

Geldenhuys, Norval. *The Gospel of Luke*. New International Commentary on the New Testament. Grand Rapids: Eerdmans, 1952.

Giblin, Charles Homer. *The Destruction of Jerusalem according to Luke's Gospel: A Historical-Typological Moral*. AnBib 107. Rome: Biblical Institute, 1985.

Gilmour, S.M. "The Gospel According to St. Luke." *Interpreter's Bible* 8:1–434. Nashville: Abingdon, 1952.

Glen, J. S. *The Parables of Conflict in Luke*. Philadelphia: Westminster, 1962.

Glombitza, O. "Der reiche Mann und der arme Lazarus: Luk.xvi 19–31, Zur Frage nach der Botschaft der Textes." *Novum Testamentum* 12 (1970) 166–80.

Godet, Frédéric Louis. *A Commentary on the Gospel according to St. Luke*. 2 vols. Translated by E. W. Schelders. Edinburgh: T. & T. Clark, 1976 [1889].

Gollwitzer, Helmut. *The Rich Christians and Poor Lazarus*. Edinburgh: St. Andrew Press, 1970.

Gooding, David. *According to Luke: A New Exposition of the Third Gospel*. Leicester: InterVarsity, 1987.

Goudoever, J. van. "The Place of Israel in Luke's Gospel." *Novum Testamentum* 8 (1966) 111–23.

Goulder, M. D. *Luke: A New Paradigm*. Journal for the Study of the New Testament Supplement Series 20. Sheffield: JSOT, 1989.

Greenblatt, Stephen. "Toward a Poetics of Culture." In *The New Historicism*, edited by H. A. Veeser, 1–14. London: Routledge, 1989.

Grensted, L. W. "The Use of Enoch in St. Luke, xvi.19–31." *Expository Times* 26 (1914–15) 333–34.

Gressman, Hugo. *Vom reichen Mann und armen Lazarus: Eine literargeschichtliche Studie*. Abhandlungen der Königlich Preussischen Akademie der Wissenschaften,

Philosophisch-Historische Klasse 7. Berlin: Königliche Akademie der Wissenschaften, 1918.

Griffith, F. L. *Stories of the High Priest of Memphis*. Oxford: Clarendon, 1900.

Griswold, Charles L., Jr. *Self Knowledge in Plato's Phaedrus*. University Park: The Pennsylvania State University Press, 1996.

Grobel, K. ". . . Whose Name was Neves." *New Testament Studies* (1963-64) 10.

Grundemann, W. *Das Evangelium nach Lukas*. 2nd Ed. THKNT 3. East Berlin: Evangelische Verlaganstalt, 1961.

Hafer, R. A. "Dives and Poor Lazarus in the Light of Today." *Lutheran Quarterly* 53 (1923) 476-81.

Hall, Edward T. *The Silent Language*. Garden City, NY: Anchor, 1973.

Hamilton, Paul. *Historicism*. New Critical Idiom. London: Routledge, 1996.

Hamm, D. "Sight to the Blind: Vision as Metaphor in Luke." *Biblica* 67 (1986) 457-77.

Hanson, R. P. C. "A Note on Luke xvi.14-31." *Expository Times* 55 (1943-44) 221-22.

Harrington, Wilfred J. *The Gospel According to St. Luke: A Commentary*. Westminster, MD: Newman, 1967.

Hart, David Bentley. *The Beauty of the Infinite: The Aesthetics of Christian Truth*. Grand Rapids: Eerdmans, 2003.

Hauck, Friedrich. *Das Evangelium des Lukas*. Leipzig: Deichertsche, 1934.

Haupt, P. "Abraham's Bosom." *American Journal of Philology* 42 (1921) 162-67.

Hauerwas, Stanley. "The Politics of Charity." *Interpretation* 31 (1977) 251-62.

———. *Unleashing The Scripture: Freeing the Bible from Captivity to America*. Nashville: Abingdon, 1993.

Heidegger, Martin. *Being and Time: A Translation of Sein und Zeit*. Translated by Joan Stambaugh. Albany: State University of New York Press, 1996 [1927].

———. "On the Essence of Truth." In *Basic Writings: From Being and Time (1927) to The Task of Thinking (1964)*, edited by David Farrell Krell, 111-137. Translated by David F. Krell. London: Routledge, 1978 [1930].

———. *On The Way to Language*. Translated by Peter D. Hertz, 1971. New York: Harper & Row, 1959.

———. "Only God Can Save Us: *Der Spiegel*'s Interview with Martin Heidegger." Translated by Maria P. Alter and John D. Caputo. *Philosophy Today* XX 4/4 (1976) 267-85.

———. "The Origin of The Work of Art." In *Basic Writings: From Being and Time (1927) to The Task of Thinking (1964)*, edited by David Farrell Krell, 139-211. Translated by David F. Krell. London: Routledge, 1978 [1964].

———. "Phenomenology and Theology." In *Pathmarks*, 39-62. Cambridge: Cambridge University Press, 1998 [1927].

———. "Plato's Doctrine of Truth." In *Pathmarks*, 155-81. Cambridge: Cambridge University Press, 1998 [1931/2, 1940].

———. "The Question Concerning Technology" In *Basic Writings: From Being and Time (1927) to The Task of Thinking (1964)*, edited by David Farrell Krell, 307-341. Translated by David F. Krell. London: Routledge, 1978 [1953].

Henderson, I. *Myth in the New Testament*. London: SCM, 1952.

Hengel, Martin. *Between Jesus and Paul: Studies in the Earliest History of Christianity*. Translated by J. Bowden. London: SCM, 1983.

Hepburn, R. W. "Demythologising and the Problem of Validity." In *New Essays in Philosophical Theology*, edited by A. Flew and A. Macintyre. London: SCM, 1955.

Heschel, Abraham Joshua. *The Sabbath: Its Meaning for Modern Man*. New York: Farrar, Straus, and Giroux, 1951.
Hintzen, Johannes. *Verkundigung und Wahrnehmung: Uber das Verhaltnis von Evangelium und der Leser am Beispiel Luk 16, 19-31 im Rahmen des lukanischen Dopplewerkes*. Athenäums Monografien, Theologie 81. Frankfurt: Hain, 1991.
Hitler, Adolf. *Hitler's Table Talk, 1941-1944: Hitler's Conversations recorded by Martin Bormann*. Translated by H. Trevor-Roper. Oxford: Oxford University Press, 1988.
———. *Mein Kampf*. Translated by Ralph Manheim. New York: Hutchinson, 1969.
Hock, R. F. "Lazarus and Dives." In *The Anchor Bible Dictionary*, 4:266-67. New York: Doubleday 1992.
Hoehner, Harold. *Herod Antipas*. Cambridge University Press, 1972.
———. "The Herodian Dynasty." In *Dictionary of Jesus and the Gospels*, 317-26. Leicester, InterVarsity, 1992.
Houlden, J. L. "The Purpose of Luke." *Journal for Study of the New Testament* 21 (1984) 53-65.
Huie, W. P. "The Poverty of Abundance: From Text to Sermon on Luke 16:19-31." *Interpretation* 22 (1968) 403-20.
Hunter, A. M. "The Interpreter and the Parables." *Interpretation* 14 (1960) 77-81.
Ingraffia, B. D., and T. E. Pickett. "Reviving the Power of Biblical Language: The Bible, Literature and Literary Language." In *After Pentecost*, 241-61. Carlisle: Paternoster, 2001.
Iser, W. *The Act of Reading: A Theory of Aesthetic Response*. Baltimore: John Hopkins University Press, 1980.
Jasper, David. *Rhetoric, Power and Community: An Exercise in Reserve*. Studies in Literature and Religion. London: Macmillan, 1993.
Jeanrond, Werner G. *Theological Hermeneutics: Development and Significance*. Studies in Literature and Religion. London: Macmillan, 1991.
Jensen, H. J. L. "Diesseits und Jenseits des Raumes eines Textes: Textsemiotische Bemerkungen zur Erzahlung 'Vom reichen Mann und armen Lazarus' (Luke 16, 19-31)." *Linguistica Biblica* (1980) 39-60.
Jenson, Robert W., and Carl E. Braaten. *Reclaiming the Bible for the Church*. Edinburgh: T. & T. Clark, 1996.
Jeremias, Joachim. *The Parables of Jesus*. Translated by Samuel Henry Hooke. London: SCM, 1963 [1947].
———. *Jerusalem in the Time of Jesus: An Investigation into Economic and Social Conditions during the New Testament Period*. Philadelphia: Fortress, 1969.
Jervell, Jacob. *Luke and the People of God: A New Look at Luke-Acts*. Minneapolis: Augsburg, 1972.
Johnson, Luke Timothy. *The Gospel of Luke*. Sacra Pagina 3. Collegeville, MN: Liturgical, 1991.
———. *The Literary Function of Possessions in Luke-Acts*. SBLDS 39. Missoula, MT: Scholars, 1977.
Johnson, Roger A. *The Origins of Demythologizing: Philosophy and Historiography in the Theology of Rudolf Bultmann*. Studies in History of Religion 28. Leiden: Brill, 1974.
Jones, Geraint Vaughan. *The Art and Truth of the Parables: A Study in Their Literary Form and Modern Interpretation*. London: SPCK, 1964.
Jouon, P. "Notes philologiques sur les Evangiles: Luc 16, 30." *Recherches de science religieuse* (1928) 354.

Jülicher, Adolf. *Die Gleichnisreden Jesu*. 2 vols. Tubingen: Mohr, 1899.
Just, Arthur A., editor. *Luke*. Ancient Christian Commentary on Scripture. New Testament 3. Downers Grove, IL: InterVarsity, 2004.
Kähler Martin. *The So-Called Historical Jesus and the Historic, Biblical Christ*. Seminar Editions. Translated by Carl E. Braaten. Philadelphia: Fortress, 1964.
Kealy, Sean P. *The Gospel of Luke*. Denville, NJ: Dimension, 1979.
Kearney, Richard, editor. *Paul Ricoeur: The Hermeneutics of Action*. Philosophy & Social Criticism. London: Sage, 1996.
Kepel, G. *The War for Muslim Minds: Islam and the West*. Harvard: Harvard University Press, 2004.
Kierkegaard, Søren. *Concluding Unscientific Postscript*. Translated by D. F. Swenson and W. Lowrie. Princeton: University Press, 1968 [1846].
———. *Fear and Trembling*. London: Penguin, 1985 [1843].
Klostermann, E. *Das Lukasevangelium*. HNT 5. Tubingen: Mohr Siebeck, 1975 [1929].
Knight, Jonathan. *Luke's Gospel*. London: Routledge, 1998.
Kolb, R., and T. J. Wengert, editors. *The Book of Concord: The Confessions of the Evangelical Lutheran Church*. Minneapolis: Fortress, 2000.
Kreitzer, L. "Luke 16:19–31 and 1 Enoch 22." *The Expository Times* 103 (1992) 139–42.
Kümmel, Werner G. *Theology of the New Testament: According to its Major Witness, Jesus-Paul-John*. London: SCM, 1974.
Kunstlinger, D. "Im Schosse Abrahams." *Orientalische Literaturzeitung* 36 (1933) 408.
Kurz, W.S. "Narrative Approaches to Luke-Acts" *Biblica* 68 (1987) 195–220.
Kvalbein, H. "Jesus and the Poor: Two Texts and a Tentative Conclusion (16, 19–31) *Themelios* 12, (1986–87) 80–87.
Lagrange, Marie-Joseph. *Evangile selon Saint Luc*. Etudes bibliques. Paris: Gabalda, 1921.
Lanham, Richard A. *The Motives of Eloquence: Literary Rhetoric in the Renaissance*. New Haven, CT: , 1976.
Leaney, Alfred Robert Clare. *A Commentary on the Gospel according to St Luke*. Black's New Testament Commentaries. London: Adam & Charles Black, 1958.
Lefort, L. T. "Le nom du mauvais riche (Luc 16.19) et la tradition copte." *Zeitschrift fur die neutestamentliche Wissenschaft* 37 (1938) 65–72.
Lemair, A. "Le Sabbat a l'Epoque Royale Israelite." *Revue Biblique* 80 (1973) 161–85.
Lenski, R. C. H. *The Interpretation of St. Mark's and St. Luke's Gospel*. Columbus, OH: Lutheran Books Concern, 1934.
Lessing, G. E. *Lessing's Theological Writings*. Edited by Henry Chadwick. London: Black. 1956.
Lincoln, Andrew T. *Ephesians*. Word Biblical Commentary 42. Dallas, TX: Word, 1990
Linnemann, Eta. *Jesus of the Parables: Introduction and Exposition*. Translated by John Sturdy. New York: Harper & Row, 1966.
Lorenzen, T. "A Biblical Meditation on Luke 16:19–31: From the Text toward a Sermon." *Expository Times* 87 (1974–75) 44–45.
Lowe, Walter. "Barth as Critic of Dualism: Re-Reading the *Romerbrief*." *Scottish Journal of Theology* 41 (1988) 377–95.
Luce, H. K. *The Gospel According to St. Luke*. Cambridge: Cambridge University Press, 1949.
Luther, Martin *The Freedom of a Christian*. In *Three Treatises*, 265–316. Rev. Ed. Philadelphia: Fortress, 1970 [1520].

———. "Small Catechism." In *The Book of Concord: The Confessions of the Evangelical Lutheran Church*, edited by R. Kolb and T. J. Wengert, 366. Minneapolis: Fortress, 2000.

———. "Treatise on Good Works." In *Luther's Works*, translated by W. A. Lambert, edited by James Atkinson, 44:15–114. Philadelphia : Fortress, 1966.

Macquarrie, John. *Heidegger and Christianity*. The Hensley Henson Lectures. London: SCM, 1994.

———. *The Scope of Demythologizing: Bultmann and His Critics*. Library of Philosophy and Theology. London: SCM, 1960.

Maddox, Robert L. *The Purpose of Luke-Acts*. Studies of the New Testament and Its World. Edinburgh: T. & T. Clark, 1982.

Manson, Thomas Walter. *The Sayings of Jesus: As Recorded in the Gospels according to St Matthew and St Luke*. London: SCM, 1957.

Manson, William. *The Gospel of Luke*. Moffatt New Testament Commentary. London: Hodder and Stoughton, 1930.

Marshall, I. Howard. *The Gospel Of Luke: A Commentary on the Greek Text*. New International Greek Testament Commentary. Exeter: Paternoster, 1978.

———. *Luke: Historian & Theologian*. Exeter: Paternoster, 1988.

———. "Luke and His Gospel." In *Das Evangelium und die Evangelien* (1983) 289–308.

Menoud, Phillipe Henri. "Jesus et ses temoins: Remaques sur l'unite de l'oevre de Luc." *Eglise et Theologie* 23 (1960) 7–20.

———. *Jesus Christ and the Faith: A Collection of Studies*. Translated by E. M. Paul. Pittsburgh Theological Monograph Series 18. Pittsburgh: Pickwick, 1978.

———. *Jesus-Christ et la foi: Recherches neotestamentaires*. Paris: Delachaux et Niestle, 1975.

———. "Le sens du verbe biazetai dans Lc 16,16." In *Melanges Bibliques*, edited by A. Descamps and A. de Halleux, 207–12. Gembloux: Duculot, 1970.

Mieses, M. "Im Schosse Abrahams." *Orientalische Literaturzeitung* 34, (1931) 1018–21.

Moltmann, Jürgen. *The Coming Of God: Christian Eschatology*. Translated by Margaret Kohl. London: SCM, 1996.

———. *The Future of Creation. Collected Essays*. Translated by Margaret Kohl. London: SCM, 1979.

———. *The Way of Jesus Christ: Christology in Messianic Dimensions*. Translated by Margaret Kohl. London: SCM, 1992.

Moore, Stephen D. *Mark and Luke in Poststructuralist Perspectives: Jesus Begins to Write*. New Haven, CT: Yale University Press 1992.

———. *Poststructuralism and the New Testament: Derrida and Foucault at the Foot of the Cross*. Minneapolis: Fortress, 1994.

Moore, W. E. "*Biazo, Arpazo* and Cognates in Josephus." *New Testament Studies* 21 (1974–75) 519–43.

Morgan Robert, and John Barton. *Biblical Interpretation*. Oxford Bible Series. Oxford: Oxford University Press, 1988.

Morris, Leon. *Luke*. Tyndale New Testament Commentary. Leicester: InterVarsity, 1992.

Müller, Paul-Gerhard. *Lukas Evangelium*. Stuttgarter kleiner Kommentar, Neues Testament 3. Stuttgart: Katholisches Bibelwerk, 1984.

Navone, John J. *Themes of St. Luke*. Rome: Gregorian University, 1971.

Newman, Carey C. *Jesus and the Restoration of Israel: A Critical Assessment of N. T. Wright's Jesus and the Victory of God*. Carlisle: Paternoster, 1999.

Neyrey, Jerome H. *The Social World of Luke-Acts: Models for Interpretation*. Peabody, MA: Hendrickson, 1991.
Nietzsche, Friedrich Wilhelm. *The Will to Power*. Translated by Walter Kauffmann and R. J. Holingdale. New York: Vintage, 1967.
Noble, P. R. "Hermeneutics and Postmodernism: Can We Have a Radical Reader-Response Theory? Part 1." *Journal of Religious Studies* 30 (1994) 419–36.
———. "Hermeneutics and Postmodernism: Can We Have a Radical Reader-Response Theory? Part 2." *Journal of Religious Studies* 31 (1995) 1–22.
Nolland, John. *Luke*. Word Biblical Commentary 35A–C. Waco, TX: Word, 1993.
———. "Luke's Use of charis." *New Testament Studies* 32 (1986) 614–20.
North, Brownlow. *The Rich Man and Lazarus: A Practical Exposition of Luke xvi, 19–31*. London: Banner of Truth Trust, 1960.
O'Donovan, Oliver. *The Desire of the Nations: Rediscovering the Roots of Political Theology*. Cambridge: Cambridge University Press, 1996.
———. *Resurrection and Moral Order: An Outline for Evangelical Ethics*. Leicester: InterVarsity, 1986.
Omanson, R. "Lazarus and Simon." *Biblical Theology* 40 (1989) 416–19.
Osborne, G. R. "Luke: Theologian of Social Concern." *Trinity Journal* 7 (1978) 135–48.
Osei-Bonsu, J. "The Intermediate State in Luke-Acts." *Irish Biblical Studies* 9 (1987) 115–30.
Osty, Emile. *La Sainte Bible traduite en francais sous la direction de l'Ecole Biblique de Jerusalem. L'evangile selon Saint Luc. Traduction, introduction et notes*. Paris: Cerf, 1961.
Pannenberg, Wolfhart. *Basic Questions in Theology: Collected Essays*. Vol. 1. London: SCM, 1970.
Patoc[insert hacek over c]ka, Jan. *Heretical Essays on the Philosophy of History*. Translated by Erazim Kohák. Edited by James Dodd. Chicago: Open Court, 1995.
Perrin, Norman. *Jesus and the Language of the Kingdom: Symbol and Metaphor in New Testament Interpretation*. London: SCM, 1976.
Pickstock, Catherine. *After Writing: On the Liturgical Consummation of Philosophy*. Challenges in Contemporary Theology. Oxford: Blackwell, 1998.
Plato. "Phaedrus." In *Plato* 1:405–679. Translated by H. N. Fowler. Cambridge: Harvard University Press, 1914.
———. *Republic*. 2 vols, Translated by P.Shorley. Cambridge: Harvard University Press, 1930.
———. "Timaeus." In *Plato* 7:1–253. Translated by R. G. Bury. Cambridge: Harvard University Press, 1929.
Plummer, Alfred. *A Critical and Exegetical Commentary on the Gospel according to S. Luke*. ICC. New York: Scribner, 1922.
Powel, W. "Parable of Dives and Lazarus." *Expository Times* 66 (1954–55) 350–51.
Rengstorf, K. H. *Das Evangelium nach Lukas*. 9th ed. NTD 3. Gottingen: Vandenhoeck & Ruprecht, 1962.
Ricoeur, Paul. "Biblical Hermeneutics." *Semeia* 4 (1975) 29–128.
———. *Essays on Biblical Interpretation*. Edited by Lewis S. Mudge. Philadelphia: Fortress, 1980.
Rienecker, Fritz. *Das Evangelium des Lukas*. Wuppertaler Studienbibel. 4th Edition. Wuppertal: Brockhaus, 1972.
Rimmer, N. "Parable of Dives and Lazarus." *Expository Times* 66 (1954–55) 215–216.

Robertson, Edwin Hanton. *The Shame and the Sacrifice: The Life and Preaching of Dietrich Bonhoeffer*. London: Hodder and Stoughton, 1987.
Robinson, J. M. *A New Quest of the Historical Jesus*. London: SCM, 1963.
Rorty, Richard. *Contingency, Irony and Solidarity*. Cambridge: Cambridge University Press, 1989.
Rumscheidt, M. "The Formation of Bonhoeffer's Theology." In *The Cambridge Companion to Dietrich Bonhoeffer*, edited by J. W. de Gruchy, 50–70. Cambridge: Cambridge University Press, 1999.
Russel, W. "The Anointing with the Spirit in Luke-Acts." *Trinity Journal* 7 (1986) 47–63.
Sabourin, Léopold. *L'évangile de Luc: Introduction et commentaire*. Rome: Gregorian University, 1985.
Saldarini, Anthony J. "Pharisees." In *The Anchor Bible Dictionary*, 5:289–303. London: Doubleday, 1992.
———. *Pharisees, Scribes and Sadducees in Palestinian Society: A Sociological Approach*. Grand Rapids: Eerdmans, 2001 [1988].
Sanders, E. P. *The Historical Figure of Jesus*. London: Penguin, 1993.
———. *Jesus and Judaism*. London: SCM, 1985.
———. *Paul and Palestinian Judaism: A Comparison of Patterns of Religion*. London: SCM, 1977.
Sanders, Jack. *The Jews in Luke-Acts*. Philadelphia: Fortress, 1987.
Safranski, Rüdiger. *Martin Heidegger: Between Good and Evil*. Translated by Ewald Osers. Cambridge, MA: Harvard University Press, 1999.
Sawicki, Marianne. *Seeing the Lord: Resurrection and Early Christian Practices*. Minneapolis: Fortress, 1994.
Saye, Scott C. "The Wild and Crooked Tree: Barth, Fish and Interpretive Communities." *Modern Theology* 12 (1996) 435–58.
Schillebeeckx, Edward. *Jesus: An Experiment in Christology*. New York: Crossroad, 1981.
Schleiermacher, Friedrich. *Hermeneutics and Criticism: And Other Writings*. Translated and edited by Andrew Bowie. Cambridge Texts in the History of Philosophy. Cambridge: Cambridge University Press, 1998.
Schmid, Josef. *Das Evangelium nach Lukas*. 4th Edition. RNT 3. Regensburg: Pustet, 1960.
Schmithals, Walter. *Das Evangelium nach Lukas*. Zurcher Bibelkommentar NT 3.1. Zurich: Theologischer, 1980.
———. *An Introduction to the Theology of Rudolf Bultmann*. London: SCM, 1968.
Schneider, Gerhard. *Das Evangelium nach Lukas*. 2 vols. Oekumenischer Taschenbuchkommentar zum Neuen Testament 3 Gütersloh: Mohn, 1977.
Scholes, R. *Textual Power: Literary Theory and the Teaching of English*. New Haven, CT: Yale University Press, 1985.
Schurhammer, G. "Eine Parabel Christi in Gotzentempel." *KM* 49 (1920–21) 134–38.
Schürmann, Heinz. *Das Lukasevangelium: Erster Teil: Kommentar zu Kap. 1,1–9, 50*. Herders theologischer Kommentar zum Nuen Testament 3/1. Freiburg: Herder, 1969.
Schweitzer, Albert. *On The Edge of the Primeval Forest*. London: Adam and Charles Black, 1955.
Schweizer, Edward. *The Good News According to Luke*. Translated y David E. Green. London: SPCK, 1984.

Scott, Bernard Brandon. *Hear Then the Parable: A Commentary on the Parables of Jesus.* Minneapolis: Fortress, 1989.
Seccombe, D. P. *Possessions and the Poor in Luke-Acts.* SNTU B/6. Linz: Fuchs, 1982.
Smail, Thomas Allan. *The Giving Gift: The Holy Spirit in Person.* London: Hodder and Stoughton, 1988.
Smith, R. A. "Sign of Jonah.'" In *Dictionary of Jesus and the Gospels*, edited by Joel B. Green, Scot McKnight, and I. H. Marshall, 754–56. Leicester: InterVarsity, 1992.
Solzhenitsyn, Aleksandr. *August 1914.* New York: Farrar, Strauss and Giroux, 1971.
Standen, A. O. "The Parable of Dives and Lazarus, and Enoch 22." *Expository Times* 33 (1921–22) 523.
Stanton, Graham N. *The Gospels and Jesus.* The Oxford Bible Series. Oxford: Oxford University Press, 1989.
Steiner, George. *Real Presences.* Chicago: Chicago University Press, 1989.
Stock, Brian. *Augustine the Reader: Meditation, Self-Knowledge, and the Ethics of Interpretation.* London: Belknap, 1996.
Strauss, Leo. *Natural Right and History.* Charles R. Walgren Foundation Lectures. Chicago: University of Chicago Press, 1953.
Strauss, Mark L. *The Davidic Messiah in Luke-Acts: The Promise and its Fulfilment in Lukan Christology.* Sheffield: Sheffield Academic, 1995.
Stronstad, Roger. *The Charismatic Theology of St Luke.* Peabody, MA: Hendrickson, 1984.
Talbert, Charles H. *Reading Luke: A Literary and Theological Commentary on the Third Gospel.* Reading the New Testament Series. New York: Crossroad, 1982.
Tanghe, V. "Abraham, son fils et son envoye (Luc 16,19–31)." *Revue Biblique* 91 (1984) 557–77.
Taylor, John V. *The Go-Between God: The Holy Spirit and the Christian Mission.* London: SCM, 1973.
Theissen, Gerd, and Annette Merz. *The Historical Jesus: A Comprehensive Guide.* Translated by J. Bowden. London: SCM, 1997.
Thiering, B. E. "Are the 'Violent Men' False Teachers?" *Novum Testamentum* (1979) 293–97.
Thiselton, Anthony. *New Horizons in Hermeneutics: The Theory and Practice of Transforming Biblical Reading.* London: Harper Collins, 1992.
———. *The Two Horizons: New Testament Hermeneutics and Philosophical Description.* Grand Rapids: Eerdmans, 1980.
Thompson, George Harry Packwood. *The Gospel According to Luke in the Revised Standard Version.* Oxford: Clarendon, 1972.
Tiede, David Lenz. *Prophecy and History in Luke-Acts.* Philadelphia: Fortress, 1980.
Tinsley, E. J. *The Gospel According to Luke.* CBC. Cambridge: Cambridge University Press, 1965.
Tomson, P. J. "Jesus and his Judaism." In *The Cambridge Companion to Jesus*, edited by Markus Bockmuehl, 25–39. Cambridge: Cambridge University Press, 2001.
Torrance, Alan J. *Persons in Communion: An Essay on Trinitarian Description and Human Participation with special reference to Volume One of Karl Barth's Church Dogmatics.* Edinburgh: T. & T. Clark, 1996.
Torrance, Thomas F. *Karl Barth: An Introduction to His Early Theology, 1910–1931.* London: SCM, 1962.
———. *Space, Time and Resurrection.* Edinburgh: T. & T. Clark, 1976.

Travis, S. "Eschatology." In *New Dictionary of Theology*, edited by S. B. Ferguson and D. F. Wright, 228-31. Leicester: InterVarsity, 1988.

Trudinger, P. "A 'Lazarus Motif' in Primitive Christian Preaching." *Andover Newton Quarterly* 7 (1966) 29-32.

Tsevat, Matitiahu. "The Basic Meaning of the Biblical Sabbath." *Zeitschrift für die alttestamentliche Wissenschaft* 84 (1972) 447-59.

Vanhoozer, Kevin J. *Is There a Meaning in This Text?: The Bible, the Reader, and the Morality of Literary Knowledge*. Leicester: Apollos, 1998.

Versenyi, Lazlo. *Heidegger, Being, and Truth*. New Haven, CT: Yale University Press, 1966.

Via, Daniel O. *The Parables: Their Literary and Existential Dimension*. Philadelphia: Fortress, 1967.

Vogels, W. "Having or Longing: A Semiotic Analysis of Luke 16:19-31." *Eglise et Theologie* 20 (1989) 27-46.

Wannenwetsch, Bernd. *Gottesdienst als Lebensform: Ethik fur Christenburger*. Berlin: Kohlhammer, 1997.

———. "Communication as Transformation: Worship and the Media." In *Media Ethics*. Studies in Christian Ethics 13(1), 93-106. Edinburgh: T. & T. Clark, 2000.

———. "'Members of One Another': *Charis*, Ministry and Representation: A Politico-Ecclesial Reading of Romans 12." In *A Royal Priesthood? The Use of the Bible Ethically and Politically: A Dialogue with Oliver O'Donovan*, edited by Craig G. Bartholomew, et al, 196-220. Scripture and Hermeneutics Series 3. Carlisle: Paternoster, 2000.

Ward, Graham. *Barth, Derrida and the Language of Theology*. Cambridge: Cambridge University Press, 1995.

———. "Barth, Modernity and Postmodernity." In *The Cambridge Companion to Karl Barth*, edited by John Webster, 274-95. Cambridge: Cambridge University Press, 2000.

———. *Theology and Contemporary Critical Theory*. Studies in Literature and Religion. London: Macmillan, 1996.

Watson, Francis. *Text, Church and World: Biblical Interpretation in Theological Perspective*. Edinburgh: T. & T. Clark, 1994.

———. *Text and Truth: Redefining Biblical Theology*. Edinburgh: T. & T. Clark, 1997.

Webb, Stephen H. *Re-figuring Theology: The Rhetoric of Karl Barth*. SUNY Series in Rhetoric and Theology. Albany: State University of New York Press, 1991.

Webster, John. "Hermeneutics in Modern Theology: Some Doctrinal Reflections." *Scottish Journal of Theology* (1998) 307-40.

———. *Word and Church: Essays in Christian Dogmatics*. Edinburgh: T. & T. Clark, 2001.

Weinert, F. D. "The Meaning of the Temple in Luke-Acts." *Biblical Theological Bulletin* 11 (1981) 85-89.

Wellhausen, J. *Das Evangelium Lucae*. Berlin: George Reimer, 1904.

Wenham, Gordon J. *Genesis 1-15*. Word Biblical Commentary 1. Waco, TX: Word, 1987.

Wehrli, E. S. "Luke 16:19-31." *Interpretation* 31 (1977) 276-80.

Westerholm, S. "Sabbath." In *Dictionary of Jesus and the Gospels*, 716-19. Leicester: InterVarsity 1992.

Witherington III, Ben. "Jesus and the Baptist—Two of a Kind?" In *Society for Biblical Literature 1988 Seminar Papers*, edited by D. J. Lull, 225-44. Alanta: Scholars, 1988.

———. *The Jesus Quest: The Third Search for the Jew of Nazareth*. Downers Grove, IL: InterVarsity, 1995.

Wittgenstein, Ludwig. *On Certainty*. Oxford: Blackwell, 1969.

Wright, N. T. *The Climax of the Covenant: Christ and the Law in Pauline Theology*. London: SPCK, 1991.

———. *Jesus and the Victory of God*. London: SPCK, 1996.

———. *The New Testament and the People of God*. London: SPCK, 1992.

———. *The Resurrection of the Son of God*. London: SPCK, 2003.

Wright, S. I. *The Voice of Jesus: Studies in the Interpretation of Six Gospel Parables*. Carlisle: Paternoster, 2000.

Yoder, John Howard. *The Politics of Jesus: Vicit Agnus Noster*. Grand Rapids: Eerdmans, 1972.

Zahn, T. von. *Das Evangelium des Lukas ausgelegt*. 4th ed. Leipzig: Deichert, 1930.

Index of Scripture References

GENESIS

2:3	214
3:4	106
4	204
6:5–6	54
11:6	106
12:2	194
12:7	194
13:16	194
15	168, 194, 195, 196, 199, 204, 226
15:2	198
15:4	206
32:22–32	138, 235

EXODUS

4:22	119

DEUTERONOMY

14:1	119
30:12–14	138

PSALMS

2	132, 191
24:9–10	108
72	132
89	132
96:10	115

PROVERBS

20:12	21
31:22	166

ISAIAH

6:9	171
11:1	132
11:4	132
11:10	132
42:1	132
42:6	132
43:6	119
49:1–6	132
55:10–11	5, 119
61:1–2	167

JEREMIAH

7:5–8	159
7:9–11	155
31:9	119

DANIEL

7	132

HOSEA

1:10	119
11:1	119

JOEL

2:28–32	153

MATTHEW

2:4–6	163
6:4	90
6:24–34	93
7:24–27	93
11:11–13	163
11:12–13	162
11:15	171
12:43–45	5
13:57	190
14:1–2	171
14:1	167
14:19	167
16:19	54
18:19–20	154
18:20	102
19:24	203
21:33–46	94
22:11–14	224
23:2–3	92
25:31–46	95, 104, 174, 181
25:40	174
26:11	65
27:11	137
27:46	153
28:20	211

MARK

6:3	189
6:4	190
6:14–16	171
10:9	99
10:25	203
15:2	137

LUKE

1:46–55	170, 223
1:50	176
1:55	176
2:34–35	162
3:8	168, 198, 204
4:18–19	167
4:22	189
4:24	162, 190
5:21	140
6:9	102
6:17–26	225
6:20–26	102, 203, 226
6:23	162
7:16	162
7:18–23	95
7:39	162
8:10	171
8:25	140
9:7–9	171
9:9	140, 171
9:23	102
9:24	102
9:31	203
10:25–37	138, 224
11:29	171, 176
11:32	66
11:47–51	162
11:52	102
13:28–30	196
13:30	102
13:31–33	163
13:33–34	162
14:7–11	224
14:15–24	223
15:1	128
15:2	169

Index of Scripture References

15:11–32	224
15:31	225
16:16–31	161–77
16:17	199
16:18	199
16:16–18	161–65, 168, 224
16:16	171, 172, 173, 175, 202
16:19	169
16:19–26	42, 100, 101, 115
16:18	202
16:21	198
16:24	198
16:25	170
16:27–28	82, 198
16:19–31	1, 19, 20, 27, 41, 50, 65, 77, 95, 100, 126, 161–77, 194–207, 221–29
16:31	41, 44, 82, 129, 171
17	206
17:1–4, 7–10	204
17:2	102
17:19	205
18:9	66
18:11	173
18:9–14	224
18:25	203
18:35–43	102
19:11–27	165
19:12–28	226
19:14	73, 122
19:15	122
20:9–19	162
23:12	191
23:21	191
23:38	224
23:45	153
24:5	125
24:13–35	21, 120, 172, 206
24:19	162
24:21	125
24:44–47	167

JOHN

1:3	115
2:19	145
4:44	190
14:17	151
16:13	151
18:14	137

ACTS

2:17–21	153
2:36	5, 131
4:25–26	120, 191
5:36–37	66
13:43	66
14:18–20	139
14:19	66
17:4	66
18:4	66

ROMANS

4:3	195
6:23	118
8:11	152
9–11	198
10:5	139
10:6–13	139
12–13	188–94
12:1	202
12:2	7, 187
12:5	7
12:6	6
14:10	45

1 CORINTHIANS

15:14	102
15:54	209

2 CORINTHIANS

3:17	152
3:18	236

GALATIANS

3:6	195
3:6–8	196
3:10	199
5:7–9	199

EPHESIANS

2:12	117
4:14	5
4:15	5

COLOSSIANS

2:15	191

HEBREWS

4	214
6:19–20	153
10:19–20	153
13:1–2	60

JAMES

2:23,26	195

REVELATION

20:11–15	45

Index of Names

Alter, Maria P, 17, 25
Andrews, Isolde, 101, 193
Aquinas, Thomas, 118, 214
Augustine, 17–18, 23–24, 92, 118, 214–15
Austin, J.L., 124

Bailey, Kenneth, E., 126
Barth, Karl, 24–31, 36, 40–41, 49, 54, 56, 81, 90, 92, 101, 105, 107, 124, 133, 142, 147, 158, 169, 174, 179–83, 193, 212, 216–19, 225, 227
Bartholomew, Craig, 2, 3, 23, 183
Bauckham, Richard, 128, 211–15, 222, 224, 226
Bede, 198
Bethge, Eberhard, 145
Blomberg, Craig, 200
Bock, Darrel L., 198
Bockmuehl, Marcus, 95, 127, 150, 205
Bonhoeffer, Dietrich, 4, 7, 34, 141–49, 153, 169, 172–73, 175, 181
Bornkamm, Gunther, 37
Brandon, S.G.F, 150
Brown, Raymond, 119, 120, 153
Brunner, Emil, 181
Buber, Martin, 5, 37, 90
Bultmann, Rudolf,, 4–8, 26–51, 76, 103, 109–11, 114, 116, 130, 194, 209–13, 218–19, 222, 225, 228, 231–32

Cadbury, Henry J., 165, 197
Caird, G.B., 198
Calvin, John, 214–16
Capron, F.H., 202
Caputo, John D., 17, 25, 96–99, 103–5, 110, 134, 143, 150
Castelli, Elizabeth, 66
Cave, C.H., 169
Chesterton, G.K., 117
Childs, Brevard,, 3
Chilton, Bruce, 163, 164, 165
Clarke, Neville, 131
Conzelmann, Hans, 115
Copplestone, Frederick, 60
Craddock, Fred B., 170
Crossan, John D., 42, 95, 135, 172, 173, 222, 224
Cullmann, Oscar, 147

Dalberg, John, E., 66
Danker, F.W., 166
Darr, John A., 165, 166, 172
Day, John, 19
Derrida, Jacques, 4–8, 18, 75–111, 116–17, 123–24, 141, 143–44, 150–51, 172–75, 208, 213, 225, 231–32
Dodd, C.H., 22, 126, 195

Index of Names

Dreyfus, Hubert, 13–14
Dunn, James D.G., 119, 146, 182

Eagleton, Terry, 59, 74
Eichhorn, J.G., 35
Eliot, George, 35
Ellis, E.E., 161
Ellul, Jacques, 59, 62
Evans, Christopher F., 195

Fiddes, Paul, 208, 215
Fish, Stanley, 4, 6–8, 18, 49–76, 94,
    110–11, 116, 123, 178, 182,
    188–90, 193. 201–3, 213, 218,
    220, 225–26, 231–32
Fitzmyer, Jospeh, 161, 165, 166, 198,
    199
Fowl, Stephen, 77, 110, 181, 182
Freedman, Samuel G., 189

Gadamer, H.G., 2, 113, 114, 116
Geldenhuys, Norval, 243
Glombitza, O., 168
Gregory of Nazianzus, 85
Gregory the Great, 198
Greene, Colin,, 3
Gressmann, H., 221–22
Griffith, F.L., 128, 222
Griswold, Charles S., 78, 83

Hamilton, Paul, 23, 111–13, 116–17
Hanson, A., 161
Harnack, Adolf von, 42
Hart, David Bentley, 104
Hauerwas, Stanley, 50, 123
Heideger, Martin, 3–33, 38–40, 43,
    45, 50–51, 54, 59, 65, 68, 69,
    73–76, 81, 84, 86–87, 90, 96, 99,
    109, 110, 139, 151, 160, 172, 176,
    179, 211, 218–20, 225, 228–30,
Hermann, Wilhelm, 29
Heschell, A.J., 213, 218
Hauerwas, Stanley, 50

Hegel, G.W.F., 39, 61, 71, 86, 87, 88,
    90, 98, 111, 112, 113, 142,
Herder, Johan Gottfried, 61, 111, 112
Hitler, Adolf, 56
Hock, R.F., 222
Hoehner, Harold, 163–66, 169, 170
Holderlin, 17–18
Horsley, Richard, 150

Ingraffia, B.D., 156–58

Jeanrond, Werner, 2, 23, 27, 40, 41,
    233
Jeremias, J., 126, 161, 166, 222, 223
Johnson, Luke, T., 66, 200
Johnson, Roger, 26, 27, 29–30, 34, 36
Jones, G.V., 126
Josephus, 164

Kahler, Martin, 35, 40–41
Kant, Immanuel, 35, 111
Kepel, Giles, 59
Kierkegaard, Soren, 27, 32, 35–36,
    39–45, 84, 86–88, 179
Kreitzer, Larry, 195, 200, 204
Kummel, Werner G., 161, 205

Lanham, Richard, 65
Leaney, Anthony, R.C., 161, 162, 170
Lessing, G.E., 36, 42, 102, 125, 128,
    216, 226
Lincoln, Andrew T., 117
Locke, John, 35
Lorenzen, T., 171
Lowth, Robert, 35
Luther, Martin, 27, 31, 34, 46, 156,
    157, 192, 214, 215

Macquarrie, John, 9, 13, 14, 24
Marshall, I. Howard, 140, 198
Marx, Karl, 59, 71
Merz, Annette, 150, 182, 196
Moltmann, Jurgen, 134, 148, 151, 152,
    175, 176, 201, 203, 211, 213, 229

Index of Names   259

Moore, Stephen D., 129
Morris, Leon, 161, 198, 200

Nietzsche, Friedrich, 12, 30, 63–64, 79, 85, 104, 179
Noble, P.R., 55
Noll, Mark, 64

O'Donovan, Oliver, 114, 115, 123, 136, 184, 189–91

Pannenberg, Wolfhart, 112
Patocka, Jan, 84–86
Perrin, Norman, 126, 161
Pickett, T.E., 156
Pickstock, Catherine, 83, 84, 93, 94
Plato, 10, 57, 60–63, 77–85, 92–98, 107, 221

Ranke, Leopold von, 61, 111
Renan, E., 35
Ricoeur, Paul, 4, 32, 86, 208
Riefenstahl, Leni, 37
Rorty, Richard, 56, 63

Schillebeeckx, Edward, 130, 144
Schmithals, Walter, 26, 27, 34
Safranski, Rudiger, 27, 68, 69
Saldarini, Anthony, 154
Sanders, E.P., 126, 127, 130, 180, 182, 190, 195, 196, 205, 214
Sawicki, Marianne, 121, 122, 123, 136
Saye, Scott C., 49–50, 54, 69
Schleiermacher, Friedrich, 137
Scholes, R, 55
Schweitzer, Albert, 1, 23, 235
Schweitzer, E.dward, 195
Scott, B.B., 100
Searle, J.R., 124
Smail, Tom, 151, 181
Solzhenitsyn, Aleksandr, 72
Stock, Brian, 23

Strauss, David F., 35, 140
Strauss, Leo, 59–63, 66–67. 70–73, 112–13

Tanghe, V., 195, 226, 227
Taylor, John V., 21, 25, 181
Tertullian, 221
Theissen, Gerd, 150, 182, 196
Thiselton, Anthony, 23–24, 27–28, 31–33, 35, 39, 52–53, 58, 67, 77, 110, 112, 115–17, 124, 139, 233
Thompson, G.T., 198
Tomson, P.J., 119
Tonnies, Ferdinand, 68
Torrance, J.B., 160
Torrance, Thomas F., 133, 134, 228
Toulmin, S., 218,
Travis, Stephen, 22

Vanhoozer, Kevin,, 3, 18, 52, 58, 77, 103, 117, 122–24, 137, 155–60, 233,
Versenyi, Lazlo, 33
Via, Otto, 126
Vico, Giambattista, 111

Ward, Graham, 56, 81, 90,
Wannenwetsch, Bernd, 7, 24, 156–58, 183–89, 192, 193, 204, 207, 224
Watson, Francis, 46, 179, 180, 181–82, 190, 193–94, 202
Webster, John,, 17, 219, 235
Wenham, Gordon, 195
Witherington, Ben, 126, 150
Wittgenstein, Ludwig, 53, 54, 64, 67, 179
Wright, N.T., 93, 94, 100, 125–32, 135, 150, 163, 195–99, 213–14, 221, 228
Wright, Stephen I., 198

Yoder, John Howard, 180

Index of Subjects

Adam, 106, 138, 175, 216
Afterlife, 221, 224, 226
Agape, 181
Aletheia, 5, 10, 12, 14–16, 96, 151
Amente, 222
Antipas, 161, 163–72, 176, 223. 224
Apperception, 19–22
Aretas, 164
Art, 9, 11, 62, 112, 126, 220
Associations, 27, 68–70, 74, 181
Authority, 7, 21, 57–60, 66. 68. 110, 142, 155, 162, 171, 183–93, 223, 230

Baal, 155
Babylon, 127
Baptism, 119, 184, 193, 198
Biblical Theology, 3
Body of Christ, 6, 50, 180–83, 187, 192–94, 207, 211, 235

Charis, 8, 178–20
Chasm, 24, 36, 41, 43, 100, 114–16, 132, 223
Chora, 95, 77, 95–101
Christology, 4, 7, 19–21, 108, 119, 140–78, 179
Communication, 3, 18–25, 54, 57, 79, 112, 156–60

Community, 7, 21, 24–25, 40, 44, 49–74, 82, 88, 94, 100, 110, 124–29, 145–47, 178–207, 221, 225–26
Consequences, 51, 53, 56–58, 64, 72, 110
Contingency, 51, 55, 179
Conventionalism, 60–61
Covenant, 88, 89, 117, 119, 127, 130, 132, 136, 139, 179–80, 194–206, 216, 217, 226
Crucifixion, 21, 105, 119–21, 130, 143, 150, 162–63, 174, 191, 234

Deconstruction, 7–9, 30, 70, 76–109, 116–24, 135–36, 141–44, 148–50, 153, 160, 173, 193, 212, 234
Didaskalos, 8, 24, 25, 151
Differance, 80
Dives, 1, 147, 157, 164–65, 191, 197, 235
Division of labor, 233

Ecclesiolatry, 207
Economy, 17–18, 66, 87–95, 101, 107, 186, 193, 219, 235
Eleazar, 168, 194–97, 198, 204, 219, 223
Eschatology, 4, 8, 19–22, 29–31, 37–41, 75, 102, 104, 114, 117, 130, 136, 151, 169, 175, 183, 194, 208–34

Index of Subjects

Ethics, 22–24, 46, 60, 75, 82–90, 95, 100, 103, 114–15, 118, 120, 123, 124, 129, 135, 147, 156, 160, 180–83, 217, 227, 232–33
Existentialism, 6, 7, 27, 33–48, 116, 145, 149, 151, 156, 209–10, 212, 225

Faith, 7, 21, 35, 39–42, 47, 59, 62, 63, 76–77, 86–88, 98–102, 106, 109, 116, 121–24, 129–33, 139, 142, 146–50, 165, 168, 194–205, 210–12, 216–17, 228–31
Freedom, 8, 11, 14, 15, 25, 34, 66, 107, 147, 149, 152, 210

Gate, 1, 20, 68, 73, 82, 88, 95, 100, 108, 127, 129, 142, 152, 164–70, 190, 197, 200, 224–25, 227
Gestell, 14–15, 18, 25, 33, 47, 74, 77, 109–10, 151, 160, 176, 208, 219, 22
Gift, 5, 38, 77–78, 84–96, 151, 181, 185–93, 215, 217, 219, 227
Gnosticism, 69, 179, 182
Grace, 17, 18, 24, 46, 87, 90, 92, 102, 127, 151, 159, 178, 180–88, 193, 204, 206, 214–20, 227–29, 235, 236

Hades, 100, 139, 200, 223
Hearing, 8, 28, 32, 33, 41, 44, 45, 50, 54, 69, 74, 82, 100, 115, 119, 125, 128, 133–39, 151, 154, 158, 160–61, 165, 170–73, 176, 180, 182, 199–205, 209, 222, 224–27, 235
Hermeneutics, 1–6, 19, 22, 23–28, 36, 40–41, 46, 55, 58, 69, 78, 106, 108, 111–24, 135, 137, 139, 154–60, 179–82, 190–93, 206, 208, 212–13, 218–20, 226–28, 231–33
  of suspicion, 156

general and special, 155, 158–59
historicist, 2, 3, 20–24, 35, 43, 61, 71–73, 111–18, 125, 132–35, 138–39, 143, 175, 211, 231, 232
Holy Spirit's role, 6, 8, 17, 24, 41, 123, 151, 153, 156–59, 175, 181, 188, 233–36
Horizons, 2, 5, 32, 66, 100, 113–16, 120, 124, 139, 149, 180, 181, 184, 193, 232–33
Meaning and Significance, 124–25
Hermes, 115–18, 138–39, 226
Herod, 140, 161–73, 191, 223, 224
Historical criticism, 35, 41, 95, 100, 132–35, 161, 235
Historicism, 2, 3, 20–24, 35, 43, 61, 71–73, 111–18, 125, 132–35, 138–39, 143, 175, 211, 231, 232
History of Religion School, 34–35
Holiness, 154–55, 230
Holy Spirit, 6, 8, 17, 24, 41, 123, 151, 153, 156–59, 175, 181, 188, 233–36
Horizons, 2, 5, 32, 66, 100, 113–16, 120, 124, 139, 149, 180, 181, 184, 193, 232–33
Humility, 3, 8, 42, 76–77, 85, 90, 99, 102–5, 118, 124, 127, 136–47, 149–77, 193, 204, 214

Individualism, 6, 21, 41, 44–47, 67, 85–86, 92, 153, 182–83, 190–94, 210, 211, 218
Infinity, 55, 80, 106
Intelligibility, 7, 9, 17, 51–54, 97, 116, 184, 203, 219, 226
Interpretive community, 7, 21, 49, 54–67, 69, 71, 73, 94, 110, 124, 183, 189, 191, 199, 225, 226
Israel, 21, 93, 105, 107, 117, 119–20, 127–32, 135, 149–50, 153, 167, 170, 173, 174, 180, 182, 195, 196–99

Index of Subjects   263

Jacob, 107, 108, 125, 138, 196, 235
John the Baptist, 95, 103, 161–64, 168, 171–72, 198

Kantianism, 27, 29, 35, 37, 86, 90, 111, 124, 232
Kerygma, 6, 31–34, 40, 48, 110, 209
Khora, 95, 77, 95–101
Kingdom of God, 30, 102, 105, 120, 126, 129, 136, 150, 162, 171, 173, 175, 189, 196, 203, 205, 224, 226

Liberation, 19, 20, 113, 148–49, 152, 201
Listening, 6, 19, 25, 37, 44, 60, 92, 94, 125, 128, 135, 137, 157–59, 165, 183, 187, 194, 207, 231, 235
Logocentrism, 81, 82, 97, 141, 143, 148, 172
Logos, 78, 81, 83, 97, 133, 141–43, 149–50, 160, 169, 172, 173, 176, 228

Magnificat, 170, 176, 223
Manichees, 214
Marcion, 46
Mary, 189
Marxism / Marxist, 59, 71
Membership, 67, 69, 178, 182, 194, 206
Messiah, 3, 7, 21, 22, 24, 40, 45, 76, 78, 87, 91, 95, 99, 101, 103–8, 110, 116–20, 128–34, 140–54, 162–69, 173–76, 184, 191, 196, 228
Metaphysics, 65, 74, 78–83, 86, 110
Modernism / Modernity, 9, 12–16, 34, 45, 68, 85, 110, 190
Mythology, 28–32, 34, 37, 209–11, 220

Neighbor, 38, 89, 117, 138, 193, 200

Objectification, 29–33, 37, 40, 71
Ontonolgy, 10–11, 14, 16, 17, 21, 52, 90, 118, 145, 220

Openness, 5–7, 40, 46, 77, 99, 107, 110, 214–15
Orgiastic, 84–85
Otherness, 5–8, 15, 20, 28, 30, 35, 44, 45, 48–51, 56, 58, 66, 69, 73, 74, 77, 78, 82, 90, 92–117, 136–51, 156, 159, 175–81, 186, 190, 193, 215, 228–35

Parousia, 102, 104, 209, 120, 213–14, 228
Pharisees, 92–93, 99, 102, 127–29, 140, 153–54, 163, 172–73
Plato, 10, 57, 60–63, 77–85, 92–98, 107, 221
  Gorgias, 63
  Phaedrus, 77–83
  Protagoras, 60
  Republic, 47, 57, 61, 221
  Timaeus, 77, 81, 96–98
Plutarch, 221
Persuasion, 49, 59, 62, 63, 65
Pharmakon, 78–81
Philanthropy, 180–81, 192, 200
Pirque Aboth, 102, 154
Poiesis, 10–16, 22, 230
Politics, 7, 9, 13, 14, 37–39, 42, 43, 47, 59, 61–65, 72, 92, 97, 98, 104, 112, 121, 126, 127, 130, 135, 136, 140, 145, 153, 154, 164, 166, 171, 183–91, 221, 223
Postmodernism, 18, 55, 56, 59, 63, 66, 81, 90, 103, 104, 123, 189, 190
Pragmatism, 50, 56–58, 73, 92, 181
Principle, 60–66, 70, 92, 111–16, 151, 159
Purple, 164, 166

Realized eschatology, 22, 30, 209–12, 221, 231
Relativism, 5, 27, 53, 56–59, 63, 69, 71, 110, 118, 148, 158, 231
Resurrection, 19, 44, 66, 74, 80, 82, 102, 122, 125, 129, 133, 144, 146,

152, 158, 167, 170–72, 176, 200, 206, 224, 226, 228
Revelation, 11, 15, 27, 31, 86, 96, 105, 124, 143, 147, 151, 158, 160, 172, 180, 193, 212, 214, 219–22
Reversal, 95, 102, 107, 128, 134–35, 173, 202, 206, 222–24, 227–28
Revolution, 61, 72, 74, 80 ,81, 112, 130, 134, 135, 150, 151, 223
Rhetoric, 6, 12, 49–53, 58–68, 73–74, 83, 97, 103, 116–17, 166, 188–89, 193

Sabbath, 209–29
Sacrifice, 84–91, 95, 101, 124, 143, 149, 183–87, 193, 202, 213, 216
Salvation history, 16, 40, 118, 129, 139, 153, 217
Shekinah, 102, 153, 154
Si-Osiris, 222
Social contingency, 51, 55, 179
Socio-pragmatic, 50, 56–58, 73, 92, 181
Socrates, 57, 78, 83, 93, 97, 98
Somatology, 21, 178–89, 193
Son of God, 119, 127
Speech (vs writing), 61, 77–82
Speech Act Theory, 153

Technology, 4–28, 33, 38, 40, 43–50, 54, 58–62, 65, 69, 70, 74, 76–78, 85–86, 95–99, 104–10, 118, 122, 137–41, 151, 155–60, 176, 178, 192, 193, 208–19, 230, 232–34
Temple, 11, 25, 93, 102, 130, 131, 153–60, 169, 170, 213, 214
Text in itself, 16, 19, 49, 52, 138, 160, 23
Textuality, 71, 80, 92, 121–22, 124, 147, 160, 174, 176, 228, 232, 234
Thamus, 78–7
Torah, 102, 123, 138, 154, 163, 164, 195, 196, 199
Transformation, 6, 13, 15, 19, 24, 45–47, 69, 70, 102, 108, 115, 136, 151, 156–58, 175, 179–80, 184, 185, 192, 194, 206, 216, 218, 220, 228, 232, 233, 235, 236
Trinity, 6, 18, 24, 141, 155, 160, 233

Wealth, 1, 42, 65, 74, 106, 117, 127, 128, 166, 169, 173, 194, 197, 201–3, 222–24
Writing, 77–82

Zacchaeus, 129

www.ingramcontent.com/pod-product-compliance
Lightning Source LLC
Chambersburg PA
CBHW050343230426
43663CB00010B/1975